All About—

Richard Burton, Eddie Fisher, Mike Todd, Nicky Hilton, the Krupp diamond, *National Velvet*, Montgomery Clift, Rock Hudson, the Betty Ford Clinic, Debbie Reynolds, Marilyn Monroe, *Cleopatra*, the early teachers, the later doctors, John Warner, *A Place in the Sun*, the contents of the drug cabinet, the great passions, the quick affairs, the immortal triumphs, the total bombs, the children and grandchildren, the early background, the illnesses, accidents, and roller-coaster weight chart, in a book that tells you—

ALL ABOUT ELIZABETH

ⓞ SIGNET BOOKS

LIVES OF THE RICH AND FAMOUS

(0451)

- [ ] **ALL THAT GLITTERED: *My Life with the Supremes* by Tony Turner, with Barbara Aria.** The sins, scandals and secrets—as written by one of the few Supremes insiders with nothing to hide. "A startling look at the Ladies, the Legend, and finally the Truth, about the Supremes." —Scherrie Payne, formerly of the Supremes (402758—$5.99)

- [ ] **GOLDEN GIRL: *The Story of Jessica Savitch* by Alanna Nash.** Who was the complex, unhappy person behind the glamorous TV image? What secret demons drove her to a tragic early death? This sensational biography gives an accurate, fascinating portrait of her public and private lives, and pays tribute to a woman who beat the odds to triumph in her profession ... but paid the ultimate price. "Compelling ... Like Bob Woodward's *Wired*, *Golden Girl* makes you feel you are inside the subject's brain."—*Glamour.* (161211—$4.95)

- [ ] **A WOMAN NAMED JACKIE by C. David Heymann.** This comprehensive and intimate portrait unravels the riddle of the world's most famous and elusive woman, Jackie Onassis, capturing the complexities and contradictions of her life and character. With a dazzling gallery of photos. (165675—$5.95)

- [ ] **THE HELMSLEY'S: *The Rise and Fall of Harry and Leona* by Richard Hammer.** "Greed and connivance in the lives of the super-rich ... read this book!"—Clifford Irving. "Absorbing, detailed and damning."—*Kirkus Reviews* (168720—$4.95)

Prices slightly higher in Canada

Buy them at your local bookstore or use this convenient coupon for ordering.

NEW AMERICAN LIBRARY
P.O. Box 999, Bergenfield, New Jersey 07621

Please send me the books I have checked above. I am enclosing $_____
(please add $1.00 to this order to cover postage and handling). Send check or money order—no cash or C.O.D.'s. Prices and numbers are subject to change without notice.

Name_____

Address_____

City _____ State _____ Zip Code _____
Allow 4-6 weeks for delivery.
This offer, prices and numbers are subject to change without notice.

All About
~Elizabeth~

ELIZABETH TAYLOR,
PUBLIC AND PRIVATE

By Caroline Latham
and Jeannie Sakol

AN ONYX BOOK

ONYX
Published by the Penguin Group
Penguin Books USA Inc., 375 Hudson Street,
New York, New York 10014, U.S.A.
Penguin Books Ltd, 27 Wrights Lane,
London W8 5TZ, England
Penguin Books Australia Ltd, Ringwood,
Victoria, Australia
Penguin Books Canada Ltd, 10 Alcorn Avenue,
Toronto, Ontario, Canada M4V 3B2
Penguin Books (N.Z.) Ltd, 182–190 Wairau Road,
Auckland 10, New Zealand

Penguin Books Ltd, Registered Offices:
Harmondsworth, Middlesex, England

First published by Onyx, an imprint of New American Library,
a division of Penguin Books USA Inc.

First Printing, December, 1991
10 9 8 7 6 5 4 3 2 1

Copyright © Jeannie Sakol and Caroline Latham, 1991

Cover photos: 2 black-and-white photos courtesy of Lester Glassner
Collection/Neal Peters. Color photo courtesy of Bob Scott/Neal Peters.

All rights reserved

REGISTERED TRADEMARK—MARCA REGISTRADA

Printed in the United States of America

Without limiting the rights under copyright reserved above, no part
of this publication may be reproduced, stored in or introduced into
a retrieval system, or transmitted, in any form, or by any means
(electronic, mechanical, photocopying, recording, or otherwise),
without the prior written permission of both the copyright owner
and the above publisher of this book.

BOOKS ARE AVAILABLE AT QUANTITY DISCOUNTS WHEN USED TO
PROMOTE PRODUCTS OR SERVICES. FOR INFORMATION PLEASE
WRITE TO PREMIUM MARKETING DIVISION, PENGUIN BOOKS USA
INC., 375 HUDSON STREET, NEW YORK, NEW YORK 10014.

If you purchased this book without a cover you should be aware
that this book is stolen property. It was reported as "unsold and
destroyed" to the publisher and neither the author nor the publisher has received any payment for this "stripped book."

For all the Elizabeth Taylor fans
who agree with us that she is still
the most beautiful woman in the world.

Introduction

Elizabeth Taylor is one of the twentieth century's most influential cultural icons. Her heart-shaped face is instantly recognizable all over the world: the thickly lashed violet eyes under dark brows, the perfectly chiseled nose, the voluptuous mouth. Since she was twelve years old, she has embodied our ideal of feminine perfection—and despite recent caviling about her weight, she still does.

But it is not just the beauty of Elizabeth Taylor that influences us. It is also her persona, that amalgam of her image on screen and her behavior in real life, that has had a significant cultural impact. Above all else, this supremely romantic creature symbolizes the human need for total, unconditional love. Today, that may seem like a cliché; we hear about it everywhere, from Oprah's TV show to Sunday morning in church. But love has not always held so paramount a position in our cultural values. For example, it used to be that public service was among our highest aspirations, and children wanted to be president when they grew up. Mike Todd encapsulated the death of that value when he told reporters that being the husband of Elizabeth Taylor was a much better job than being president.

Elizabeth Taylor reflects our cultural commitment to the emotion of love. Watching her on the screen, in such movies as *Butterfield 8* and *Cleopatra*, we have learned that true love is worth any sacrifice. Reading about her painful divorce from first husband Nicky Hilton, after seven months of marriage, and observing the long slow death of her relationship with Richard Burton, we have learned that true love is hard to find, and even harder to keep. And following sympathetically her recent struggles with her addictions, we have learned that without true love, all the riches and fame the world can offer are no more than ashes in the mouth.

This book is a catalog of all that Elizabeth Taylor has meant to us over the years, on the screen and off, and all that we have learned from her life and love.

All About Elizabeth

-A-

Academy Award Nominations

Elizabeth Taylor has been nominated for an Academy Award as Best Actress five times:

- 1957 for *Raintree County*. She lost to Joanne Woodward for her performance in *The Three Faces of Eve*.
- 1959 for *Cat on a Hot Tin Roof*. She lost to Susan Hayward for her role as the condemned murderess in *I Want to Live*.
- 1960 for *Suddenly Last Summer* (along with her costar, Katharine Hepburn). Both Taylor and Hepburn lost to Simone Signoret for *Room at the Top*.
- 1961 for *Butterfield 8*. For the role of Gloria Wandrous, Elizabeth Taylor won her first Oscar.
- 1966 for *Who's Afraid of Virginia Woolf?*. This role gave Taylor her second Oscar.

Accident Prone

In addition to her many illnesses, Elizabeth Taylor has also sustained numerous injuries through accidents. Twisted ankles, broken fingers, even a metal splinter that blew into her eye—she seems to be accident prone. Director Richard Brooks said of Taylor, "If she opens a beer can, she cuts herself; if there is a chair in the middle of the set, she falls over it while talking over her shoulder to someone."

Actors Who Have Played Elizabeth Taylor's Father

- Hugh Herbert in *There's One Born Every Minute*
- Donald Crisp in *National Velvet*
- George Murphy in *Cynthia*
- Leon Ames in *A Date with Judy* and *Little Women*
- Walter Pidgeon in *Julia Misbehaves*
- Percy Waram in *The Big Hangover*
- Spencer Tracy in *Father of the Bride* and *Father's Little Dividend*
- Shepperd Strudwick in *A Place in the Sun*
- Tom Tully in *Love Is Better Than Ever*
- Felix Aylmer in *Ivanhoe*
- William Powell in *The Girl Who Had Everything*
- Louis Calhern in *Rhapsody*
- Paul Fix in *Giant*
- Michael Hordern in *The Taming of the Shrew*

Actors Who Have Played Elizabeth Taylor's Husband

- Peter Lawford in *Julia Misbehaves* and *Little Women*
- Robert Taylor in *Conspirator*
- Don Taylor in *Father of the Bride* and *Father's Little Dividend*
- John Ericson in *Rhapsody*
- Peter Finch in *Elephant Walk*
- Van Johnson in *The Last Time I Saw Paris*
- Rock Hudson in *Giant*
- Montgomery Clift in *Raintree County*
- Paul Newman in *Cat on Hot Tin Roof*
- Richard Burton in *The V.I.P.s*, *Who's Afraid of Virginia Woolf?*, and *The Taming of the Shrew*
- Marlon Brando in *Reflections in a Golden Eye*
- Peter Ustinov in *The Comedians*

- Michael Caine in *X Y & Zee*
- Laurence Harvey in *Night Watch*
- Henry Fonda in *Ash Wednesday*
- Burt Lancaster in *Victory at Entebbe*

Actresses Who Have Played Elizabeth Taylor's Mother

- Peggy Moran in *There's One Born Every Minute*
- Anne Revere in *National Velvet*
- Selena Royle in *Courage of Lassie*
- Mary Astor in *Cynthia* and *Little Women*
- Greer Garson in *Julia Misbehaves*
- Fay Holden in *The Big Hangover*
- Joan Bennett in *Father of the Bride* and *Father's Little Dividend*
- Frieda Inescort in *A Place in the Sun*
- Josephine Hutchison in *Love Is Better Than Ever*
- Judith Evelyn in *Giant*
- Mercedes McCambridge in *Suddenly Last Summer*
- Mildred Dunnock in *Butterfield 8*

Adopting a Child with Richard Burton

It was a source of sorrow to Elizabeth Taylor during her marriage to Richard Burton that she could no longer bear children—she wanted to have his baby as a symbol of their love. Taylor began to consider the alternative of adoption. She said she wanted to adopt a Jewish child, then suggested an African child, finally a Vietnamese child. But the idea never got beyond the dream stage. One reason might have been the reluctance of her husband. Burton pronounced, "To adopt a child requires more thought and more preparation than the probable accident of conception. We have the money to indulge ourselves with pets but we can take no risk at all with a child that is going to bear our name."

James Agee on Elizabeth Taylor

In his 1944 review of *National Velvet*, famed writer and movie critic James Agee ruminated on his feelings about young Elizabeth Taylor. He frankly stated, "Ever since I first saw the child two or three years ago in I forget what minor role in what movie, I have been choked with the peculiar sort of admiration I might have felt if we were both in the same grade of primary school." This statement prefaced his reluctant conclusion that she wasn't particularly gifted as an actress. Sadly, he opined, "She seems rather to turn things off and on, much as she is told, with perhaps a fair amount of natural grace and of a natural-born female's sleepwalking sort of guile, but without much, if any, of an artist's intuition, perception or resóurce. She strikes me, however, if I may resort to a conservative statement, as being rapturously beautiful."

Alfalfa Costars With Elizabeth

In her first screen appearance, in 1942, Elizabeth Taylor played opposite Carl Switzer, the boy who created the role of Alfalfa in the *Our Gang* series. At that time, he was a well-known face and she was a newcomer. Four years later, Elizabeth Taylor was the star of *Courage of Lassie*, receiving top billing, and Alfalfa played the minor role of "First Youth." Switzer was shot to death in a brawl in 1959, at the early age of thirty-two.

All-Star Tribute to Elizabeth Taylor

In 1977, Elizabeth Taylor was the subject of a CBS-TV program called *All-Star Tribute to Elizabeth Taylor*. In addition to an appearance by Taylor, there were speeches by Paul Newman and Joanne Woodward, as well as former MGM stars June Allyson and Margaret O'Brien. The event raised money for the new wing named after Taylor of a Los Angeles hospital.

Alvin

Alvin was a green parrot that accompanied Elizabeth Taylor while she was on the road with the stage production of *Private Lives* in 1983.

Amebic Dysentery

In the winter of 1975, Elizabeth Taylor went to Leningrad to film *The Blue Bird*. She promptly came down with amebic dysentery, which she called wryly "a hell of a way to diet."

American Foundation for Aids Research

Elizabeth Taylor, in the forefront of support for the victims of AIDS, was the first—and so far the only—National Chairman of the American Foundation for AIDS Research, a cause she supports with her own time and money. Taylor revealed that taking the chairmanship cost her a lucrative contract for a soft-drink commercial, and she also commented on the problems facing AIDS fund-raisers. "It was extraordinary how many people didn't want their names connected with [AIDS]. It would blow your mind who wouldn't help. I was both terribly frustrated and incensed." Thanks in large part to Taylor's leadership, the cause has achieved respectability in Hollywood.

Taylor told an interviewer what motivated her efforts. "AIDS is a cruel and tragic disease that indiscriminately consumes our friends, family, and loved ones. The only solution is care—for all of us to take an active role and eradicate this disease before it eradicates the world. AIDS should be everyone's priority, because as long as we do not have a cure, it is a time bomb that threatens our children, our society—even our economy."

American or English?

At the beginning of Elizabeth Taylor's career, she was continually labeled by MGM's publicity machine as English. That image was appropriate to her roles as an orphan in an English institution (*Jane Eyre*), as Roddy McDowall's playmate in an idyll of the English countryside (*The White Cliffs of Dover*) and as a Duke's granddaughter (*Lassie Come Home*). It was reinforced by her success as the English girl, Velvet Brown, in *National Velvet*. But even when Taylor's roles were American, like the girl she played in *A Date with Judy*, MGM called their young star "as British as they make them."

But Elizabeth Taylor was born an Amercian citizen. Even though her birth took place in a London suburb, her parents were American citizens, both born in a little town in Kansas not far from Dodge City, and they registered their daughter as an American citizen. The Elizabeth Taylor who rode the Pi and spoke with an English accent in *National Velvet* was in real life visiting her maternal grandparents on their chicken farm in Pasadena. Her "Britishness" was simply a myth that helped launch her career.

Years later, when Taylor was married to Richard Burton, there was constant complaint about her too-American accent and attitude. In such vehicles as *Cleopatra, Doctor Faustus*, and *Under Milk Wood*, critics pounced on the flat American tones of her voice, and claimed that she could turn any locale into Beverly Hills just by walking onto the set. Ironically, that was the time in her life when she renounced her American citizenship. Taylor was motivated primarily by the wish to shelter her large earnings from U.S. taxes; calling her house in Gstaad her principal residence allowed her to pay taxes at the lower Swiss rate. So at the time she was perceived as being almost obnoxiously American, she was no longer a U.S. citizen and had to limit the number of days she stayed in the country in order not to fall afoul of the tax laws.

Today, Taylor is considered one of America's national treasures, and she is once again a resident of the United States. At last, the image and the reality have coalesced.

AMFAR Benefit Masquerade

One of the biggest social events of the 1989 winter season in New York was the December benefit masquerade to raise money for the American Foundation for AIDS Research (AMFAR). Hostess of the gala event was Elizabeth Taylor, a tireless worker for the organization of which she is the national chairman. Escorted by cohost Malcolm Forbes, Taylor looked beautiful in a dazzling white silk dress, embroidered with gold thread and sparkling stones, designed by David Emanuel (the man who created Princess Diana's wedding dress). She stood amid vases of lavender roses—chosen in tribute to her eyes—and told the assembled guests at the thousand-dollar-a-plate dinner, "There isn't a spot in the world that hasn't been touched by AIDS." Later in the evening, Taylor and Forbes watched a group of transvestites dance in costumes made of feathers and flounces, and then accepted a one million-dollar check from industrialist John Kluge and his wife Patricia. *The New York Times* labeled the evening, "*La Cage aux Folles* meets the Fortune 500."

Miss Birdine Anderson

Miss Birdine Anderson was the teacher assigned by the Los Angeles County Board of Education to tutor Elizabeth Taylor at the school on the MGM lot. According to Hollywood legend, it was "Andy" for whom Elizabeth wrote her little essay about her chipmunk Nibbles, and Andy who suggested that Elizabeth send it to a publisher.

Miss Anderson even accompanied sixteen-year-old Elizabeth Taylor to London, when MGM sent her to make *Conspirator* on location, playing opposite Robert Taylor. Five days a week, Miss Anderson spent three hours giving Elizabeth her lessons. The star complained to her friend Roddy McDowall, "How can I concentrate on my education when Robert Taylor keeps sticking his tongue down my throat?"

Anniversary Gesture

For a wedding anniversary gift, Richard Burton one year planned to treat Elizabeth Taylor to a few days of privacy and relaxation at their house in Puerto Vallarta, Mexico. As a sentimental gesture, he arranged for Elizabeth's favorite Hollywood florist to fill the house with her favorite orchids. Unfortunately, their departure was delayed while the couple shot retakes for a movie they were wrapping up. By the time they finally arrived in Puerto Vallarta, the house was full of dead flowers.

Around the World in 80 days

The reason Elizabeth Taylor's third husband, Mike Todd, was both rich and famous at the time they met was that he was the producer of the very successful 1956 movie, *Around the World in 80 Days*. He had purchased the rights to the Jules Verne classic novel because he thought the story of a trip around the world was the perfect basis for a movie shot in Todd-AO, the wide-screen process he pioneered. He hired humorist S. J. Perelman to write the screenplay; Perelman, who complained that getting his checks out of Todd was a major excavation project, was to win an Academy Award for his work.

Mexican comedian Cantinflas, to whom Todd was introduced by his then-fiancée, Evelyn Keyes, was signed to play the role of Passepartout, and suave David Niven was cast in the role of Phileas Fogg, the Englishman who tries to win a club bet by traveling around the globe in just eighty days. With the leads in place, Todd set about persuading his Hollywood friends, including Marlene Dietrich, to appear in cameo roles, another of his innovations. Thus he was able to list many big names in the credits, yet spend only modest amounts of money.

The movie was a box-office smash the moment it was released, and Todd subsequently devoted many months to promoting and publicizing both the film and himself. One indirect result was that in 1957, *Around the World in 80 Days* won the Oscar for Best Picture, beating out the film that starred his by-then wife, Elizabeth Taylor, *Giant*. Even after the film disappeared from the U.S. market, Todd continued to make deals for foreign rights, and the momentum of the movie's enormous earning power was not lost until Todd died in 1958. The wide-screen process used to film the movie made it visually unsuccessful on the small screen, so it is currently seen only occasionally in revival theaters.

"Around the World in 80 Days": The Song

Rights to the hit song, "Around the World in 80 Days," from the movie of the same name, were owned by Mike Todd, the movie's producer. Shortly before his death in a plane crash, he assigned the lucrative rights to his wife, Elizabeth Taylor, as "a little nest egg."

Around the World with Mike Todd

In 1968, ten years after the death of Mike Todd, Mike Todd, Jr. produced a TV special about his father's life, called *Around the World with Mike Todd*. There were photos and film clips of Todd, and many famous people, including Orson Welles, Ethel Merman, Gypsy Rose Lee, and Jack E. Leonard, talked about their memories of the entrepreneur. So did his widow, Elizabeth Taylor, by then married to Richard Burton but still visibly moved by the memory of the love she shared with Todd.

"Arrivederci Roma"

While Elizabeth Taylor and Richard Burton were involved in their romance on the set of *Cleopatra* in Rome, her husband Eddie Fisher returned to the United States for a series of nightclub appearances. The singer opened each one with "Arrivederci Roma." Later, he teamed up with singer-dancer Juliet Prowse, who came onstage singing a song entitled "I'm Cleo, the Nympho of the Nile." Taylor was not amused.

Art against Aids

In 1987, Elizabeth Taylor presided over a benefit called Art Against AIDS, for which art dealers and galleries offered a percentage of their sales receipts to help AIDS research. The benefit was kicked off with a glamourous evening in New York, with Taylor in attendance. *The New York Times* commented, "Never underestimate the power of a movie star. Especially a superstar like Elizabeth Taylor. Once she attached her name to the American Foundation for AIDS Research, it became not only acceptable but desirable for other celebrities to become involved in the cause."

Art Collection

Elizabeth Taylor has a small but choice collection of art that hangs on the walls of her Bel Air home. It includes paintings by Renoir, Van Gogh, Degas, Rouault, and Monet. Some of the collection was a legacy from her father, an art dealer, and she has continued to add to it, buying with a knowledgeable eye.

Ash Wednesday

In 1973, Elizabeth Taylor costarred in *Ash Wednesday*, opposite Henry Fonda. The plot was pure soap opera, about an aging woman who undergoes extensive plastic surgery (face, breasts, buttocks, even hands are lifted) in the hope of winning back her straying husband (Fonda). Some audiences objected to the graphic reality of the surgical scenes, many of which were filmed during actual plastic surgery by the doctor who served as a technical consultant.

Ash Wednesday was one of Taylor's best performances of the decade. Rex Reed enthused, "She's subtle, sensitive, glowing with freshness and beauty, fifty pounds lighter in weight; her hair is coiffed simply, her clothes ravishing, her makeup a symphony of perfection. For those who grew up in love with Elizabeth Taylor (I assume we are legion) this movie is pure magic. She is once again the kind of star marquees light up for." *Variety* thought she carried the film single-handedly, and *Cue* praised her for acting well. But her reputation had fallen so low that even critical praise did not draw audiences to the box office, and the film went down as one more failure on her record.

Mary Astor Plays Mother

In two MGM movies, veteran actress Mary Astor played the mother of Elizabeth Taylor. In *Cynthia*, Astor rebelled against her husband (George Murphy) to help her sickly daughter lead a normal life, and several critics commented on the two actresses' excellent portrayal of a mother-daughter relationship. Astor was once again cast as Taylor's mother in *Little Women*, where she played the long-suffering Marmee.

In her memoirs, *A Life on Film*, Astor wrote about her recollections of the young Elizabeth. When they made *Cynthia*, said Astor, Taylor "was just beginning to turn into an exquisite beauty. A figure just beginning to blossom, beautiful skin that needed no makeup, and those violet eyes with lashes that needed no mascara." Astor also remembered Elizabeth Taylor as being very bright and good at concentrating on her work. Despite all the compliments, Astor apparently did not grow really fond of Elizabeth Taylor. "Elizabeth was cool, and slightly superior," she wrote. "More than slightly. There was a look in those violet eyes that was somewhat calculating, as though she knew exactly what she wanted and was quite sure of getting it. Maybe all she wanted was that great big hunk of a diamond ring. It seems to symbolize what she got."

Atoka Farm

Atoka Farm was John Warner's Virginia estate, near Middleburg, where Elizabeth Taylor lived during their marriage. A 2,700-acre cattle ranch, Atoka Farm had been part of Warner's divorce settlement from his first wife, heiress Catherine Mellon. The estate boasted a beautiful old stone house, along with two tennis courts, a pool, and stables. Elizabeth said it reminded her of the Kentish countryside where she had spent weekends as a child, and opted to hold her wedding to Warner, her seventh marriage ceremony, on the grounds of the estate.

Author

Elizabeth Taylor, herself the subject of scores of books, has four books to her credit as an author. They are:

- *Nibbles and Me*, 1945. New York: Duell, Sloan and Pearce
- *World Enough and Time* (with Richard Burton) 1964
- *Elizabeth Taylor*, 1965
- *Elizabeth Takes Off*, 1988

-B-

Baby-Blue Cadillac

On Elizabeth Taylor's sixteenth birthday, her parents gave her a new baby-blue Cadillac, presenting her with a gold key to the car at a party on the MGM set. The gesture loses some of its charm when you realize that they bought the car with money that came from her salary . . . and they wouldn't even let her take driving lessons. Taylor didn't learn to drive until 1989.

Banana Plantation

One of the many investments made by Elizabeth Taylor and Richard Burton in the years they were among the highest-paid of all movie stars was a 685-acre banana plantation on Tenerife, one of the Canary Islands.

Beau Brummel

Beau Brummel, a 1954 MGM release, was an unsatisfactory period piece costarring Elizabeth Taylor and Stewart Granger (good friend of her then-husband, Michael Wilding), with Peter Ustinov, in the role of the future King George IV, stealing all his scenes. As the earlier *Ivanhoe* and later *Cleopatra* were to demonstrate, Elizabeth Taylor was never comfortable in a role that wasn't essentially modern. In this Regency drama, based on a play written in 1890, she played Lady Patricia, the aristocrat who is beloved by Beau Brummel (Stewart Granger). In the end, she chooses to marry her dull fiance (played by James Donald) because Brummel falls out of favor with the Prince of Wales and goes to debtor's prison.

The film was shot in England and displayed the lavish MGM touch in its elaborate sets and gorgeous costumes. But as a drama it did not hold together, and critics were generally biting about all the actors, with the exception of Ustinov's portrayal of the Prince of Wales and Robert Morley as George III, his father. Some contrasted it unfavorably with the 1924 Warner Brothers movie based on the same play, which starred John Barrymore as Brummel and Mary Astor as Lady Patricia. Otis L. Guernsey, Jr. called Taylor "decorative, but something less than useful," and *The Monthly Film Bulletin* was even meaner, calling her "barely articulate."

Beautiful Women: Elizabeth Taylor's List

Although many of us believe Elizabeth Taylor is the most beautiful woman in the world, she considers herself only pretty. Her top choice for truly beautiful? Ava Gardner. Two other women she has mentioned as being particularly beautiful are Jacqueline Kennedy Onassis and Taylor's own daughter Liza.

Before Passion . . .

Before Elizabeth Taylor introduced her own scent, Passion, she was known to wear Femme, by Rochas, and Caleche from Hermes.

Belching Competitions

Richard Burton reported that on the set of *Who's Afraid of Virginia Woolf?*, Elizabeth Taylor and costar Sandy Dennis often held belching competitions. "Elizabeth is a good belcher," he announced, "but Sandy nearly always won."

Jeanne Bell

Jeanne Bell (real name Anna Morgan) was a beautiful model who had the distinction of being the first black woman to pose for *Playboy*. She met Richard Burton first on the set of *The Klansman* in 1973, a movie in which she had a bit part. He then helped her get another small part in his film *Jackpot*, which was shot on location in Nice in late 1974. Burton at the time was engaged to Princess Elizabeth of Yugoslavia, but she broke off the engagement when she learned of his relationship with Bell. Jeanne Bell then moved into Burton's rented villa, where she stayed until August 1975, when Elizabeth Taylor (who had been in Russia shooting *The Blue Bird*) and Richard Burton announced their reconciliation. Burton publicly gave Bell the credit for helping him quit drinking during the period they were together.

Belushi Does Taylor

A sketch on *Saturday Night Live* in 1978 featured John Belushi, padded to look especially tubby and wearing heavy eye makeup, in the role of the campaigning Elizabeth Taylor. Belushi's Taylor, majestic and campy, chokes on a chicken bone while she is stuffing her face (alluding to a real-life incident that sent Taylor to the hospital). Taylor later revealed that she saw the sketch and thought it was funny.

Ron Berkeley

Ron Berkeley was Richard Burton's makeup man, who traveled with Burton and Elizabeth Taylor during the 1960s. Burton admitted he needed help because he couldn't even draw a straight line. His wife traveled with a hairdresser but always did her own makeup. Berkeley left Burton's employ after the star's marriage to Suzy Hunt, who learned to do her husband's makeup herself.

Bessie Mae

Montgomery Clift liked to call his friend Elizabeth Taylor "Bessie Mae." "The whole world calls you Elizabeth Taylor," he complained, so he made up a name that would be all his own.

Best Feature

Elizabeth Taylor once claimed she thought her best feature was her gray hairs, and went on to joke, "They're all called Burton." That was during the time she was married to Richard; who knows what she called those gray hairs after the divorce!

Betty

Betty was the pony given to little Elizabeth Taylor by family friend Victor Cazalet when the Taylors lived in England before World War II.

The Betty Ford Center

On December 5, 1983, just one month after *Private Lives* closed, Elizabeth Taylor entered the Betty Ford Center, near Palm Springs, California, for treatment of her dependence on prescription drugs and alcohol. "I realized I was taking far too many pills, even though they were prescribed," the star later told the press. "I would try to say something and the thought from my brain wouldn't reach my tongue. I was stuttering. I was stumbling, and it terrified me."

The Betty Ford Center was established as a facility within the Eisenhower Medical Center, at Rancho Mirage, in 1982, through the efforts of the former first lady and industrialist Leonard Firestone. The treatment program, which has room for sixty patients, includes a stay of four to six weeks, followed by outpatient care for as long as a year afterward. The program includes daily meetings and lectures as well as group therapy sessions. Explained Taylor, "In group therapy, you're up for grabs. People call you on everything. You can tell when somebody is hiding behind lies. After awhile, all of your gimmicks and tricks are stripped away. You're raw, defenseless. That's when it starts being constructive. That's when you learn who you are." Another important feature of the Ford Center's program is its family counseling. Taylor's children were all very supportive of her decision to enter the program and participated fully in the counseling.

Elizabeth Taylor was one of the first celebrities to go to Rancho Mirage, and it was in helping her that the Center developed its policy of treating famous patients like any other. She was assigned her share of work, such as doing laundry, washing dishes, and scrubbing floors. By an ironic coincidence, Peter Lawford entered the Center at about the same time, and he told a reporter, "We have our own jobs, like vacuuming, taking out the garbage—Elizabeth did that for a while until it got too heavy for her back." Celebrities who later followed in Taylor's footsteps at Betty Ford included Mary Tyler Moore, Liza Minnelli, and Johnny Cash. The most famous fictional alumna is TV's Murphy Brown.

Elizabeth Taylor is outspoken in her admiration for founder Betty Ford, who also acted as a personal counselor for Taylor. "Betty Ford and I discussed what it would be like to go public. She had done it and was the better for it. I just hoped the public would understand." Taylor also says of Betty, "What she's done for women alcoholics is just phenomenal. She's lifted the stigma." The star credits the Ford Center with restoring her to psychological health, although she adds, "Stopping the addiction is basically an ongoing process. Although the rate of cure at Betty Ford is about 75 percent, it's not like seven weeks there undoes years of drugs and alcohol. You have to recreate what you learned every day."

Between Friends

Between Friends was a 1983 TV movie that starred Elizabeth Taylor in the role of a Jewish princess and Carol Burnett as her overachieving best friend. The two mature divorcees meet and share their woes, and eventually they are both the better for it. Taylor explained the movie's premise more succinctly: "She [Carol Burnett] plays a slut and I play a lush." Based on the book *Nobody Makes Me Cry* by Shelley List, the script was adapted for the little screen by List and collaborator Jonathan Estrin. The movie was produced by HBO, who believed in the vehicle and the stars enough to put up $4 million, about twice the amount usually budgeted for a TV movie.

Both Taylor and Burnett were enthusiastic from the moment they read the script, and they had a good time making the movie on location in Toronto. Burnett told an interviewer, "We were like two girls in Sunday school. Sometimes the director would have to say to us, 'Now folks, we have to be serious.' " The good relationship between the stars came across on the screen; as *New York Times* reviewer John J. O'Connor noted, the chemistry between the two actresses worked splendidly. The ratings were good, and both Burnett and Taylor got favorable reviews (even though most critics apparently felt obliged to mention Taylor's recent failure on stage in *Private Lives*.)

Beverly Hills House

After young Elizabeth Taylor signed her contract with Universal Studios, the Taylor family bought a Spanish-style house on Elm Drive in Beverly Hills. It was stereotypical Hollywood, white stucco with a red tile roof. Elizabeth's menagerie there consisted of three dogs, a cat, eight chipmunks, and a squirrel. Her two horses were boarded elsewhere. She attempted to keep a lion cub, but her father vetoed the idea. Although the house was on a quiet tree-lined street, it was modest by neighborhood standards—it didn't even have a swimming pool. Taylor lived in this house until she left it as a bride, when she married first husband Nicky Hilton.

Bibliography

Adler, Bill, *Elizabeth Taylor: Triumphs and Tragedies*. New York: Ace Books, 1982.

Agee, James, *Agee on Film*. Boston: Beacon Press, 1958.

Alpert, Hollis, *Burton*. New York: G. P. Putnam's Sons, 1986.

Astor, Mary, *A Life on Film*. New York: Delacorte Press, 1977.

Bosworth, Patricia, *Montgomery Clift*. New York: Harcourt Brace Jovanovich, 1978.

Bragg, Melvyn, *Richard Burton: A Life*. Boston: Little, Brown & Co., 1989.

Brodsky, Jack and Nathan Weiss, *The Cleopatra Papers*. New York: Simon and Schuster, 1963.

Burton, Philip, *Early Doors: My Life and the Theatre*. New York: Dial Press, 1969.

David, Lester, and Jhan Robbins, *Richard and Elizabeth*. New York: Funk & Wagnalls, 1977.

Eames, John Douglas, *The MGM Story: The Complete History of Fifty Roaring Years*. New York: Crown Publishers, 1979.

Greene, Myrna, *The Eddie Fisher Story*. Middlebury, VT: Paul S. Eriksson, Publisher.

Hirsch, Foster, *Elizabeth Taylor*. New York: Galahad Books, 1973.

Joseph, Joan, *For Love of Liz*. New York: Manor Books, 1976.

Kelley, Kitty, *Elizabeth Taylor: The Last Star*. New York: Simon and Schuster, 1981.

Keyes, Evelyn, *Scarlett O'Hara's Younger Sister*. Secaucus, NJ: Lyle Stuart, 1977

LaGuardia, Robert, *Monty*. New York: Arbor House, 1977.

Maddox, Brenda, *Who's Afraid of Elizabeth Taylor?* New York: M. Evans & Co., 1977
Nickens, Christopher, *Elizabeth Taylor: A Biography in Photographs*. New York: Doubleday (A Dolphin Book), 1984.
Taylor, Elizabeth, *Elizabeth Takes Off*. New York: G. P. Putnam's Sons, 1987.
Taylor, Elizabeth, *Elizabeth Taylor*. New York: Harper & Row, 1964.
Vermilye, Jerry and Mark Ricci, *The Films of Elizabeth Taylor*. Secaucus, NJ: Citadel Press, 1976.
Waterbury, Ruth, *Elizabeth Taylor: Her Life, Her Loves, Her Future*. New York: Appleton-Century, 1964.

Bicentennial Ring

In 1976, Elizabeth Taylor accepted an engagement ring from future husband John Warner. He had designed the unusual piece himself, as a commemoration of America's Bicentennial year. It was made of rubies, diamonds, and sapphires—red, white, and blue.

The Big Hangover

The Big Hangover, an MGM release in 1950, costarred Elizabeth Taylor and Van Johnson, playing a noble lawyer, in a blend of farce and romance. The unbelievable plot centered on Johnson's inability to tolerate even a whiff of alcohol without becoming drunk. Elizabeth, his boss's daughter, helps him overcome his problem and live happily ever after. It was a foolish story, and the weak script wasted the talents not only of Taylor and Johnson but of the excellent supporting cast, which included Leon Ames, Selena Royle, Rosemary DeCamp, Fay Holden, and Gene Lockhart.

Most of the reviews were justifiably lukewarm. *Variety* called Taylor warm and appealing, but the reviewer for *The*

New York Herald Tribune commented that she "hovers on the edge of this comedy, dressed up like a mannequin." Perhaps the meanest comment was the snippy one in *The New Yorker*: "Miss Taylor is beautiful and cannot act. This puts her one up on Mr. Johnson." In this picture Elizabeth Taylor was, incidentally, dressed for the first time by Helen Rose, who was to make many costumes for many of her future MGM movies as well as the wedding dresses for Taylor's first three marriages.

Bill

In the 1943 movie, *The Courage of Lassie*, the dog referred to as Lassie in the publicity stills is called "Bill" throughout the movie. In fact, the title was a last-minute attempt to reach Lassie fans with a story about the life of a collie named Bill who has every sort of adventure, including serving in the army during World War II and returning as a shell-shocked veteran.

Birth of a Star

Elizabeth Taylor was born in London, to American parents, on February 27, 1932, weighing in at eight and a half pounds. Her mother recalls that for the few first weeks of her life, little Elizabeth was a very ugly baby, covered with dark hair, with eyes that didn't open for days.

Birthplace

When Elizabeth Taylor was born, her parents were living in a house at 8 Wildwood Road, in London. The street faced fashionable Hampstead Heath, but was actually located in the suburb called Hendon, usually thought of as a working-class suburb. The house itself was a comfortable neo-Georgian, given the name "Heathwood."

Birthday Party at Studio 54

In February 1978, Elizabeth Taylor's friend Halston gave a birthday party for the star at Studio 54. The entertainment featured the Rockettes, and Taylor's birthday cake was a more-than-life-size creation that was shaped like Taylor and weighed more than 500 pounds. As photographers snapped away, she cut a breast off the cake and fed it to her host. Husband John Warner left early.

The Black Panthers

Although Elizabeth Taylor did not approve of the radical political organization called the Black Panthers, which was active in the turbulent 1960s, she and then-husband Richard Burton did contribute $3,000 apiece to a defense fund for the Panthers. Their contribution helped to pay for lawyers hired to defend Panthers, such as Huey Newton and Bobby Seale, in their various court cases.

Claire Bloom Disenchanted

Claire Bloom first met Richard Burton in 1949 when they both appeared in the London stage production of *The Lady's Not for Burning*. Later they costarred in the movies *Alexander the Great* and *Look Back in Anger*, and, according to most accounts, became involved in an off-screen romance as well. In 1965, Bloom costarred with Burton again, in *The Spy Who Came in from the Cold*. She told reporters that Elizabeth Taylor and Richard Burton ignored her, and never invited her to dinner. She added that she now found Richard boring, "as people are when they have got what they wanted . . . a beautiful wife, money, and a great career."

The Blue Bird

The Blue Bird was a lavish screen version of the 1908 play written by Maurice Maeterlinck, which starred Elizabeth Taylor playing four roles: Mother, Light, Maternal Love, and Witch. The 1976 version of this allegorical story, which had previously been turned into a 1940 vehicle for little Shirley Temple, also starred Jane Fonda as Night, Ava Gardner as Luxury, and Cicely Tyson as Cat. Others in the all-star cast included George Rose, Will Geer, Mona Washbourne, and Patsy Kensit in the Shirley Temple role. Russian ballerinas Maya Plisetskaya and Nadezhda Pavlova also appeared. The movie was directed by Hollywood veteran George Cukor. The cost was reported to be more than $15 million.

Most of the film was shot on location in Leningrad during a bitter Russian winter, and most of the cast and crew suffered from the cold and the bad food served at the commissary of Leninfilm, the official Russian movie company that coproduced the film. Taylor, who was accompanied by then-boyfriend Henry Wynberg, told a reporter, "My stomach is groaning for some chili or a good steak," but after awhile, it was just groaning . . . as Taylor and others came down with amebic dysentery.

Elizabeth Taylor, thanks to her years of experience with movie scripts, understood that her roles as written were a problem. "Light can't be saccharine or a Girl Scout leader. In the play she's a goddam bore, but she will not be a goddamn bore the way I play her. I think I'll put in a few swear words . . . Give 'em a little cleavage. We can spritz it up." But the problems turned out to be more serious than some cleavage and swear words could fix. *Variety* accurately predicted, "Elusive box office prospects are ahead."

Florinda Bolkan

In 1968, the media reported that Richard Burton was becoming involved with Brazilian actress Florinda Bolkan, one of the actresses in *Candy*, in which Burton played a cameo role. If it was true, the affair didn't last long, for Elizabeth Taylor was soon by his side.

Bonus for National Velvet

After *National Velvet* was released, it was obvious that young Elizabeth Taylor was going to be a major star. MGM, who had her under contract at the salary of $75 a week, decided that she deserved some additional compensation for her part in making the movie such a success at the box office—and no doubt they also wanted to keep their new young star happy. So they gave her a bonus of $15,000, as well as the gift of the horse she had ridden in the movie.

Boom!

Boom! was a 1968 movie starring Elizabeth Taylor and Richard Burton that was made with good intentions and bad results. Taylor and Burton each received salaries of about $1 million, which proved to be a total loss for the producer and distributor. The script was written by Tennessee Williams, based on his play *The Milk Train Doesn't Stop Here Anymore,* a success on Broadway five years earlier. The movie was directed by Joseph Losey and the supporting cast included Noel Coward and Michael Dunn. But somehow it all added up to a failed film.

Taylor played much-married heiress Sissy Goforth, who knows she is nearing death and intends to spend her last months dictating her memoirs. Sissy was a character created on stage by Hermione Baddeley and later revived by Tallulah Bankhead, and it was a role for which Elizabeth Taylor was quite unsuited. She was too young and much too vital to be believable as the dying Sissy. Burton was also miscast opposite his wife, playing the role of Sissy's mysterious young secretary, because no one could believe for a moment that he was younger and healthier than Taylor. (The role had been originated by the young blonde Tab Hunter.)

The movie was negatively received by critics, and generally ignored by ticket buyers. A Chicago critic commented, "Elizabeth Taylor and Richard Burton remain the nearest thing we have in the movies to a reigning royal family, no matter how uneven their acting abilities. We know so much about them—or think we do—that there is a gruesome satisfaction at the sight of them bogged down in Tennessee Williams's belabored script, especially since its broad lines seem to resemble the Burton and Taylor private lives." And that was one of the best reviews! *Life* said unkindly, "She is fat and will do nothing about her most glaring defect, an unpleasant voice which she cannot adequately control."

"Boozy"

Elizabeth sometimes called Richard Burton "Boozy"—usually in an affectionate manner.

Born without a Sense of Time

Elizabeth Taylor's second husband, Michael Wilding, complained that she was born without any sense of time. Her habitual lateness may also have been in part due to her great concern over her looks. When you are frequently called the most beautiful woman in the world, you don't want to disappoint your audience—so Taylor often spends two or three hours getting ready to face the world, doing everything from changing clothes numerous times to plucking her eyebrows in front of the magnifying glass.

Taylor admits of herself, "I still have no sense of time. It's like a disease. If I could conquer it, I would be fairly disciplined. It isn't deliberate. It isn't a subconscious rebellion. I think it began during my younger days when I had to go both to work and to school, and I would much rather have been out riding a horse."

Bottle of Pool Water

At a 1989 celebrity benefit auction, one of the items offered was a bottle of water from Elizabeth Taylor's swimming pool. There was a label, autographed by the star, that warned, "Don't drink this." The purchaser was New York interior designer Vincente Wolf, who bought it as a present for his former partner Bob Patino, a Taylor fan.

Box-Office Ratings

Between 1958 and 1968, Elizabeth Taylor was a dominant box-office attraction. Here's how she rated, in terms of comparative ticket sales:

1958–2	1964–Not on list
1959–Not on list	1965–9
1960–4	1966–3
1961–1	1967–6
1962–6	1968–10
1963–6	

Claudie Bozzacchi

Claudie Bozzacchi was for years Elizabeth Taylor's personal live-in hairdresser. The two women were friends as well, and Elizabeth and then-husband Richard Burton once traveled with Claudie to the little Corsican village of Guar Guale to visit her seventy-four-year-old grandmother.

Marlon Brando

According to Richard Burton, Elizabeth Taylor and Marlon Brando were very similar screen presences. "She has the same qualities I use to describe Marlon," he explained. "Slow moving, quiet, with a suggestion of infinite power." Burton added, "Both of them never move directly toward an object . . . They are evasive and you can't quite catch them. That is why they are such remarkable stars." Although Brando and Taylor did costar in one movie, *Reflections in a Golden Eye*, it regrettably showed neither of them at the peak of their talent.

Breaking Away from MGM

By 1960, Elizabeth Taylor had been under contract to MGM for seventeen years. But the studio that once virtually dominated Hollywood had fallen on hard times. It made only a handful of movies each year, and could not afford either to raise its stars' salaries or to showcase them in lavish productions. Taylor's contract had nearly run out, and she had already accepted her role in *Cleopatra* from 20th Century-Fox, at a salary of $1 million. She assumed that MGM would allow her to make that movie before she fulfilled her contractual obligation to them with one final picture.

MGM execs were not as obliging as Taylor had hoped. They had cast her as Gloria Wandrous in *Butterfield 8*, and they didn't want to delay the production. They were even less willing to cast another actress in the role of the call girl, at a time when the publicity surrounding Taylor's marriage to Eddie Fisher was at its height. Despite the best efforts of batteries of lawyers hired by Taylor, she was forced to make the MGM movie; otherwise, the studio would have put her on suspension and prevented any other studio from hiring her for two years.

Or course, the story had a happy ending. In return for her acquiescence, Taylor received her first Oscar for her portrayal of Gloria.

Michelle Breeze

Michelle Breeze has been Elizabeth Taylor's stand-in since 1971. Hollywood insiders say "she looks more like Liz than Liz does." Interestingly, she also looks like the late Natalie Wood, who often asked Breeze to work with her. Breeze, committed to Elizabeth, had to turn her down—until a period came when Elizabeth made few movies and Breeze was able to act as Wood's stand-in on *Brainstorm*, which turned out to be the star's last picture before her accidental drowning.

The British Film Award

In 1966, when *Who's Afraid of Virginia Woolf?* was released, Elizabeth Taylor was the winner of the British Film Academy award for Best Actress of the Year.

Broken Finger

In 1973, while Elizabeth Taylor was filming *Night Watch* in London, she fell off a platform and broke a finger. It was badly set and later had to be rebroken to repair the damage.

Carol Burnett

In 1983, Elizabeth Taylor costarred with Carol Burnett in the TV movie, *Between Friends*. Burnett told reporters that when she was growing up in Los Angeles, she used to stand in the crowd outside movie premiers to watch the stars arrive, and that the star she remembered most vividly was the young Elizabeth Taylor, so carefully dressed and poised and beautiful. Taylor in her turn confessed to a great admiration for Burnett's comedic talents. She had been a regular viewer of Burnett's TV show.

With a beginning like that, it is no surprise that the two became the best of friends. They discovered they had a number of things in common: a hatred of tabloid newspapers, a devotion to Rock Hudson, a natural tendency to mother their friends, and a rabid interest in soap operas. On the set, they spent their lunch hours glued to the TV set. "I've watched *All My Children* for ages," explained Burnett, "and Liz likes *One Life to Live* and *General Hospital*. I'd fill her in on the background, and she'd fill me in, so we'd know what was going on." They also shared a particular brand of raucous humor that found expression on location—as, for example, when Carol Burnett broke Taylor up by suddenly flipping the elegant fur coat she wore in one scene to reveal a pair of long johns stenciled with the words "Blue Moon."

In a more serious vein, Burnett paid tribute to Taylor's skills as an actress. "I was eager to do a movie with Elizabeth. I always like to play tennis with a better tennis player. Because that's how I learn. And here was a woman who grew up in film. She knows the camera and her way around a character and a set as well as the best in the business."

The two women remain the best of friends, and agree they would love to find another opportunity to work together. Said Burnett, "There are people you can know for years without feeling close, and then people you meet and feel you know at once. Elizabeth and I talked on the phone a few years ago, when she was fund-raising for Wolf Trap. I had a premonition then: This is a lady I could have as a friend."

Jessica Burton

Jessica Burton is the younger daughter of Richard Burton and his first wife, Sybil. Jessica was born severely retarded, and her future was always a source of great concern to Richard Burton. In 1962, she was sent to a private institution for the handicapped in Pennsylvania, where she still lives.

Jessica was one of the reasons it was so difficult for Richard Burton to decide to leave his family for Elizabeth Taylor. Taylor, in her turn, understood his guilt and for a time broke off the affair so he could return to the family that needed him.

Kate Burton

Katherine Burton, named after the heroine of *The Taming of the Shrew* but always called Kate, is the daughter of Richard Burton and his first wife, Sybil, born in Switzerland in September 1957. After her parents' divorce, she lived with her mother and stepfather, Jordan Christopher, in New York City. Kate told an interviewer for *Us*, "I've had a relatively normal childhood—mostly because I didn't live with my father." In 1984, she commented, "I'm so much my mother's child, but I love, understand, and feel very close to my father." She also established a good relationship with her new stepmother. "She's a caring person, that's one of her problems. She doesn't act like a star up close, she's very approachable. I love Elizabeth, I always have." She still sees Taylor frequently, and Taylor's four children as well.

Kate was educated at the United Nations International School and Brown University. She decided to become an actress and attended Yale Drama School. Her father was initially disapproving. "That was the big showdown," she recalled. But Burton eventually became a wholehearted supporter of his daughter's career.

Her first New York stage appearance came in 1982, with a part in Broadway revival of Noel Coward's play, *Present Laughter*. Then she had the title role in Eva LeGallienne's *Alice in Wonderland*, which was later taped as a special for PBS-TV, for which Richard Burton made a cameo appearance as the White Knight. Near the end of her father's life, Kate again worked professionally with him, when she appeared in the TV miniseries *Ellis Island* as the daughter of a rich senator; Richard Burton agreed to take the role of her father. He summed up the characters pithily: "You're playing a person with no humor and I'm playing a pompous ass." Kate subsequently played Pegeen Mike in *Playboy of the Western World* and J.J. in the musical *Doonesbury*, based on the cartoon characters of Garry Trudeau. Her most recent stage appearance was her 1989 role as Isabella in the Lincoln Center production of *Measure for Measure*.

In 1987, Kate married Michael Ritchie, a Broadway stage manager, whom she had met during the production of *Present Laughter*. In 1988, they had a son, Morgan.

Maria Burton

Elizabeth Taylor first saw her future adopted daughter Maria in 1960, in Germany. Taylor never forgot her first sight of the girl. "She was covered with abscesses, suffering from malnutrition, and had a crippled hip . . . She did not cry, she did not laugh . . . She had very dark eyes and she watched everything." Taylor had wanted to give new husband Eddie Fisher a child, but after a tubal ligation she was no longer able to conceive; thus the idea of adoption arose. But American adoption agencies were opposed to the placement of children with entertainers, especially those with no permanent address. So Taylor's friend, actress Maria Schell, looked for a child in her native Germany. She found a baby who had been born with a crippling hip deformity, to a poor family, the Heisigs, who could not afford the multiple operations that would be necessary to correct the girl's problem. Elizabeth and Eddie adopted the baby in late 1961 and named her after Maria. As part of the divorce agreement that ended the Taylor–Fisher marriage, Eddie agreed to allow Taylor's fourth husband Richard Burton to adopt Maria and give her his name.

Maria underwent a series of operations to correct her hip deformity, and then was privately tutored to catch up on the education she had missed while ill. In 1965, Maria's parents turned up at the Burtons' hotel in Paris, protesting what they said was the immoral conduct of Taylor and Burton. Elizabeth's lawyers made a hefty settlement, and no more was heard on the subject. Maria spent much of her childhood in Switzerland, where she attended the International School in Geneva.

Maria modeled before she retired to marriage and motherhood. She married agent Steve Carson, with Phoenix Artists, in February, 1982, and the couple has one daughter, Eliza, born in late 1982. The Carsons live in New York City.

Philip Burton

Philip Burton was a high-school teacher in Port Talbot, Wales, in the 1940s. Himself Welsh-born, Burton was a graduate of the University of Wales, had been a writer for the BBC, and had done some directing in small theaters. One of his students was young Richard Jenkins, the son of a coal miner in nearby Pontrhydfen. Burton took the young man under his wing, taught him to appreciate great literature, and helped him acquire a standard British accent (the Jenkins family spoke nothing but Welsh at home). In order to help Richard enter Oxford for a term, he made the boy his legal ward and invited him into his home. Thereafter Richard officially changed his name to Richard Burton as a mark of his gratitude. The actor later said in tribute to Philip Burton, "His impact on me was decisive but not immediate. It was cumulative, not a blinding moment of revelation. I felt with him that my mind broadened with every step I took."

The close relationship between the two men was impaired for a time when Richard left his wife Sybil to live with Elizabeth Taylor: Philip Burton disapproved of the scandal and sympathized with Sybil's plight. The rift was healed by Elizabeth Taylor, who telephoned Philip Burton to tell him how much Richard missed him, and to ask him to come to Burton's opening on Broadway in *Hamlet* in 1964. Burton later moved to the United States and lived in retirement for many years in Key West, Florida.

Tony Palmer, maker of a documentary film about Burton's life, arrived at the conclusion that the role Philip Burton played in Richard's life damaged the younger man. "I believe," said Palmer, "that the source of his tragedy was that he was given away, effectively sold, by his father when he was fourteen. Philip Burton, who adopted him and gave him his surname, was and is a kind, generous, noble man. No praise can be too high for what he managed to do with this rather strange lad. But I am certain that the fact that he was given away left Richard with a deep emotional scar which he spent most of his life trying to heal."

Richard Burton

Actor Richard Burton, Elizabeth Taylor's fifth husband, was born Richard Walter Jenkins in Pontrhydfen (the name means "the bridge across the valley") Wales, on November 10, 1925. According to local legend, he was a twelve-pound baby. Richard's father, also named Richard, was a hard-drinking coal miner who could not afford to raise all of his thirteen children after his wife Edith Maude Thomas, a former barmaid, died five days after the birth of the couple's last child, in 1927. Richard, the second youngest, was sent by "Daddy Ni" to live with an older married sister in nearby Port Talbot. After World War II military service in the Royal Air Force, he began to establish himself as one of the great stage actors of his day. Richard Burton started making films in England in the late 1940s and made his first Hollywood movie, *My Cousin Rachel*, in 1952. Other early films included *The Robe* (1953), *The Rains of Ranchipur* (1955), *Alexander the Great* (1955), and *Bitter Victory* (1958).

20th Century-Fox asked Richard Burton to play Mark Antony in *Cleopatra* after his Broadway triumph in the role of King Arthur in *Camelot*, for which he won the 1961 Tony for Best Actor in a Musical. Ironically, Burton was the studio's second choice for the role. They had initially signed Stephen Boyd for the part, but he had to drop out during the delay caused by Elizabeth Taylor's near-fatal illness. Thus fate brought Taylor and Burton together on the set in Rome, and a torrid romance was immediately kindled.

At the time, Richard was married to his Welsh-born wife of twelve years, Sybil Williams, with whom he had two daughters, Kate and Jessica. Although he was known for his habit of having affairs with his leading ladies, including Jean Simmons and Claire Bloom, Richard had always eventually returned to Sybil and the children. But the romance with Taylor was so all-consuming that he eventually asked Sybil for a divorce.

As soon as Elizabeth Taylor obtained her own divorce from Eddie Fisher, on March 6, 1964, the press began to watch for signs of wedding plans. Burton was then appearing in a stage production of *Hamlet* in Toronto, and

Taylor was with him. She told reporters that they would take their time to plan a traditional Jewish wedding, but instead they chartered a plane and flew to Montreal for a private ceremony. It was conducted in a suite in the Ritz-Carlton Hotel, by a Unitarian minister.

Burton subsequently appeared in a number of movies costarring his wife Elizabeth Taylor. They included *The V.I.P.s* (1963), *The Sandpiper* (1965), *Who's Afraid of Virginia Woolf?* (1966), *The Taming of the Shrew* (1967), *The Comedians* (1967), and *Boom!* (1968). His solo credits during the years of their marriage included excellent performances in *The Night of the Iguana* (1964), and *The Spy Who Came in from the Cold* (1965). He was nominated for an Academy Award seven times: *My Cousin Rachel* (1952, for Best Supporting Actor), *The Robe* (1953), *Becket* (1964), *The Spy Who Came in from the Cold* (1965), *Who's Afraid of Virginia Woolf?* (1966), *Anne of the Thousand Days* (1969), and *Equus* (1977). He was never a winner. His last loss was particularly painful: he joyfully started to get out of his seat when the winner was announced as "Richard . . . Dreyfuss." In the last years of his life, Burton appeared in a series of undistinguished vehicles. One of the bright spots for him was a cameo role in the TV miniseries *Ellis Island*, playing the senator father of his own actress daughter, Kate Burton.

Richard Burton and Elizabeth Taylor were divorced in June 1974, and remarried a little over a year later, on October 10, 1975. They separated again within months, and were divorced again in 1976. Burton promptly remarried. His third wife was Suzy Hunt. The marriage ended in divorce in 1982, and Burton was married again in 1983, to his fourth wife Sally Hay. The same year, he and Elizabeth Taylor were reunited professionally in the stage production of Noel Coward's *Private Lives*.

Richard Burton died of a cerebral hemorrhage on August 5, 1984. He was buried in the churchyard of a Protestant church in the Swiss village of Celigny, near Geneva. At his funeral, daughter Kate recited lines from the Dylan Thomas poem, "Do Not Go Gentle into That Good Night." Amid the many flowers on his coffin was a single red rose, without a message—sent by Elizabeth Taylor.

The Burtons' Film Grosses

According to one estimate, in the years between 1963 (when *Cleopatra* was released) and 1966, pictures that starred one or both of the Burtons grossed about $167 million.

Burton's First Remark to Taylor

Elizabeth Taylor has frequently told of meeting Richard Burton when he arrived in Rome to start filming *Cleopatra*. His first remark to her was not startlingly original: "Has anybody ever told you that you're a very pretty girl?" In a later interview, Burton claimed that this type of tried-and-true remark was one of the reasons he was so successful with the opposite sex, but at the time Taylor found it unbearably trite, and said so to a number of crew members on the set.

"The Bus Boy"

Some of those close to Elizabeth Taylor referred to her fourth husband, Eddie Fisher, as "The Bus Boy," a snide reference to his willingness to do anything he could to help his wife.

Butterfield 8

Elizabeth Taylor won her first Oscar for her performance in the 1960 MGM movie, *Butterfield 8*. Surely it was a result unexpected by either star or studio. The movie, based on a novel by John O'Hara that had been published twenty-five years earlier, focused on the life and death of a high-priced call girl, aptly named Gloria Wandrous. She makes the mistake of falling deeply in love with one of her clients (Laurence Harvey). Erroneously concluding that he will never divorce his wife (Dina Merrill), Gloria hops in her car and recklessly drives into a fatal crash. (In the book, she throws herself off a cruise ship.)

After the good scripts of *Cat on a Hot Tin Roof* and *Suddenly Last Summer*, Elizabeth Taylor found this melodrama badly written and exploitative. She complained bitterly about appearing in it, and did her best to persuade MGM to release her from her contractual obligation to take the assignment. But the studio wouldn't budge, and warned her that if she didn't cooperate she wouldn't be released to play 20th Century-Fox's Cleopatra, a role she badly wanted. Taylor finally acquiesced with bad grace, giving interviews throughout the movie's production that criticized its bad taste and shoddy script. "The role they want me to play is little better than a prostitute. Doing this picture gripes the hell out of me . . . It's too commercial, it's in bad taste. Everybody in it is crazy, mixed-up sick." It seemed that her only victory was in getting a part for husband Eddie Fisher as the piano player who was not a lover but a platonic friend—amateur psychologists could have a field day with *that* casting choice!

But when the Oscar nominations were announced that year, Elizabeth Taylor learned that she had won another victory; for the fourth year in a row, her name was on the list. Perhaps it was her resentment that helped her give an emotionally touching performance. Initially, few insiders expected her to win the coveted award for so slight a vehicle. Then, just as Academy members were casting their votes, Taylor got pneumonia and nearly died. It made people in Hollywood reflect on her career, and recognize the fact that she had indeed turned from a movie star into an actress. Barely recovered by the time of the ceremony, a frail Elizabeth Taylor joyfully accepted the golden statuette.

Whatever the motives of Academy members might have been, Taylor's performance in *Butterfield 8* was a competent one. *Variety* called her the picture's major asset, adding, "While the intensity and range of feeling that marked several of her more recent endeavors is slightly reduced in this effort, it is nonetheless a torrid, stinging overall portrayal with one or two brilliantly executed passages within." Paul Beckley spoke of Taylor's "crackling effect on the screen." In this movie, where she has to work against an unconvincing script, we can see just how far she has come in projecting a kind of passion and intensity, how she can dominate the screen even when the words she has to say are foolish or bathetic. Taylor may have gotten the Oscar for the wrong picture—certainly, the performances in *Cat on a Hot Tin Roof* and *Suddenly Last Summer* are more satisfying—but her acting deserved the recognition the Academy finally gave it. As time has passed, the movie's standing with critics and fans alike has increased. For example, in 1989, it was one of a short list of films sponsored by the magazine *New York Woman* in a series intended to depict the range of lives women in New York may live.

Byron House

The first school Elizabeth Taylor attended was the London private school, Byron House. She left in 1939, when her father Howard Taylor sent his wife and children to the safety of America on the eve of World War II.

— C —

Call Her Anything but Liz

If there's anything Elizabeth Taylor hates, it's being called "Liz."' You can call her "Tubby," as did her husband Richard Burton; or even "Chicken Fat," a pet name used by John Warner; and she will smile graciously. But "Liz"—the name used by the media in their pseudo-familiarity—makes her see red. Her friends bend over backward to insure that the dread syllable never leaves their mouths.

Callaway Went Thataway

Elizabeth Taylor appeared in a cameo role, as herself, in the 1951 movie, *Callaway Went Thataway*. It was a lighthearted MGM musical, starring Fred MacMurray and Dorothy McGuire as Hollywood promoters trying to revive the career of a faded Western star. One scene takes place on the MGM lot, where the cowboy actor (actually, Howard Keel playing a real cowboy who is masquerading as the actor, who is also played by Howard Keel, because the actor is AWOL at the critical moment—you get the drift of the plot) is introduced to real MGM stars. They included June Allyson, Esther Williams, Clark Gable, Dick Powell, and

Elizabeth Taylor. The fact that MGM execs asked Taylor to make a guest appearance in the movie was an index of their esteem for her star power.

Although this movie is special to Taylor fans because it is the only time she appeared on screen as Elizabeth Taylor, it seems to have vanished from circulation. Too bad, for it was a bright and funny vehicle for some of MGM's most reliable talents.

Camillo's

Camillo's was a restaurant in Manhattan that was a favorite place in the early 1950s for Elizabeth Taylor and friend Montgomery Clift to spend entire evenings, sitting at their table drinking and talking until everyone else had left and the owner was ready to lock up.

Campaigning for John Warner

At the time Elizabeth Taylor married John Warner, his ambition was to run for the Senate seat from Virginia that would be vacant in 1978. In this endeavor, Elizabeth Taylor proved to be a loyal and valuable assistant. She traveled to small towns on buses, she shook so many hands her own had broken blood vessels, she wore silly hats and even hairnets, and she kissed babies. She ate rubber chicken (and once nearly choked to death on a bone) and pizza and hamburgers and drank milkshakes. Of course, she always attracted crowds. And even though her past was controversial and her tastes and values were not those of the ordinary American citizen—and in fact, she wasn't even an American citizen anymore but had adopted British citizenship—Elizabeth

Taylor was warmly received. Most political observers agree that Warner could not have won the election without the help of his wife. He was sworn into office on January 3, 1979, with Taylor by his side.

Can't Sleep Alone

Immense publicity surrounded the romance of Elizabeth Taylor and Eddie Fisher, most of it hostile toward Taylor. One of the most damaging articles published at the time was written by gossip columnist Hedda Hopper. Hopper said she had talked to Taylor intimately, and quoted the star as defending the relationship with Fisher by saying, "What do you expect me to do, sleep alone?" Taylor later asserted that she "never said, or even thought" any such thing. Viewed from the vantage point of thirty years later, the remark has the ring of truth. But how foolish it was of Taylor to tell prudish Hedda Hooper the truth!

Elizabeth Diane Carson

Elizabeth Diane Carson is Elizabeth Taylor's granddaughter. Taylor's third grandchild was born on November 5, 1982, to her daughter Maria Burton and husband Steve Carson. The baby, called "Eliza," weighed eight pounds, ten and a half ounces. Ironically, she was born on the day that Taylor's divorce from John Warner became final.

The Cartier Diamond

The single most expensive piece of jewelry ever owned by Elizabeth Taylor was the sixty-nine-carat Cartier diamond. In 1969, Richard Burton paid $1,050,000 for this gift to his wife. The Cartier was a huge emerald-cut stone that had formerly belonged to the sister of Walter Annenberg, former U.S. Ambassador to Great Britain and close friend of Ronald and Nancy Reagan. Not content to stop there, Burton also bought his wife a $100,000 diamond necklace, from which to hang the Cartier diamond as a pendant.

Taylor had learned about the diamond when it was to be auctioned off by Parke-Bernet in New York, and her lawyer Aaron Frosch bid on it for her. But Cartier outbid Taylor, which made her depressed. So Burton went straight to the jewelers and purchased it from them. One of the terms of the sale was that the diamond, an inch long and about the same thickness, would be displayed in the window of Cartier's Fifth Avenue store before it went to Taylor.

Elizabeth Taylor put the diamond on the market in 1978, when she was married to John Warner, and sold it a year later. According to rumor, the star accepted a price considerably below her announced asking price of $4.5 million—$3 million is the figure generally given.

Casa Kimberley

Elizabeth Taylor and husband Richard Burton first discovered Puerto Vallarta, Mexico, when he went there to shoot *The Night of the Iguana*. Her former husband Michael Wilding, then Burton's Hollywood agent, had arranged for them to rent a four-story white stucco house there, called Casa Kimberley. They liked the Spanish-style hacienda, with its six guest bedrooms, huge terrace, and walled privacy so much they bought it for $40,000. They used it as a vacation home, to get away from the pressures of Hollywood. It was decorated with pre-Columbian artifacts that were the gift of the Mexican government to the superstars who gave the country so much publicity.

Casa Kimberley was originally two quaint old houses, standing high enough above town to afford a view of the blue waters of Banderas Bay, that together formed one large comfortable residence. According to Taylor's biographer Kitty Kelley, Burton had a bridge built between the two buildings, so he could retire to one when he was angry with Elizabeth. She responded by following him and knocking loudly on his door until he opened it and a reconciliation would take place. The couple called it their "bridge of love."

Cat on a Hot Tin Roof

Elizabeth Taylor has cited *Cat on a Hot Tin Roof* as the high point of her film career. It was her husband Mike Todd who convinced her to take the part of Maggie the Cat in 1958. According to producer Pandro Berman, "You had to go to Mike if you wanted anything. She was plastic in his hands. She had no thoughts of her own in those days." *Those days* came to a sudden end: Two weeks after the film started shooting, Todd was killed. Taylor believes she retreated into the character of Maggie the Cat as a way of dealing with her grief. "When I was Maggie was the only time I could function. The rest of the time I was a robot." When she returned to work several weeks after Todd's funeral, the stagehands—many of them men who had known Taylor since her childhood days at MGM—sent her a touching bouquet of violets to express their sympathy. Helen Rose, who designed Taylor's wardrobe for the film, quickly discovered that all the star's clothes would have to be altered, because grief had caused her to lose so much weight.

The screen version of Tennessee Williams's play costarred Paul Newman as Maggie's husband Brick, Burl Ives in the role of Big Daddy and Judith Anderson as Big Momma, with Jack Carson and Madeleine Sherwood as Brick's brother and fecund sister-in-law. MGM originally intended to shoot the movie in black and white, much to the distress of director Richard Brooks. It was Mike Todd who intervened, selling the producer and top studio execs on the need for color in a film that would surely be a major MGM release.

The focus of Williams's plot is the trouble between Brick and Maggie about having the child Big Daddy insists they produce if they are to inherit any of his money. Brick seems reluctant to perform his husbandly duties, in large part due to his homosexual inclinations (only vaguely hinted at in the film version). He drinks to forget the problem, and she becomes as jumpy as a cat on a hot tin roof. Taylor turned in a superb performance in the role of the distraught wife. She may have been helped by drawing on the experiences of her own past, in particular her marriage to Nicky Hilton—like Brick the son of a rich and powerful father, and also like Brick, given to ignoring her and forcing her to plead for his attention and affection. Or maybe we only look for these parallels because her acting is so good we can't believe it isn't "real."

Critics could compare Taylor to two previous Maggies, Barbara Bel Geddes on the New York stage and Kim Stanley in London. For the most part, they came down in favor of Liz. *Variety* said, "Elizabeth Taylor has a major credit with her portrayal of Maggie. The frustration and desires, both as a person and as a woman, the warmth and understanding she molds, the loveliness that is more than a well-turned nose—all these are part of a well-accented perceptive interpretation." *Time* said Taylor played with "surprising sureness," while Bosley Crowther called her "terrific as a panting, impatient wife, wanting the love of her husband as sincerely as she wants his inheritance." *Life* summed it up: "Elizabeth Taylor gives the best performance of her career as Maggie the Cat."

The positive critical judgment was echoed by members of the Motion Picture Academy, when they nominated Elizabeth Taylor for Best Actress. Although she lost to Susan Hayward for her performance in *I Want To Live* (a role Taylor had wanted to play), Elizabeth Taylor was still happy just to be on the list. In fact, *Cat on a Hot Tin Roof* failed to win a single Oscar, despite six nomimations.

Victor Cazalet

Victor Cazalet was a well-to-do Englishman, also a member of Parliament, who befriended the Taylor family when they moved to London in 1929. Cazalet, nicknamed "Teenie" in reference to his slight stature, was one of Howard Taylor's gallery customers, unusual because he was adding to the family collection rather than selling it. Another bond was the Christian Science Church, to which both the Taylors and Cazalet belonged. Cazalet was well connected: his sister Thelma was able to take Sara Taylor to the coronation of King George VI in 1936. Thelma later talked to writer Brenda Maddox about the Cazalet family's devotion to the Taylors. "Francis and Sara were absolute charmers. And these two lovely children would come dancing in! My mother and brother absolutely adored them. We all did. We took them straight in. They became a part of us." Victor Cazalet often invited the Taylors to visit his country house in Kent, called Great Swifts, and eventually lent them a cottage on the estate. They named it "Little Swallows" and spent most of their weekends there. Cazalet gave little Elizabeth her first pony. Elizabeth in turn often called Cazalet her godfather, which was not literally true, but it was certainly the case that the English bachelor acted the role in the Taylors' lives.

Sara Taylor always credited Victor Cazalet with helping Elizabeth recover from scarlet fever. She was very ill, running a high fever, and suffering from abscessed ears, when Cazalet came to visit. He held the little girl in his arms and talked to her about the power of God. According to Sara Taylor, "A wonderful sense of peace filled the room. I laid my head down on the side of the bed and went to sleep for the first time in three weeks. When I awakened, she was fast asleep! The fever had broken."

Cazalet enlisted in the Army at the outbreak of World War II and attained the rank of major. He was killed in a plane crash near Gibraltar in 1943, along with Polish General Sikorski. Members of his family remain among Elizabeth Taylor's close friends.

CBE

In 1970, Richard Burton was honored by Queen Elizabeth II with the title of Commander of the British Empire and invited to Buckingham Palace for the formal presentation. Although Burton had hoped for a knighthood like Laurence Olivier's, which would have entitled him and his wife to be called Sir Richard and Lady Burton, he was nevertheless thrilled to escort his wife (wearing an extremely becoming silver fox hat) and his sister Cissie to the ceremony at "Buck House." Thereafter, he was permitted to add the initials C.B.E. after his name.

Celebrating Maria's Adoption

Elizabeth Taylor and husband Eddie Fisher adopted a baby, whom they named Maria, late in 1961, while Taylor was in Rome filming *Cleopatra*. To help the couple celebrate the event, Taylor's costar Richard Burton and his wife Sybil threw a lavish party. It was only days later that Burton and Taylor began their affair.

Characters Played by Elizabeth Taylor in Her Movies

Among the memorable names of characters played by Elizabeth Taylor in her movies are:

- Helen of Troy *(Doctor Faustus)*
- Helen *(Jane Eyre)*
- Helen Ellsworth *(The Last Time I Saw Paris)*
- Gloria Twine *(There's One Born Every Minute)*
- Gloria Wandrous *(Butterfield 8)*
- Mary Skinner *(Life with Father)*

- Mary Belney *(The big Hangover)*
- Catherine Holly *(Suddenly Last Summer)*
- Katharina *(The Taming of the Shrew)*
- Martha *(Who's Afraid of Virginia Woolf?)*
- Martha Pineda *(The Comedians)*
- Leonora Penderton *(Reflections in a Golden Eye)*
- Leonora *(Secret Ceremony)*
- Elizabeth Taylor has also been Jimmie Jean Jackson, Lady Patricia, Velvet Brown, Anastacia Macaboy, Leslie Lynnton Benedict, Sissy Goforth, the Blue Fairy, and, of course, Cleopatra.

Chateau Ariel

During Elizabeth Taylor's marriage to Eddie Fisher, he bought her a chalet that they called Chateau Ariel, in Gstaad, Switzerland, for $350,000. Ownership allowed her to become a legal resident of Switzerland, a move that had tax advantages at a time she was earning high salaries for each movie. Later, Taylor and Richard Burton used this house as a retreat, a place to sleep, exercise, and diet before returning to the highly public world of the entertainment business. They kept no permanent staff there, and often did their own cooking and cleaning. Chateau Ariel has continued to be a favorite getaway spot for Elizabeth Taylor.

"Chicken Fat"

John Warner occasionally referred to his wife Elizabeth Taylor as "Chicken Fat."

Chicken Feathers and Tar

After her second wedding to Richard Burton, Elizabeth Taylor made public her feelings about the occasion in an article she wrote for *Ladies' Home Journal*: "We are stuck like chicken feathers to tar—for lovely always."

The Child in the Body of a Woman

In the painful period following her divorce from first husband Nicky Hilton in late 1950, Elizabeth Taylor explained some of her marital problems by saying she had the emotions of a child in the body of a woman. That quote was picked up worldwide and used to describe the star for at least twenty more years. Decades later, much to Taylor's irritation, some skeptic announced that Taylor herself never made the remark, that it was invented by her press agent. She threatened, "You want to meet whoever said that and give them a knuckle sandwich."

Chili from Chasen's

One of Elizabeth Taylor's favorite foods is the chili served at Chasen's restaurant in Hollywood. When the mood strikes her, she simply telephones Chasen's to order the chili—and has it flown to her, wherever she is.

Christian Science

Elizabeth Taylor's mother was a devout Christian Scientist, who believed that "divine love always has met and always will meet every human need." Before little Elizabeth went to auditions, her mother would hand her a Christian Science prayer book and tell her to think good thoughts.

Sybil Williams Burton Christopher

On February 5, 1949, Welsh actress Sybil Williams married Richard Burton at a registry office in London. They had met when Sybil was an extra on the set of Burton's first movie, and they were introduced by his mentor, Welsh actor and playwright Emlyn Williams (no relation to Sybil). Within months of their marriage, at Burton's request, Sybil (then just twenty) gave up her own career to help concentrate on his. She read Richard's scripts, bought his clothes, worried about his health when he drank too much. They had two children, Kate and Jessica, who was born retarded.

Sybil had been married to Richard Burton for more than twelve years when he met Elizabeth Taylor on the set of *Cleopatra*. Sybil told a close friend that she had noticed the strong attraction between the two almost immediately. "I suddenly looked at Rich and saw him looking at Elizabeth. It was the way he kept his eyes on her—and I thought: hello!" At first, Sybil chose the course of waiting it out. Burton had been involved with his leading ladies before, without any threat to the continuation of the marriage. But Sybil's position became less and less tenable, especially after Burton started to live openly with Taylor at London's Dorchester Hotel during the filming of *The V.I.P.s*, rather than at home with Sybil and the children in Hampstead. Although Sybil publicly stated that she expected to get Richard back—and when she did, he would be a much richer man, thanks to the publicity value of his affair with Taylor—in the end she bowed to the inevitable and gave her husband the divorce he sought, in Guadalajara, Mexico, on December 5, 1963, on the grounds that he had been "in the constant company of another woman." She retained custody of their daughters and received a settlement in excess of $1.5 million. Two years went by before Richard saw either of his daughters, and Sybil never saw or spoke to her ex-husband again.

After the divorce, Sybil moved to New York, where she became part of the glamourous Manhattan social scene and a celebrity in her own right. She was a coproducer and casting director of the Establishment Theater Company, on East Fifty-forth Street, and then turned the site into one of Manhattan's trendiest disco clubs, Arthur.

In 1965, Sybil married British rock star Jordan Christopher, twelve years her junior. He was a member of the Wild Ones, a group Sybil auditioned to appear at her disco. Sybil later admitted she was very anxious about the difference in their ages and their backgrounds. "What I kept saying to myself all the time was: 'Sybil, what *are* you doing, you a simple Welsh Methodist lass, with . . . rock and roll?'" But the marriage has endured. In the 1980s, they moved to southern California and became active as agents and producers; according to a 1989 interview, they are planning a return to New York in the near future. Sybil and Jordan have one daughter, Amy, born in 1968.

Cleaning up Liz's Language

From the time Elizabeth Taylor was a bobbysoxer, her salty language was notorious in Hollywood. MGM did its best to persuade her to speak like a young lady, without much success. It was not until she married Richard Burton that any progress was made, thanks to his efforts. On one notable occasion, Burton proudly told a reporter he had stopped his wife's use of profanity and turned to her for confirmation.

"Haven't I, darling?" Burton asked.

"You bet your ass," she answered.

Cleopatra

At the time of its release in 1963, *Cleopatra*, starring Elizabeth Taylor, was the most expensive movie ever made. It cost 20th Century-Fox about $40 million to bring the spectacle to the screen, a staggering sum that threatened to bankrupt the studio. Among other things, the budget included the building of a twenty-acre set for Cleopatra's palace, the hiring of 6,000 extras for Cleopatra's triumphant entry into Rome, and the creation of the $6,500 solid-gold dress Taylor wore for the occasion. Expenses also included an initial $1,000,000 salary for its star, Elizabeth Taylor, a sum that she forced Fox to double before the shooting was finished. Some of the budget incidentals are most amusing. For example, Fox had to defend itself against a lawsuit brought by the owner of elephants used in one of the scenes, because someone at the studio had described the elephants as "wild" after they charged the extras and destroyed the set.

Initially, the film was directed by Rouben Mamoulian. But he had trouble getting the mammoth production organized. Sets were being constructed and the script rewritten while the movie's star, Elizabeth Taylor, was in bed with a cold, then an abscessed tooth, followed by a possible case of meningitis. The studios outside London, where production began, were so cold that it was impossible for the cast to wear the costumes appropriate to sunny Rome and Egypt without looking pinched and blue. After one month of production, the studio had already spent $2 million. Then, in February of 1961, Elizabeth Taylor nearly died of pneumonia. Fox shut down production until she was able to carry on, despite a demand from the studio's insurance company that she be replaced. Fox executives stood firm—by this time, it was clear that only Taylor had the box-office appeal that could rescue the film from disaster and the studio from bankruptcy. The fact that Taylor won the Oscar that spring, for *Butterfield 8*, fortified their determination that Taylor must play the Queen of the Nile.

During the hiatus, Mamoulian was replaced by Joseph L. Mankiewicz, the Oscar-winning director of *A Letter to Three Wives* and *All About Eve*. Mankiewicz also won Academy

Awards for writing the scripts of those pictures, and *Cleopatra* was a project he was especially interested in writing as well as directing. He had several years earlier adapted Shakespeare's *Julius Caesar* for the screen, and had read a great deal of relevant history as part of his preparation. His intention was to go back to historical sources to draw authentic portraits of the three central characters, Cleopatra, Caesar, and Antony. As Foster Hirsch in his book on the films of Elizabeth Taylor has commented, the result of Mankiewicz's contributions to the script was that "Cleopatra, Caesar and Antony often sound like the bitchy actresses in *All About Eve*."

When filming first began, Taylor's costars were to have been Peter Finch in the role of Caesar and Stephen Boyd as Antony. (The studio's first choice for Antony had been Burt Lancaster, who was committed elsewhere.) But by the time Elizabeth Taylor was well enough to resume work, neither Finch nor Boyd was available. Rex Harrison and Richard Burton were signed in their stead. Production was moved to the warmer climate of Rome, in deference to Taylor's health, and work finally began in earnest.

Elizabeth Taylor and Richard Burton, each married to other people at the time, met on the *Cleopatra* set and began a passionate love affair. The publicity about their illicit romance overshadowed the movie itself, which proved a mixed blessing. The public was not disposed to take the movie seriously, but at least they were attracted to the theater to watch the real-life lovers on the screen.

One major obstacle to *Cleopatra*'s success with audiences was the length of the film. According to one report, its first rough cut was twenty-six hours long! Then the director cut it down to a five-hour version and told studio execs they should release two movies, one called *Caesar and Cleopatra*, the other called *Antony and Cleopatra*; the executives refused. Eventually the film was edited down to a final version that ran just over four hours. Chief victim of the compression was Richard Burton. Most of the scenes that illustrated the gradual disintegration of Antony's character were cut. As Elizabeth Taylor complained, "They cut the film so that all you see is him drunk and shouting all the time, and you never know what in his character led up to that."

Cleopatra was for the most part a critical disaster. Although some reviewers praised Rex Harrison's portrayal of Caesar, the general reaction to script and performances was negative. Elizabeth Taylor especially came under attack. She had never looked comfortable or secure in period pieces, and the role of the cunning ruler of Egypt was not really well suited to her screen persona. She could handle the spoiled, petulant, wheedling aspects of Cleopatra's character, but not the power of a reigning monarch. Taylor was unfavorably compared to actresses who had starred in earlier screen versions: Theda Bara, Claudette Colbert, and Vivien Leigh. She was also negatively compared to her costars, Rex Harrison and Richard Burton, two well-trained classical actors; even her accent seemed to offend many purists. The damage the picture did to Taylor's reputation as a serious actress was immense.

Only a few major reviewers were kind. One was Brendan Gill at *The New Yorker*. He called Taylor "less an actress than a great natural wonder, like Niagara or the Alps," and added, "It was right of the director to treat her as the thing she had become—the most famous woman of her time, and probably of all time, who, perfectly made up, her nakedness picked out in cloth of gold (and the camera never failing, from scene to scene, to make obeisance to that justly celebrated bosom) is set pacing from bed to bath and from Caesar to Mark Antony not as the embodiment of a dead ancient queen but as, quite literally, a living doll, at once so sexy and so modest that her historical predecessor, seeing her, might easily have died not from the sting of an asp but from the sting of envy." Bosley Crowther of *The New York Times* paid Taylor a backhanded compliment: "For me, her handsome bearing, her strongly imperious air, her power to convey a conviction of a woman in various states of love offset the distraction of her plumpness and the somewhat grating quality of her voice."

Most reviews ranged from polite carping to rank hostility. *Time* said, "The 'infinite variety' of the superb Egyptian is beyond her, and when she plays Cleopatra as a political animal she screeches like a ward heeler's wife at a block party." Stanley Kauffman opined, "Miss Taylor is a plump, young American matron in a number of Egyptian costumes and makeups. She need do no more than walk around the throne room to turn Alexandria into Beverly Hills." *The Monthly Film Bulletin*'s critic, John Peter Dyer, said, "Elizabeth Taylor, in the past an underrated actress, here proves herself vocally, emotionally and intellectually overparted to a disastrous degree." And *Cue* concluded, "Despite her great beauty, Miss Taylor simply does not possess the emotional range—in voice control or movement—to match consistently the professional perfection of [Rex Harrison and Richard Burton]."

Another major victim of *Cleopatra* was 20th Century-Fox. Before the picture was finished, the company's stockholders had fired the president, and his successor fired both the movie's producer, Walter Wanger, and its director, Joe Mankiewicz. He then had Fox's lawyers file suit against Elizabeth Taylor and Richard Burton for $50 million, claiming that their off-the-set conduct had damaged the film. The suit was finally settled with a payment from Taylor for about $2 million. She subsequently remarked that the film was "like a disease . . . an illness one had a very difficult time recuperating from." Although the studio teetered on the edge of bankruptcy, box-office receipts (and sales of foreign licenses) eventually proved adequate for a rescue.

Cleopatra Competition

When 20th Century-Fox first began to cast *Cleopatra*, they had a number of actresses in mind for the coveted role. Among the possibilities they considered:

- Brigitte Bardot
- Joan Collins
- Susan Hayward
- Audrey Hepburn
- Jennifer Jones
- Gina Lollobrigida
- Sophia Loren
- Dolores Michaels
- Marilyn Monroe
- Kim Novak

- Suzy Parker
- Millie Perkins

Eventually, all other actresses fell by the wayside and it was agreed that only Elizabeth Taylor could be the perfect Cleopatra.

The Cleopatra Contract

Producer Walter Wanger of 20th Century-Fox felt from the beginning that Elizabeth Taylor was the only star who could play the role of Cleopatra in the studio's planned epic. She had the Queen of the Nile's fatal beauty and imperious disposition—and the fact that the publicity about her marriage to Eddie Fisher was at fever pitch didn't hurt, either. Taylor initially asked for $1 million to make the movie, and Wanger (who incidentally was married to Joan Bennett, who had played Taylor's mother in *Father of the Bride*) agreed. Then she shrewdly increased her demands as the time of production drew near. She wanted $4,500 a week living expenses for herself and Eddie; a penthouse suite in London's luxurious Dorchester Hotel; a Rolls-Royce limousine to drive her back and forth to the set; her choice of hairdressers (Sidney Guilaroff) and costume designers. She also asked to have the movie filmed in Todd-AO, the process developed by her late husband Mike Todd, on which she would receive a royalty.

20th Century-Fox agreed to all Taylor's requests.

Cleopatra's Chair

In the spring of 1989, a designer named Vincent Jacquart began selling copies of the throne from which Elizabeth Taylor reigned over Egypt in the movie *Cleopatra*. Jacquart had bought the chair at a sale held by 20th Century-Fox and then produced a line-for-line copy. The price tag for the copy was $5,400.

Montgomery Clift

Montgomery Clift and Elizabeth Taylor became friends when they costarred in *A Place in the Sun*. Even before production began on the Paramount picture, the studio insisted that they go on a "date" to the premiere of Clift's latest movie, *The Heiress*. The actor was annoyed, the seventeen-year-old Taylor thrilled. She borrowed a dress and a little white mink stole from the MGM wardrobe to make a good impression on him, but it was actually her earthy curses that turned him into an instant friend.

Montgomery Clift was born in Omaha, Nebraska, in 1920; he had a twin sister, Roberta. His initial Broadway appearance came at fourteen, and his first big success was in the 1940 Robert Sherwood play, *There Shall Be No Night*. Clift's screen debut came in *The Search* (1948) and in the same year, he costarred with John Wayne in the Howard Hawks classic Western, *Red River*. He received an Oscar nomination for his performance in *A Place in the Sun*, but many consider that his best work came in *From Here to Eternity*, for which he also received a nomination but lost the Academy award to William Holden for *Stalag 17*.

According to a biography of Clift written by Robert LaGuardia, Taylor fell for Clift and pursued him on the set of *A Place in the Sun*, writing him gushing letters that went as far as proposing marriage. Clift's response was ambiguous. LaGuardia quotes Taylor as saying (years later), "For three days Monty played the ardent male with me and we became so close. But just as he'd overcome all of his inhibitions about making love, he would suddenly turn up on the set with some obvious young man that he had picked up. All I could do was sit by helplessly and watch as he threw this in my face." Shortly thereafter, she married Nicky Hilton.

In the early months of 1951, after her brief marriage to Hilton ended, Elizabeth Taylor again turned to Montgomery Clift. People who knew the two at the time have later revealed that it was obvious they were in love with one another and that Elizabeth Taylor hoped to persuade Montgomery Clift to marry her. He loved her in return, but knew that he was not a good candidate for marriage—partly because he loved his freedom and partly because he could not alter his homosexual preferences. Monty called Elizabeth his "twin," and indeed the two beautiful and famous young people did seem like two halves of a single soul. Eventually, the romance settled down into a long, intense friendship that was ended only by Clift's death in 1966.

Clift was always there for Elizabeth. He helped her through the pain of her divorce from Nicky Hilton, he took her out when she was pregnant with her first child, and he doted on young Michael, Jr., buying a special little chair and table for the boy to use when he came visiting Clift's apartment. During the time her marriage to Wilding was falling apart, Elizabeth and her two sons often stayed in Clift's New York duplex, and Monty held her in his arms to comfort her while he gave her glasses of soothing hot milk for her nerves.

In return, Elizabeth Taylor was a fiercely loyal friend to Clift. She helped him through the final stages of *Raintree County*, after his near-fatal car accident, and did all she could to make the filming of *Suddenly Last Summer* endurable to him, at a time when drugs and alcohol made him nearly nonfunctional. Thereafter, Clift became unemployable in Hollywood. The ravages of his addictions had made him look thin and ill and old, and producers all feared he would never be able to finish any movie that he started. Taylor wanted him for her costar in *Reflections in a Golden Eye*, and when Warner Brothers said they would not sign him because they couldn't get insurance on the production if he was in it, Taylor announced that she would personally put up the $1 million they needed. Clift biographer Patricia Bosworth quotes Clift as saying, "Elizabeth Taylor is the greatest friend. She keeps on trying to help—everybody else has deserted me." Clift was looking forward to working on the film and proving to Taylor that her confidence in him was justified.

Sadly, before shooting could begin, Montgomery Clift was found dead of a heart attack on the morning of July 22, 1966, a few months short of his forty-sixth birthday. Taylor told the press the next day, "I am so shocked I can barely accept it. I loved him. He was my brother—he was my dearest friend." She sent two huge bouquets of chrysanthemums to his funeral.

Clip in The Last Picture Show

In *The Last Picture Show*, the movie set in the 1950s that was directed by Peter Bogdanovich and based on a novel by Larry McMurtry, the high school kids in a small Texas town go to the movies to play out their own sexual fantasies. The film Bogdanovich used in the dating scene at the theater was *Father of the Bride*, starring Elizabeth Taylor at her most gorgeous. As critic Pauline Kael commented, "Looking at Elizabeth Taylor might well make anyone dissatisfied with his lot—she really *was* the most beautiful girl in the world."

Cocktails for Giant

In *Elizabeth Takes Off*, Elizabeth Taylor revealed that she and Rock Hudson invented a cocktail that they drank nightly while on location in Marfa, Texas, for the filming of *Giant*. It was made of vodka, Hershey's chocolate syrup, and Kahlua.

Art Cohn

Art Cohn was a journalist who began to write a biography of Mike Todd in 1957. Todd had agreed to cooperate, and Cohn had interviewed him numerous times. Cohn was planning to travel to New York on business in late March 1958, so when Todd called him and invited him to fly east on Todd's private plane, Art immediately agreed. He thought the trip would be a good opportunity for another interview, uninterrupted by the constantly ringing phone that was such a problem in Todd's office.

Art Cohn died in the same plane crash that killed Todd.

At the time, he had finished all but the last two chapters of his book; his wife Marta completed the work and turned it over to the publisher. In her epilogue, she wrote, "There is no doubt in my mind they had a rendezvous with Death in New Mexico on the 22nd of March, 1958. Nothing, nothing on this earth, could have kept them from that Appointment."

Collecting Art Deco

Elizabeth Taylor is fond of the style called Art Deco, popular in the 1930s, and has for a number of years been collecting Deco art and *objets*. For example, Taylor owns an original Erté drawing (given to her by Michael Caine) and a Deco belt buckle.

Collie Puppy

In the spring of 1989, at the ceremonies in which she received the Hope Award, Elizabeth Taylor was presented by her friend Charles Bronson with an eight-week-old collie puppy. Nestled in Taylor's arms, the puppy began to lick her bejeweled throat. The star cooed, "Oh, a girl after my own heart. She likes diamonds, rubies, and emeralds. We are going to get along *fine*."

The Comedians

In 1965 Elizabeth Taylor again made a movie costarring with husband Richard Burton, *The Comedians*. It was the chilling story of life in Haiti during the dictatorship of "Papa Doc" Duvalier, based on a novel by Graham Greene, who also wrote the screenplay. Taylor played the relatively small role of wife of an ambassador (Peter Ustinov), and Burton was the cynical hotelier with whom she has a long-standing affair. Taylor offered to take the part at a reduced salary, in order to be near her husband; the producers, who had originally wanted Anouk Aimee to play the ambassador's wife, found Taylor had made them an offer they couldn't refuse. The supporting cast was excellent, including such stars as Alec Guinness, Lillian Gish, James Earl Jones, and Cicely Tyson. The movie was shot on location in Dahomey, West Africa, since of course the Haitian government of Duvalier refused to cooperate.

But most critics were not impressed by the direction, and also found fault with the performances of both Taylor and Burton—perhaps because they felt the couple, cast once again as lovers, were endlessly playing themselves in their movies. *Newsweek* commented unkindly, "Aside from them, as if anything could be aside from them, *The Comedians* might have been a good film." Judith Crist complained that the movie was brought "to a dead halt by the Burtons' cinematic amours and maulings, which are becoming not only boring but slightly less esthetic (the years are taking their toll, as they do on all sex symbols, especially from the chin-line down)." *The Monthly Film Bulletin* characterized the Burtons as mooning "glumly, plumply, passionlessly through their romantic routine."

Conspirator

In 1949, Elizabeth Taylor costarred with Robert Taylor in *Conspirator*, a melodrama of little distinction that was shot on location in England. Her role was that of a young American woman who visits London, falls in love with a British officer and marries him. She then discovers that her new husband is a Communist traitor, and when he knows that *she* knows, he becomes so desperate he even considers killing her. In the end, he proves to be a British gentleman after all: He does the honorable thing and takes his own life.

The movie is notable chiefly because it was the first time

Elizabeth Taylor played a fully adult role. At seventeen, she certainly looked the part of the young wife. According to costar Robert Taylor, she also acted the part. "They told her to kiss, and she kissed!" he later recalled. "The only thing I had to teach her was to powder down her lips."

As its plot indicates, *Conspirator* was not the romantic romp in which MGM typically cast its young stars. The assignment was intended to give Elizabeth Taylor a chance to grow as an actress, but the script was weak and trite, and costar Robert Taylor seemed wooden and dull as the villain. *The New York Herald Tribune* dismissed the movie by saying, "An attempt to make capital of a topical theme has failed dismally on the screen. The hero is handsome and the heroine is pretty. The script merely serves as a background for another screen romance." A few critics felt Elizabeth had done well in a difficult assignment—*Variety*, for example, said she was given "a big opportunity for an emotional and romantic lead and comes out with flying colors"—but most reviews were negative. Perhaps the most valuable aspect of the role was the fact that at seventeen Elizabeth Taylor was able to play such an adult role believably.

A Consummate Movie Actress

Most Hollywood insiders agree that Elizabeth Taylor is one of the industry's most accomplished screen actresses. One reason, of course, is that fabulous face, which the camera loves from every angle and at any distance. Taylor's years of experience before the cameras also help, and she seems to know how to get the most out of the slightest change of expression, as the movie close-up demands. Richard Burton freely acknowledged that he had learned much about the craft of acting for the camera from his wife. When they first worked together, in *Cleopatra*, he was uneasy because he thought she was underplaying their scenes together. But when he saw the rushes, he realized that she had learned from such economy that she could project intense feeling through changes of expression that were nearly imperceptible in real life but showed up dramatically on the screen, where her face was so magnified. One veteran cinematographer, Harold Salemson, who worked with Taylor on *Suddenly Last Summer*, talked about her professionalism. "She knows how to play to the camera. She will blink on the same syllable every time. She will do each scene letter perfect, and she will do it exactly the same way each time for hours on end. Every one of her takes match."

Conversion to Judaism

After Elizabeth Taylor married Mike Todd in 1957, in a civil ceremony, she expressed an interest in studying his religion, Judasim. She began to study it seriously in the sorrowful days after Todd's death, under the tutelage of Rabbi Max Nussbaum. The rabbi later said of her, "She was a good pupil. She has a good understanding of Jewish life and has read extensively in Jewish history. She is very intelligent."

In March 1959, about a year after Todd's death, Elizabeth Taylor went through the conversion ceremony. The solemn ritual took place at Temple Israel in Hollywood, under the supervision of Rabbi Nussbaum. After answering questions about the Jewish faith, Elizabeth pledged her loyalty in a vow that ended, "Hear, O Israel: the Lord our God, the Lord is One." Talking to reporters afterward, she said, "This is something I've wanted to do for a long time. I felt that it should bring me happiness and fulfillment. It has nothing to do with my marriage plans."

Several months later, Elizabeth Taylor married her fourth husband, Eddie Fisher, in a Jewish ceremony. At about the same time, she donated $100,000 to the state of Israel. Although her three subsequent marriages—two to Richard Burton and one to John Warner—were not Jewish ceremonies, Taylor has remained a staunch supporter of the nation of Israel, donating her time to fund-raising efforts and giving her own money to Israeli causes as well.

County Wicklow

During Elizabeth Taylor's marriage to Richard Burton, the couple owned a farmhouse on ten acres of rich pasturage in Ireland's County Wicklow. They used it to breed horses.

The Courage of Lassie

In 1946, Elizabeth Taylor, who had appeared in the first Lassie movie, *Lassie Come Home*, starred in *The Courage of Lassie*. In fact, the only connection the second movie had to Lassie was its title. It was actually a story about a dog named Bill whose adventures included enlisting in the army and fighting in Japan. Taylor played the young girl who adopts Bill when he is an abandoned puppy and raises him, and then welcomes him back from the war, even though he seems to have turned mean and vicious. She pleads for Bill's life in court, assuring the judge he is just another shell-shocked vet. Of course, she wins the case, and soon her love and care nurse Bill back to his old happy self.

This postwar movie had several other titles before someone had the bright idea of taking the name of Lassie in vain (MGM had already turned out one popular sequel to the first movie, starring Peter Lawford as the grown-up version of the boy played by Roddy McDowall in the original). Audiences must have been quite confused about the Lassie connection. The reviewers certainly were, some referring to the star of the movie as Lassie and others as Bill. Whatever the questions about the dog's name, there was no question about its being the star of the movie; nearly one-fourth of the picture was over before any human appeared on the screen.

The Courage of Lassie was clearly one of MGM's B movies, but the reviews were surprisingly kind. *The New York Times* critic said, "Elizabeth Taylor is refreshingly natural as Lassie's devoted owner," while the *New York Daily News* pronounced, "Elizabeth Taylor, very beautiful and charmingly sincere, has the leading role as Bill's devoted mistress." Alton Cook, writing in the *World Telegram*, voiced a slight complaint: "Young Miss Taylor does a pleasant enough job, although her dialogue is limited to endless cries of 'Oh, Bill!' " One curmudgeon, writing for *The New York Herald Tribune*, claimed that "Lassie walks off with all the acting honors," but for the most part, reviewers considered that Taylor had acquitted herself well.

A point of minor interest about the movie for Taylor fans is that during production she persuaded MGM to film a scene where she plays with her pet chipmunk Nibbles, about whom she had just written a book. Alas, the scene was edited before the movie was released, putting an end to Nibbles's theatrical career.

A Cowboys Fan

Elizabeth Taylor is a good friend of Jerry Jones, the owner of the Dallas Cowboys football team. In the fall of 1989, she attended a game in Dallas as Jones's guest, and went down on the field with him for the opening coin toss. Taylor met the referee, Pat Haggerty, and then called heads as he tossed the coin. She was interrupted by a Washington player complaining to the referee that Washington, as the visitors, had the right to call the toss. The embarrassed Haggerty told Taylor, "You've got me all shook up."

Crowds Outside the Theater

In 1964, Richard Burton played the role of Hamlet in a Broadway production of the Shakespeare classic. Every night after the performance, Elizabeth Taylor arrived in a limousine to pick up her husband at the theater named after another famous show-business couple, the Lunt-Fontanne, on West Forty-sixth Street. Crowds numbering about 5,000 gathered there at eleven o'clock every evening, just to watch Elizabeth dash out of the limo to the stage door and back again on Richard's arm.

Cruise on the Borrowed Yacht

In the fall of 1989, Elizabeth Taylor borrowed a yacht from producer Dodi Fayed for a planned cruise of the Mediterranean, accompanied by Larry Fortensky. There were reports that she had packed a wedding gown designed by Yves St. Laurent, fanning the rumors of a marriage to her current beau. Yet Taylor ended up in Morocco, acting as hostess at Malcolm Forbes's birthday party, while Fortensky returned alone to California. If the star did pack a wedding dress, it returned to California still in its tissue paper.

George Cukor

George Cukor directed Elizabeth Taylor in *The Blue Bird* and was impressed by her talent and professionalism. The man who directed such film stars as Greta Garbo, Katharine Hepburn, and Judy Holliday said of Taylor, "She's capable of enormous concentration. Also, she's a very accomplished actress; she knows what she's doing . . . she's really a very gifted actress and she tries all the time."

George Cukor was born in 1899 and started his professional career on Broadway. In 1929 he went to Hollywood, where he acquired the reputation of being a "woman's director." Among his best-known films are *Camille*, *The Women*, *The Philadelphia Story*, and *A Star Is Born*. In 1964, he won the Oscar for his direction of *My Fair Lady*. Cukor died in 1983.

Cynthia

Cynthia, starring fifteen-year-old Elizabeth Taylor, was released in 1947. It became a sentimental favorite, especially with servicemen, who wrote thousands of letters to its star. She played the role of an ailing and overprotected young girl who fights to have a normal life and eventually achieves it. As several critics noted, the theme moved the film closer to tragedy than comedy, and certainly set it apart from the run-of-the-mill high school and college movies popular at the time. Taylor, the teenager with the fully adult face, was ideally cast as the frail but determined heroine. Her parents were played by George Murphy and Mary Astor, and S.Z. Sakall was the kindly old music teacher who helps her believe she has the strength she needs to overcome the obstacles of her ill health.

According to Mary Astor's amusing memories of her acting career, *Cynthia* was planned as a B movie—although as Astor put it, "Metro never stinted on their B-type movies." As an example, she cited the apron she wore in one scene set in the family kitchen. "Just the ordinary bib-type checked apron with a pocket on it and rickrack around the borders," explained Astor. "The pocket was appliqued, and the rick-rack was handstitched. At so much a yard, and so many hours of hand work by the union wardrobe seamstresses—you figure it out." And, Astor added, "Of course, there was a duplicate also, in case I spilled ketchup or something on it." This little detail sheds light on the vast sums generated—and spent—in the heyday of the movie studio.

In the final analysis, *Cynthia* will always be best remembered as the movie in which Elizabeth Taylor received her first screen kiss. The kisser was actor James Lydon, previously the star of the *Henry Aldrich* series when it moved from radio to the movies. MGM had originally intended to capitalize on the event by calling the movie *First Kiss*, but in the end adopted the blander *Cynthia*, although they did use "Her First Kiss" as a promotional tag. Taylor later said that she was very anxious about filming that scene, apparently fearing she would be awkward or inadequate. It was hardly a passionate moment, but that first sweet kiss, like the movie in which it occurred, did have a certain youthful charm.

Her first screen kiss put teenaged Elizabeth Taylor on the cover of *Life* for the first—but definitely not the last—time. For a mere B movie, *Cynthia* got a lot of attention. *Variety* praised her performance: "Miss Taylor breathes plenty of life into the title role as a sheltered young girl who has never had a date or other fun generally accepted as a matter of fact by teen-agers." Howard Barnes opined, "Miss Taylor does a brilliant job with the title role. In vivid contrast to Hollywood's general conception of the bobby-soxer, she plays an unwilling invalid with grave charm. The scenes in which she has her first taste of the rich full life are interpreted with subtle authority." Bosley Crowther in *The New York Times* said, "Played by Elizabeth Taylor in a dewy-eyed, fluttery style, little Cynthia will chew her way softly, like a moth, into susceptible hearts."

-D-

"Daddy Ni"

Richard Burton's father was called by his children "Daddy Ni." As an adult, Burton displayed an enormous ambivalence toward his father, an unemployed coal miner who first sent Richard to live with an older sister and then agreed to let another man become the boy's guardian. In some interviews, he spoke of his mentor, Philip Burton, as his only father; at other times, he seemed to view his father with affection and even admiration. Daddy Ni was never impressed by Richard's fame and wealth, but he did seem proud—and perhaps slightly envious—of the fact that Richard had won so beautiful a woman as Elizabeth Taylor.

Daisy

Daisy was a gift to Elizabeth Taylor from English actor Sir John Gielgud. She was a black and white Shih Tsu, and she later had a puppy that Taylor kept, naming it Papillon. According to journalist Liz Smith, "Their only function in life is to look up adoringly at Elizabeth."

Vic Damone

Before Elizabeth Taylor met her first husband Nicky Hilton, she dated singer Vic Damone.

Dancing for the Royal Family

At the age of three, Elizabeth Taylor appeared in a short dance program before the British royal family. The two golden-haired princesses, Elizabeth and Margaret, were fellow students at Madame Vacani's Dance School, and a recital had been arranged for their parents, the then Duke and Duchess of York. Taylor, costumed as a butterfly, did not leave the stage with the rest of the beginner's group, but stood alone to take an extra curtain call. She later said, "It was a marvelous feeling on that stage—the isolation, the hugeness, the feeling of space and no end to space."

Daniels and Demerol

Elizabeth Taylor told reporters in 1987 that she was sure she would have died had she not entered the Betty Ford Center to get help for her addictions, citing Jack Daniels bourbon and the prescription drug Demerol as the biggest threats to her life. "I was drinking Jack Daniels and soda along with Demerol, and of course I was higher than a kite."

Peter Darmanin

Peter Darmanin was an advertising executive from Malta who had a brief fling with Elizabeth Taylor in the winter of 1975–76. He told reporters that they met in a hotel bar in Gstaad, Switzerland. "I felt a pair of devastating eyes staring at me as I turned around," he recalled. "It was Elizabeth Taylor. She told me she was very happy to see me." Taylor was alone because Richard Burton, whom she had remarried only months earlier, had gone to New York without her. The meeting ended with Darmanin staying at Taylor's house for weeks of skiing. When the ski season was over, so was the romance. So, of course, was Taylor's second marriage to Richard Burton.

A Date with Judy

In 1948, Elizabeth Taylor costarred in a colorful musical typical of MGM's best workmanship, *A Date with Judy*. Based on the radio series of the same name, the movie was an amusing but illogical confection that starred young singer Jane Powell in the title role, Wallace Beery as her father, Robert Stack as the older man she thinks she's in love with, and Scotty Beckett as the boy she eventually recognizes as the right one for her. Elizabeth Taylor played Judy's best friend, the sophisticated and spoiled daughter of the town's rich banker (Leon Ames), who criticizes her father for only being interested in the price of AT&T stock and snatches Robert Stack away right under Jane Powell's nose. The cast also included Xavier Cugat as the leader of the band that plays for the school dances, and Carmen Miranda as the band's singer, stealing scenes with her brassy musical numbers and her wonderfully outrageous costumes.

A Date with Judy was the first time Elizabeth Taylor played a young woman on the screen; her character is a younger and (as yet) more innocent version of Angela Vickers, the spoiled and dangerous heroine of *A Place in the Sun*. Previous roles, even when they had some element of romance, characterized Taylor as a *winning child* rather than an emotionally mature female. Perhaps that is why so many people believe Robert Stack gave Taylor her first screen kiss (although it was really James Lydon in *Cynthia*, released the previous year). The impact of her scenes with Stack can be judged from the comment of reviewer Otis Guernsey, Jr. "The big surprise in *A Date with Judy* is Elizabeth Taylor as the petulant dark-eyed banker's daughter. The erstwhile child star of *National Velvet* and other films has been touched by Metro's magic wand and turned into a real, 14-carat, 100-proof siren with a whole new career opening in front of her. Judging from this picture, Hedy Lamarr had better watch out, with Elizabeth Taylor coming along." *Variety* said, "Elizabeth Taylor makes a talented appearance. Her breathtaking beauty is complimented by the Technicolor lensing." Critic Alexander Williams said, "The surprise of *A Date with Judy* is Miss Taylor, who has turned into a ravishing beauty."

One amusing index of Elizabeth Taylor's success in the movie was that she immediately received 1,065 invitations from college boys to be their date to the prom!

David Di Donatello Award

In 1972, Elizabeth Taylor won the David Di Donatello award, Italy's version of the Oscar, for her performance in *Hammersmith Is Out* Husband Richard Burton won the Best Actor award for his role in the same film.

Glenn Davis

Glenn Davis was a tall, handsome sports hero newly graduated from West Point when he was introduced to Elizabeth Taylor in 1948 by an MGM publicist trying to arrange a date for the teenaged star. Davis has been co-captain of the Army football team, while setting records for yardage as a halfback that stood for many years. An all-around athlete, he was also on West Point's basketball and baseball teams.

At the time he met Taylor, Davis was an army officer about to be sent to Korea, but he was able to stay in California for most of the summer in 1948, and Elizabeth was sure she was in love. Davis later emphasized that their conduct was always prim and proper, and the sixteen-year-old Liz was probably too young for genuine passion. But when Glenn went to Korea, she promised to "wait forever," and wore his gold All-American football around her neck as a token that they were engaged: "I love Glenn and want to be with him."

Davis returned six months later, bringing her a pearl necklace as a present for her seventeenth birthday, and an engagement ring he planned to give her soon thereafter. But to his consternation, Taylor seemed more interested in wealthy Floridian Bill Pawley, who threw Davis a "Welcome Home" party as a ploy in his own pursuit of the lovely young star. Glenn escorted Elizabeth to the 1949 Academy Awards, but within a few weeks, he became discouraged in his pursuit. *Time* summed it up in the magazine's inimitable style: "Suddenly it was all over and Glenn was gone, deftly recovering his fumbled gold football." Taylor kept the pearl necklace he had given her, which somehow ended up in her parents' estate and was willed to her daughter Liza Todd. In 1951, Glenn Davis married actress Terry Moore, but the couple was divorced one year later. He remarried and went into business in Texas, later moving back to southern California.

James Dean

James Dean was Elizabeth Taylor's magnetic costar in *Giant*, the last film he ever made. The two became friends on the set, and Taylor was an outspoken admirer of Dean's acting talent.

The star who was to become a symbol of the 1950s was born James Byron (after the Romantic poet) Dean in Marion, Indiana in 1931. After a midwestern childhood that was shadowed by the death of his mother when he was nine, Dean studied for a year at UCLA and then went to New York to try for a career as a stage actor. After some critical successes in supporting roles on Broadway, he was voted the Most Promising Newcomer of 1953. He then met director Elia Kazan and was signed to the movie role of the rebellious Cal in *East of Eden*. That single screen performance was all it took to make James Dean a film star of the first magnitude.

Giant was shot in early 1955. Director George Stevens said of Dean as a screen presence, "He is what the young people believe themselves to be." Dean's work on the film was finished before Taylor's; on his last day on the set, she gave him a tiny Siamese kitten as a farewell gift. Four days later, Dean died in the crash of his silver Porsche Spyder in Paso Robles, California. His legend began to evolve almost instantaneously—and by the time *Giant* was released at the end of the year, the drama of his short life and untimely death threatened to swamp all publicity about the movie itself. Dean was nominated posthumously for an Oscar for his performance in the role of ranch hand-turned-millionaire Jett Rink, but did not win the coveted award.

Elizabeth Taylor was strongly affected by her costar's death. "He was so young, so full of life," she said—about the actor who was a year older than she was. Taylor found herself unable to stop sobbing as she worked to complete her own scenes in *Giant*. George Stevens tried to push her to complete the film, with the result that she collapsed and had to be rushed to the hospital, for what turned out to be a two-week stay. Thus Taylor didn't attend Dean's funeral, but she did send flowers. And she was openly critical of the Academy of Motion Picture Arts and Sciences for refusing to give Dean a special Oscar in posthumous recognition of his amazing screen presence.

Death of Mike Todd

On March 22, 1958, Mike Todd boarded his private plane, *The Lucky Liz*, to fly from Hollywood to New York to accept an award as Showman of the Year from the prestigious Friars Club. His wife, Elizabeth Taylor, decided at the last minute not to accompany him as planned because she was in bed with a bad cold. The plane, a Lockheed Lodestar, could hold twelve passengers, and Todd invited several of his friends to come along to keep him company. Only two were free to accept: Art Cohn, who was working on a biography of Todd and thought the trip would be a good chance for an extended interview; and James Bacon, a reporter for the Associated Press. Minutes before the scheduled takeoff at 10:20 PM, Bacon canceled because he didn't want to fly in the heavy rainstorm that had come up. The plane took off with Todd, Cohn, the pilot, and the copilot aboard.

Heading toward a refueling stop in Tulsa, the *Lucky Liz* flew into a terrible storm. Somewhere over the Zuni Mountains of New Mexico, the plane crashed, killing all four men on board.

Death Scenes

Elizabeth Taylor's movies have featured two traditional deathbed scenes. They were:

- The scene in *Jane Eyre* where she is the saintly young Helen who dies after being punished by the sadistic minister who runs the Lowood School orphanage where she and Jane become friends
- The scene in *The Last Time I Saw Paris*, where she is also named Helen, this time Van Johnson's betrayed wife, who dies of pneumonia caught from standing in the rain

In *Cleopatra*, we watch her commit suicide by putting her hand in a basket containing a poisonous asp. In *Butterfield 8*, she drives her car into a wall.

Debbie's Final Verdict on Eddie

Years after her divorce from Eddie Fisher, Debbie Reynolds described him as being "like an elevator that can't find the floor."

Sandy Dennis

Sandy Dennis was the Broadway actress selected to costar with Elizabeth Taylor in *Who's Afraid of Virginia Woolf?* Both women received Academy Award nominations for their work, and Dennis won the Oscar for Best Supporting Actress the same night that Taylor took home her second Best Actress award. On the set, the two actresses became good friends when they adopted Abyssinian kittens that were littermates. Both adore animals, although Dennis has pulled ahead in her pet count, now at twelve cats and two dogs. In a 1989 interview in *People*, Dennis reminisced about the Burtons as she got to know them on the set of *Virginia Woolf*: "They were at a wonderful time in their life. He read mysteries and she just wanted to go out and eat Mexican food."

Sandy Dennis, born in Nebraska in 1937, had already won two Tonys at the time she appeared in *Virginia Woolf*: one for her work in *A Thousand Clowns* and one for *Any Wednesday*. Oddly, after she won the Oscar, her career did not seem to benefit. Dennis played a leading role in *Up the*

Down Staircase in 1967, but her subsequent films were few and found little support at the box office. Her most recent screen success was in a supporting role in *The Four Seasons*, with Alan Alda and Carol Burnett.

John Derek

When eight-year-old Elizabeth Taylor enrolled in Hawthorne School in Hollywood in 1940, she got an immediate crush on one of her classmates, named Derek Hansen. Taylor recalls that the boy ignored her totally. When he grew up, he changed his name to John Derek—and became an actor and connoisseur of beautiful women.

Diamond Salad

Not long after Richard Burton bought the sixty-nine-carat Cartier diamond for his wife Elizabeth Taylor in late 1969, the couple went out for dinner at the Beverly Hills Hotel, where show biz folk go to see and be seen. Liz, wearing her new diamond pendant, became aware that the other patrons were all staring at the fabulous gem. She summoned the headwaiter, nonchalantly removed the diamond and placed it on top of her salad, and told him to take it around the room and let everyone look at it. When he returned, Taylor picked up the diamond, wiped off the salad dressing, and put it back around her neck.

"Dickenliz"

During Elizabeth Taylor's marriage to Richard Burton, the famous couple was often referred to by the press as "Dickenliz."

Diet Tips from "Miss Lard"

In her 1988 book *Elizabeth Takes Off*, Elizabeth Taylor gives excellent advice to people who want to follow her example and lose weight. Among her tips:

- Set reasonable goals and expect to lose weight gradually.
- Whatever your diet allows you to eat should be cooked with care and presented in an attractive fashion.
- Post a picture of yourself at your fattest for motivation. (Taylor generously adds, "If you think a picture of me as Miss Lard will inspire you, go ahead and put it on your refrigerator.")
- Don't keep the clothes you wore before you started to lose weight, and don't buy new clothes with elastic waists and no shape. Make your clothes fit your body, so you will always be aware of it.
- Allow yourself an occasional binge without guilt.

Marlene Dietrich: A Rival in Love

Early in 1951, Elizabeth Taylor began dating British actor Michael Wilding while she was in London for the production of *Ivanhoe*. She fell in love with the suave older man instantly. Although he had not yet proposed marriage, she went so far as to buy herself a huge sapphire ring and announce their engagement. Movie fans went wild and the press jumped on the story.

Wilding, however, was reluctant. He was still married (although separated from his wife); he was nearly twenty years older than Taylor; and most important of all, he was very much in love with Marlene Dietrich. He was happy to squire the German actress, eight years older than himself, anywhere she wanted to go, from a night on the town to a trip to the hairdresser, and he always seemed animated and happy in her company. Perhaps it was Dietrich's elusiveness that made Wilding pursue her so devotedly. Marlene was still married to her husband of thirty years, and had no intention of changing the situation. Once Taylor became interested in Wilding, it was only a matter of time before her persistence won out over Dietrich's mystery.

Interestingly, Taylor's next husband, Mike Todd, was also an ex-boyfriend of Marlene Dietrich, who agreed to appear in a cameo role in his movie, *Around the World in 80 Days*.

The fascinating Marlene Dietrich was born in Berlin in 1901, and much of her early life is shrouded in mystery. She first appeared on screen in a Czech film in 1923 and then married the director, Rudolf Sieber, with whom she had one daughter, actress Maria Riva. Dietrich never divorced Sieber, but began to live apart from him shortly after the birth of their child. He died in 1975.

Dietrich's screen success is linked with her discovery by German-born Hollywood director Josef von Sternberg, who cast her in *The Blue Angel*. Together, they made six more films that turned the sultry Marlene, with her deep voice and her long legs, into a legend. In 1948, when her daughter Maria had a child, the press hailed Dietrich as "the world's most glamorous grandmother"—a title later transferred to Elizabeth Taylor.

Marjorie Dillon

Marjorie Dillon was for many years the stand-in for Elizabeth Taylor at MGM. They became friends when they were still girls attending the school on the back lot, and "Margie" was one of Taylor's bridesmaids at her wedding to Nicky Hilton. Later, Margie provided a temporary place of refuge after the marriage collapsed. The star treated her stand-in generously. When Margie married, Elizabeth not only gave her an elegant suit to be married in, but also a frilly negligee for the wedding night and a matched set of luggage for the honeymoon.

Dinner with Aristotle Onassis

In 1972, Elizabeth Taylor became jealous of husband Richard Burton's attraction to several of his gorgeous costars in the movie *Bluebeard*; they included Raquel Welch, Virna Lisi, and Joey Heatherton. Director Eddie Dmytryk, a friend of both Taylor and Burton, observed that Richard's leading ladies were all falling in love with him, and Taylor feared that he might be reciprocating. Her way of striking back was to have dinner (in Rome) with Aristotle Onassis. Photographers had a field day snapping pictures of Elizabeth Taylor dining with Jacqueline Kennedy's husband at the famed Hostaria Dell'Orso.

Dior in Duplicate

One of the most famous photos of 1961 shows Elizabeth Taylor at that year's Moscow Film Festival, talking to Gina Lollobrigida. The photo revealed that the two women were wearing identical Dior gowns. Taylor later told reporters,

"I don't think Gina was amused, but I was. Mine is the original." She meant that she bought hers from the designer, whereas Gina's turned out to be a copy run up by her Italian dressmaker.

Divorce from Eddie Fisher

Elizabeth Taylor asked Eddie Fisher for a divorce in April 1962, sending her agent Kurt Frings and former stepson Mike Todd, Jr. to tell Eddie her request and negotiate a settlement. Fisher, surprised and humiliated, was in no mood to make the process easy for Taylor. He dragged his feet, meanwhile releasing nasty remarks to the press about Taylor and Burton. Fisher initially asked for a large settlement, but eventually agreed to take $750,000, along with the use of another $250,000 for ten years. Once the agreement had been reached, Taylor filed for a divorce while she was in Puerto Vallarta, Mexico, on location where Richard Burton was shooting *The Night of the Iguana*. Fisher did not contest her action, so the divorce was granted on March 6, 1964. By that time, Taylor had already left Mexico and was in Toronto, where Burton was appearing on stage in *Hamlet*. She and Burton were married days later.

Divorce: His/Divorce: Hers

In 1973, ABC-TV aired a pair of ninety-minute movies, starring Elizabeth Taylor and Richard Burton, called *Divorce: His* and *Divorce: Hers*. The concept was to show two different views of the disintegration of a marriage, but the scripts failed to deliver the strong differentiation that would have justified such a lengthy dual production. Directed by Waris Hussein, both stories moved slowly, and there was little plot development in either. In costumes by Edith Head and hairdos by Alexandre of Paris, Taylor looked ravishing, but she failed to surmount the skimpy material and the overblown production that featured far too many flashbacks and instant replays. *Variety*'s critic lamented, "Miss Taylor wallowed in suds to a point where the many close-ups between her ample bazooms failed even in distracting from the nonsense."

Divorcing Burton: The First Time

On June 26, 1974, Elizabeth Taylor obtained a divorce from Richard Burton. The action was filed in Switzerland, and the divorce granted in a court in Saanen, near Taylor's home in Gstaad. Taylor was present, wearing dark glasses, but a medical certificate was presented as evidence that Burton was not well enough to travel from the United States to Switzerland. Taylor's petition cited "irreconcilable differences," and she told the judge that her life with Richard had become intolerable. Taylor had provided a lengthier explanation of the divorce in an interview some weeks earlier:

> A woman will try and dominate a man. But really, inside herself, she wants to be dominated . . . And she wants to lean on him—not have him lean on her. If he does lean on her, everything goes slightly off-key, like a bad chord. She hopes it will pass, that the guy will come through. When he doesn't, she begins to needle him. If nothing happens, she goes on needling—until he stops listening. At that moment, she becomes bitter and he goes deaf. Finally there is no more dialogue.

The divorce settlement had the Burtons dividing all their joint property equally. Taylor kept her jewelry, all the art except a small Picasso, the house in Puerto Vallarta, their yacht *Kalizma*, and custody of their adopted daughter Maria. When it was all over, Burton issued his own statement, saying, "Frankly, she'll be better off without me. I intend to roam the globe searching for ravishing creatures."

Divorcing Burton: The Second Time

Elizabeth Taylor's second—and final—divorce from Richard Burton was granted in Switzerland in early 1976. The property settlement was the same as it had been in the Burtons' first divorce.

Edward Dmytryk

Edward Dmytryk was the director of *Raintree County*, starring Elizabeth Taylor and Montgomery Clift. He was one of the guests at the home of Taylor and then-husband Michael Wilding the night of Monty's near-fatal accident, and knew that the star would need all the support he could get to finish the film. The studio urged Dmytryk to replace Clift and reshoot all his scenes, but after the director talked to Elizabeth Taylor, he decided to wait until Clift was able to return to work.

Years later, Dmytryk directed Richard Burton in *Bluebeard* and had the chance to get reacquainted with Elizabeth Taylor. He was one of the guests at her fortieth birthday bash, and recalled it as one of the best parties he had ever been to in his life.

Do Blondes Have More Fun?

In 1984, after leaving the Betty Ford Center, Elizabeth Taylor startled fans by going blonde. Although she had been a blonde in several movies, including *Little Women* and *Hammersmith Is Out*, in real life Taylor had always stuck to her natural dark hair. She confessed that she had long wanted to see what she would look like as a blonde, but was afraid the public would react negatively to such a drastic change in her appearance. The self-confidence the star gained at the Ford Center helped her decide to try being a blonde. Apparently, blondes do *not* have more fun than Elizabeth Taylor for she soon switched back to being a brunette (albeit a gray-streaked one).

Doctor Faustus

Doctor Faustus was a 1967 movie produced and directed by Richard Burton, which starred him in the title role. It was a film version of a performance of the classic play by Christopher Marlowe that Burton had given in Oxford as a benefit for the Oxford University Dramatic Society. Unable to find financial backers to help bring it to the screen, Burton used his own money. His personal investment was estimated to be more than $1 million.

Burton's wife, Elizabeth Taylor, agreed to play (both at Oxford and on the screen) the role of Helen of Troy, the temptress who stands for all the weaknesses of the flesh. It was a nonspeaking part, which some reviewers snidely suggested was her husband's way of keeping his classy English production from being sabotaged by her Beverly Hills accent. Other parts were played by Oxford undergraduates who had participated in the earlier production, and the codirector was Burton's old drama teacher at Oxford, Nevill Coghill. More than one reviewer likened *Doctor Faustus* to a home movie and complained that the Burtons should never have inflicted it on theater audiences. In point of fact, audiences mostly avoided the experience. The total gross was just over a half million dollars.

Stanley Donen

Stanley Donen, born on April 13, 1924, was a dancer and choreographer who got his first chance to direct in a collaboration with Gene Kelly, on the witty and inventive *On the Town*. Although Donen choreographed the 1948 movie, *A Date with Judy*, in which Elizabeth Taylor had one of the leading roles, he didn't get to know her until 1951, when he was selected by MGM to direct *Love Is Better Than Ever*, right after he finished working with Kelly on the musical hit *Singin' in the Rain*.

During the production of the film, romance blossomed between Donen and his star, who was in the process of getting divorced from Nicky Hilton. Donen was attentive to Taylor and a sympathetic listener; he also had the aura of authority that good directors know how to assume. Their affair became so public that Donen's wife filed for divorce, claiming her husband's affections had been alienated by another woman. MGM worried about negative public reaction to the relationship between Taylor and Donen, who was ten years older; and according to Hollywood rumor, Taylor's mother was also dead set against Elizabeth's involvement with Donen, on the grounds that he was Jewish and not yet very successful in Hollywood. Whether coincidentally or by design, Elizabeth Taylor was quickly cast as Rebecca in *Ivanhoe*, which was scheduled to be shot on location in England. The separation, combined with Elizabeth's introduction to British actor Michael Wilding, the man who was to become her second husband, ended her romance with Stanley Donen.

In 1972, Donen married French actress Yvette Mimieux. In addition to a string of movie musicals codirected with Gene Kelly, Donen also directed *Charade, Two for the Road, Bedazzled*, and, most recently, *Lucky Lady*, with Liza Minnelli and Burt Reynolds.

Don't Get Her Irish Up!

When Elizabeth Taylor talks about losing her temper, she often refers to herself as Irish. It's a plausible contention to judge by her looks, with the typically Celtic combination of fair skin, dark hair, and blue eyes. But in fact, she hasn't a drop of Irish blood in her veins. On her father's side, her ancestors were Scottish and English; on her mother's side, they were German.

"Dr. Feelgood"

Dr. Max Jacobson, a New York physician, treated a number of celebrity patients. His special treatment was a series of "health shots" that were later revealed to be a combination of vitamins and methamphetamine, or "speed." Jacobson, nicknamed "Dr. Feelgood" by the media in the 1970s, when he faced indictment, had an impressive roster of celebrity clients. It included President John F. Kennedy, as well as, on occasion, his wife Jacqueline; Andy Williams; Eddie Fisher; and, very briefly, Fisher's wife Elizabeth Taylor.

Drinking Bouts

As a popular young star at MGM, Elizabeth Taylor did not drink any kind of alcoholic beverages. It was not until she was married to Nicky Hilton that she started to drink, and by the time she was in her thirties, she was indulging in epic drinking bouts in the company of husband Richard Burton. Burton's ability to drink was legendary. One reporter recalled watching him, in Puerto Vallarta while filming *Night of the Iguana*, drink twenty-three shots of tequila along with innumerable chasers of Carta Blanca beer. The same reporter, Mike Todd's friend Jim Bacon (who turned down Todd's invitation to travel with him in the plane that crashed, killing all aboard), said of Taylor, "She can outdrink any man I have ever known, including Burton."

Drinking Man's Diet

To play the role of Martha in *Who's Afraid of Virginia Woolf?*, Elizabeth Taylor gained twenty-five pounds. Of course, after her award-winning performance, she had to lose them again. She told readers of *Elizabeth Takes Off* that she decided to go on the Drinking Man's Diet, popular in the 1970s, and husband Richard Burton agreed to do the same. Taylor confessed ruefully, "It worked for awhile and then we dropped the 'diet' and just continued drinking."

Drug Journal

When Elizabeth Taylor entered the Betty Ford Center for treatment of her drug dependency in late 1983, she was required to keep a "drug journal," or record of her experiences with drugs and her efforts to stop using them. For a *New York Times* interview a year after she left the center, Taylor read her first entry in the drug journal:

> Today is Friday. I've been here since Monday night, one of the strangest and most frightening nights of my life. Not to mention lonely. But I am not alone. There are people here just like me, who are suffering just like me, who hurt inside and out just like me, people I've learned to love. It's an experience unlike any other I've known.
>
> Nobody wants anything from anybody else, except to share and help. It's probably the first time since I was 9 that nobody's wanted to exploit me. Now the bad news. I feel like hell. I'm going through with-

drawal. My heart feels big and pounding. I can feel the blood rush through my body. I can almost see it, running like red water over the boulders in my pain-filled neck and shoulders, then through my eyes and into my pounding head. My eyelids flutter. Oh, God, I am so, so tired.

The Duke and Duchess of Windsor

During the decade that Elizabeth Taylor was married to Richard Burton, they enjoyed a close friendship with another famous married couple, the Duke and Duchess of Windsor. Taylor had met the Windsors years earlier, in 1950, when she was on her honeymoon with Nicky Hilton aboard the *Queen Mary*. But it was not until her romance with Burton made international headlines that a real friendship developed with the former king and the woman for whom he gave up his throne. The Burtons often dined at the Windsors' home outside Paris, and Elizabeth still keeps photos of those occasions in her living room. And of course she is reminded of her friend the duchess every time she wears the diamond pin she bought from the Windsor estate.

Dwindling Box-Office Appeal

Elizabeth Taylor was one of the top ten box-office draws from the early 1950s until the late 1960s. She did not fall off the list until 1968, the year after she won her second Oscar. Although she remains a legendary star, she has never regained her box-office draw or bankability.

-ℰ-

Eddie and Debbie

When Eddie Fisher married Debbie Reynolds in the fall of 1955, the whole world agreed they were an adorable couple. Fisher was a teen idol, whose records seemed to sell as fast as they could be released, and Reynolds was the all-American girl next door, who just happened to be singing and dancing in MGM musicals. Columnist Hedda Hopper enthused, "Never have I seen a more patriotic match than these two clean-cut clean-living youngsters. When I think of them, I see flags flying and hear bands playing." The couple had two children: Carrie Francis, now an actress and author, and Todd Emmanuel, named after Eddie's best friend, Mike Todd.

But the reality differed from the public image. Almost from the beginning, there had been strains in the marriage. Fisher was urban, Jewish, accustomed to staying up all night and sleeping all day. Reynolds was a homebody, an outdoor type, adjusted to a schedule at MGM that required getting up very early in the morning and going to bed early at night. The couple's problems were further exacerbated by Fisher's drug dependence at the time.

Debbie and Eddie had spoken of divorce on numerous occasions, and were planning to separate, when she discovered she was pregnant with their second child. Both agreed to stay married for an unspecified time. Mike Todd was killed just two months after Todd Fisher was born, and even though Debbie knew Eddie was spending a great deal of time with Elizabeth, she was not prepared for Eddie's open defection. Debbie first told reporters that she and Eddie were still very much in love and had never been happier than in the past year. "Don't blame Eddie for this," she added, implying that Taylor was the responsible party.

In February 1959, Debbie appeared in a Los Angeles courtroom and cited her husband's interest in another woman as the reason for the failure of the marriage. She got custody of their two children, as well as a settlement valued at $1 million, and child support payments of $40,000 a year. That divorce would not become final for a year; meanwhile, Eddie Fisher established residence in Las Vegas and obtained a fast divorce on the same terms, a step to which Debbie reluctantly gave her consent. Later, she said contemptuously of her former husband, "I had two children by him who could have been sired by anybody . . . I raised them, supported them, and took care of them. He didn't help at all."

"Eddie's Eden"

During Eddie Fisher's marriage to Elizabeth Taylor, he bought property in rural Jamaica, where he loved to go to get away from it all. Elizabeth nicknamed the property "Eddie's Eden" but was indignant when he wanted to keep the property in the divorce settlement.

Eddie's Phone Call to Elizabeth

In the spring of 1962, when rumors were flying about the relationship between Elizabeth Taylor and Richard Burton on the set of *Cleopatra*, Eddie Fisher flew back to New York, where he claimed he had a singing engagement. In reality, he entered Gracie Square Hospital, reportedly suffering from a nervous breakdown. When he emerged, he held a press conference in his hotel room at the Pierre. Reporters demanded to know if his marriage was over;

Eddie denied it, saying the only romance between his wife and Richard Burton was through their roles as Mark Antony and Cleopatra. Faced with the obvious disbelief of the reporters he had convened, Eddie then made a call to his wife in Rome to ask Elizabeth to speak to the reporters and deny the rumors herself.

"Well, Eddie," Taylor said truthfully, "I can't do that because there is some truth in the story. I just can't do that."

Eddie said, "Wait a minute, what do you mean you won't do that?"

Elizabeth answered, "I can't do that because it is true. There is a foundation to the story."

Eddie and Elizabeth never lived together again after that fatal phone call.

E'en So

One of the dogs in the Taylor–Burton menage was a one-eyed Pekinese named E'en So. Richard had trained the dog to respond to commands given in Welsh.

Elephant Walk

When Elizabeth Taylor was a little girl, her mother thought she should be cast as Vivien's Leigh's daughter in *Gone with the Wind*. In 1954, Taylor was Leigh's replacement in *Elephant Walk*. It was a Paramount picture that had been slated to costar Laurence Olivier and his then-wife, Vivien Leigh, as two members of a steamy romantic triangle (Dana Andrews was the third) on a tea plantation in Ceylon. But when it came time to begin production, Olivier could not get out of other pressing commitments, so Peter Finch was cast in his role, and shooting began on location in Ceylon, one of the hottest, muggiest, most uncomfortable places in the world. By the time the cast returned to Hollywood to complete the movie, Vivien Leigh was ill and exhausted, and she promptly suffered a severe nervous breakdown. To save the picture in which it had already invested a substantial sum, Paramount had to find a new leading lady—preferably someone about the same size, shape, and coloring as Vivien Leigh, so that the expensive background footage shot in Ceylon could still be used.

Elizabeth Taylor was the obvious choice. In fact, she had initially been considered for the part before Vivien Leigh, but she had been pregnant with her second child at the time the movie was first cast. Arrangements were made to borrow Taylor from MGM, which charged a stiff price for the services of their star. The movie's producer, Irving Asher, later commented on how grateful he felt for Taylor's professionalism on the set. Apparently, Peter Finch had fallen in love with Vivien Leigh in Ceylon, and was moping over her departure; the other male lead, Dana Andrews, was drinking heavily. Said Asher, "Elizabeth was a dream to work with. She arrived on time, knew her lines, and was really quite patient and helpful with Dana. Sometimes he was in such bad shape that we had to shoot him from behind, and in their scenes together, Elizabeth led him."

Taylor played Ruth Wiley, the recent bride of a plantation owner in Ceylon (Peter Finch). On her arrival at her new home, she quickly learns that she is in for a hard time. Her husband has a terrible temper, the servants are willful, a cholera epidemic is raging, and her life is threatened by a herd of wild elephants. She finds comfort and support from the handsome and manly overseer (Dana Andrews). And she displays a certain independent spirit throughout.

Although the location scenes were striking and unusual, critics panned *Elephant Walk* for its turgid melodrama. Once again, Elizabeth Taylor looked breathtakingly beautiful, but was required to do very little acting. Her own reviews ranged from lukewarm to hostile. *The New York Times* called her performance "petulant and smug," while the *Monthly Film Bulletin* said she "failed to convey much in the way of character." *Variety* was content to note that Edith Head's costumes complemented Taylor's natural beauty. One of the most interesting analyses came in the course of a long review in *Look*: "The producers of MGM's *Rhapsody* and Paramount's *Elephant Walk* have placed Elizabeth Taylor . . . in the incredible position of being rejected by a total of four men she chooses to love. Elizabeth puts up a game fight, though. She wins their reluctant hearts by means of sheer grit, rather than through her natural charms—a most unsatisfactory arrangement for any girl. These woeful tales, however, have a curious power in the hands of Miss Taylor—an indication of her growing talents as an adult and honest actress, who can make an audience believe just about anything."

Elisheba

When Elizabeth Taylor went through the rituals of conversion to Judaism, she adopted a Hebrew name. The one she chose was Elisheba, which means "dedicated to God." For her second name, she chose Rachel, because she loved the story of Jacob's long love for her.

The Elizabeth

In 1968, Richard Burton paid just under $1 million to buy a small private jet plane he named *The Elizabeth*. The twin-engine de Havilland carried ten passengers comfortably, with a kitchen, a bar, and a movie projector and screen. Burton joked to reporters, "I bought it so we could fly to Nice for lunch."

Elizabeth in Doonesburyland

In early 1979, after Elizabeth Taylor's husband John Warner had been elected to the Senate, the couple began to appear in Garry Trudeau's comic strip *Doonesbury*. The cartoonist was anything but flattering, calling Warner "Senator Elizabeth Taylor" and implying that he bought his party's nomination. Taylor was always drawn with a huge bosom and rolls of fat, and the strip's characterization of her as "a tad overweight but with violet eyes to die for" became so well known it was even turned into a bumper sticker.

Elizabeth Takes Off

In 1988, Elizabeth Taylor authored a book about her battle to keep her weight under control, called *Elizabeth Takes Off*. Published by Putnam in February, the book was one of the most successful celebrity diet books of the last decade. It sold 512,750 copies in hardcover, making it number six on the list of the year's best-selling nonfiction.

Part of the success of the book was due to Taylor's frankness in talking about her own problems with weight. She told her readers, "You saw how badly I let myself go and how I fought my way back. If I could win my battle to lose weight and regain my self-esteem, you can too." She traced some of her problems to the rapidity of her rise to stardom while she was still a child. "One minute I was kissing a horse and the next I was kissing Bob Stack."

Elizabeth Taylor

In 1964, Elizabeth Taylor signed a contract with prestigious publishing house Harper & Row to write her autobiography, and received an advance of $150,000. The book retold the stories of her romances and her illnesses, her stardom and her work as a serious actress, and was illustrated with photos of the star taken by her friend Roddy McDowall. Taylor dedicated it to "The Lady from Pismo Beach," her term for the ardent fan who loves to read all the gossip about her favorite stars. Although the book got snippy reviews, it sold well; apparently Elizabeth knew what the ladies from Pismo Beach wanted to read.

Elizabeth Taylor in London

In 1963, Elizabeth Taylor starred in a one-hour special for CBS-TV, called *Elizabeth Taylor in London*. She conducted a tour of the famous city, standing in front of historic locales, such as the Tower of London and the houses of Parliament, in her Dior wardrobe. Taylor was paid $500,000 for her work, which made her the highest-paid television entertainer for a single special.

Elizabeth Taylor Paper Dolls

In 1945, Elizabeth Taylor agreed to let her name and face be used on a book of "Elizabeth Taylor Paper Dolls." There was also an Elizabeth Taylor coloring book released the same year.

The Elizabeth Taylor Story

In 1982, ABC-TV announced it was planning to produce a "docudrama" on the life of the most famous actress in the world. Called *The Elizabeth Taylor Story*, it was slated to star Christina DeLorean as Taylor. The real Elizabeth Taylor promptly filed a lawsuit against ABC. She told reporters, "My career is at stake and I'm angry. I am my own industry—someday I may write an autobiography or I may even do a film autobiography—and their project is taking away from my income." The suit never went to court, as ABC soon announced that it was dropping the project.

Elizabeth the Fat

One of Richard Burton's less affectionate nicknames for his wife, generally used in public when he was displeased, was "Elizabeth the Fat."

The Elizabeth Theater Group

The Elizabeth Theater Group was a theatrical production company formed by Elizabeth Taylor and Broadway producer Zev Bufman in order to mount *Private Lives* on the stage. The play opened in Boston, went on to Broadway, and then embarked on a national tour. Audiences flocked to see Taylor as Coward's heroine Amanda, acting opposite former husband Richard Burton, but critics panned their performances. The Elizabeth Theater Group got its money back—and meanwhile Taylor received a salary reported to be as high as $70,000 a week.

Elmer

According to Hollywood legend, the young Elizabeth Taylor was found one day in the garden of the family's London home, carrying on a conversation with "Elmer." When her mother asked the girl who Elmer was, Elizabeth handed her a wiggly fat worm—her pet of the moment.

The Empress's Diamond

For his wife's fortieth birthday, in 1972, Richard Burton gave Elizabeth Taylor a diamond with a sentimental history. It had been given by Mogul Emperor Shah Jehan to his wife in 1621, the year of her death. (That's when he built the Taj Mahal as her memorial.) The Empress's diamond was inscribed on the back with words of love from her adoring husabnd, making it a suitable present for the Queen of the Screen from her then-consort. Burton was the one who displayed it to photographers, posing with the diamond dangling on his forehead. He joked, "I set out to buy the Taj Mahal, but it was a little difficult to transport to Switzerland."

Engagement Present from Eddie Fisher

When Elizabeth Taylor became engaged to Eddie Fisher, he gave her a bracelet studded with fifty diamonds to mark the event. Some insiders noted its similarity to the bracelet given Taylor as a wedding present several years earlier by third husband Mike Todd, Fisher's best friend.

The Engagement Ring Taylor Bought Herself

In late 1951, Elizabeth Taylor was trying to convince Michael Wilding that they should be married. Since he appeared unconvinced and continued to see Marlene Dietrich, Taylor bought herself a large sapphire and diamond ring and began to wear it on her engagement finger, telling the press it was a gift from Wilding. Within weeks, they were husband and wife.

Engagement Rings: The List to Date

Being engaged to Elizabeth Taylor has been an increasingly expensive proposition. Here's a list of the rings she has worn during her official engagements.

- Bill Pawley's: 3.5-carat diamond, in 1949
- Nicky Hilton's: 5-carat diamond, in 1950
- Michael Wilding's: sapphire and diamond, in 1952
- Mike Todd's: 29.7-carat diamond, in 1956
- Victor Luna's: 16.5-carat cabochon sapphire, surrounded by diamonds, in 1983
- Dennis Stein's: 20-carat sapphire, in 1984

Entebbe Hostages

In 1976, the world watched as Ugandan dictator Idi Amin held 104 Jewish passengers on an international flight hostage at the Entebbe airport. Elizabeth Taylor immediately telephoned Israel's ambassador to the United States, Simcha Dinitz, and offered to go to Entebbe to negotiate with Amin. As it turned out, the Israelis had other plans: They stormed the airport and rescued the hostages.

Entry into Rome

One of the key scenes in *Cleopatra* is the Queen of the Nile's entry into Rome. Elizabeth Taylor, wearing a gold dress that weighed more than 20 pounds, was to ride atop a 3-story sphinx, pulled by 300 extras in fanciful costumes, as it went through a high archway and into a replica of the Forum, where 6,000 Romans had been hired to create a crowd. In a televised interview, Richard Burton revealed that just as the director was about to shout "Action" and start the whole procession in motion, he noticed an ice cream vendor doing great business in the thick of the crowd!

The entry scene was a pivotal point in the plot of the movie, the moment when Cleopatra would learn whether the crowd's reception would encourage the hopes that her son by Caesar could one day rule Rome. As it happened, the scene was shot at a pivotal moment in the life of Elizabeth Taylor. Her romance with Richard Burton was open knowledge, and there had been harsh criticism of her morals by many sources, including the official newspaper of the Vatican. The studio had received bomb threats against Taylor, and policemen were scattered throughout the crowd to protect the star. Elizabeth Taylor was, understandably, extremely nervous before the shooting began, but also determined to carry on.

As the action began and the sphinx rolled slowly into the crowded Forum, she saw people rushing toward her, and for a moment it seemed as if her worst fears were coming true. Then she realized the crowd was shouting her name and asking her to throw a kiss; she was simply being received with an excess of enthusiastic admiration.

Envy: Shelley Winters Tells It Like It Is

Shelley Winters costarred with Elizabeth Taylor in *A Place in the Sun* in 1951. The plot demanded that the two young women exhibit a startling contrast: the blonde Winters a blowzy nag with a shrill voice and no future; the glossily perfect Taylor every man's dream of the ideal rich and beautiful wife. Winters later confessed that it made her physically ill to look at pictures of herself beside Taylor in that movie. And even though the role netted her an Oscar nomination, a distinction denied Taylor, Shelley says it was not enough to abate her envy. For years, she bought herself new white Cadillac convertibles, because that was the car that Elizabeth Taylor drove in *A Place in the Sun*.

Yet Shelley, whose second husband, Vittorio Gassman, was Taylor's costar in *Rhapsody*, was generous in her praise of Taylor's performance in *A Place in the Sun*. "She had a depth and simpleness which were really remarkable," she said.

Shelley Winters was born in St. Louis in 1922, making her ten years older than Taylor. She had small roles in several Broadway plays and then went to Hollywood in the late forties. In 1948, she attracted attention in a supporting role in *A Double Life*. Although Winters didn't win an Oscar for *A Place in the Sun*, she later took home two of the gold statuettes—for her supporting role as the terrified Mrs. Van Daan in *Diary of Anne Frank*, and for her performance as the blind girl's slatternly mother in *A Patch of Blue*. She was also nominated for the 1972 disaster film, *The Poseidon Adventure*. Shelley Winters's two published memoirs have both shocked and amused the public with their sexual candor and bluntly worded opinions, earning their place on the best-seller lists.

Epitaph

Elizabeth Taylor in 1973 suggested to an interviewer how she would like her epitaph to read: *Here lies Elizabeth Taylor Burton. Thank you for every moment, good and bad. I've enjoyed it all.*

"Erotic Vagrancy"

The love affair of Elizabeth Taylor and Richard Burton began on the set of *Cleopatra*—and thus in the Catholic city of Rome. When the liaison of the two film stars hit the media, the Vatican quickly issued a derogatory comment, calling their love affair a case of "erotic vagrancy" and publicly chiding Taylor for breaking up the marriage that was itself founded on the dissolution of her husband's marriage to Debbie Reynolds.

Estate of Mike Todd

When Mike Todd died in a plane crash in March 1958, he left an estate valued at approximately $5 million. The heirs were his son, Mike Todd, Jr., and his widow, Elizabeth Taylor. But through complicated provisions in the will, all taxes owed on *Around the World in 80 Days*, the movie that was the estate's chief asset, were to be deducted from Taylor's half. Without Todd's continuing efforts to publicize the movie, box-office receipts dropped off quickly. Thus Taylor ended up with very little financial gain.

"E.T."

Carol Burnett likes to call her friend Elizabeth Taylor "E.T."

Extra in Anne of the Thousand Days

In 1968, Richard Burton starred in *Anne of the Thousand Days*, opposite young Genevieve Bujold. Elizabeth Taylor accompanied her husband on location in Canada, and for a lark, she donned a costume as an extra in a masked ball scene. The young woman whose place she took, Charlotte Selwyn, complained to the studio about losing a day's pay to Taylor, and the studio issued a statement explaining that Taylor hadn't gotten a credit for it but had done it as "a fun thing." There was no report as to whether the news made Miss Selwyn feel any better.

The Extra Twenty-Eight Minutes for Hamlet

When Richard Burton was starring in a 1964 production of *Hamlet* in Toronto, wife Elizabeth Taylor would often attend his performance. According to Burton, Taylor's presence in the theater would add an extra twenty-eight minutes to the running time of the play. What caused the slowdown? "The ladies would come right down to her seat and stare at her . . . and talk about her, saying, 'Her eyes are blue, not violet.'"

-F-

The Failed Adoption

Early in 1982, Elizabeth Taylor visited a day-care center in Tel Aviv, while she was in that city on her brief Middle East peace mission. She saw an adorable one-year-old, Karen Peretz, and was told that the baby's mother had died two weeks earlier. Enchanted by little Karen, Taylor made inquiries about adopting the child. Initially, the father seemed receptive, but when he realized that Karen would be taken away from Israel to live, he changed his mind and refused.

Family Intervention

Elizabeth Taylor says she went to the Betty Ford Center in December 1983, as a result of family intervention. She was in a Santa Monica hospital, being treated for the effects of her consumption of alcohol, Demerol and Percodan, when family members decided on the classic confrontation recommended by therapists who treat drug and alcohol abusers. Her brother Howard and his wife, and three of her four children went to the hospital to tell her that she was killing herself, and to suggest that she choose to enter the Betty Ford Center instead.

Taylor later told an interviewer, "I was in such a drugged stupor that when they filed into my room I thought, 'Oh, how nice, my family are all here to visit.' Then they sat down, and each read from papers they had prepared, each saying they loved me, each describing incidents they'd witnessed of my debilitation, and each saying if I kept on the way I was with drugs, I would die." Taylor also described her reaction to the intervention. At first, she admitted, she was defensive. "Then I realized my family wouldn't have come unless I'd really reached the bottom. I didn't get angry with them. I was astonished. Then, after feeling this overwhelming sense of guilt, I realized that I had to get help. I became a drunk and a junkie with great determination, and with the same great resolve that got me to that point, I could turn it to work for me." She asked for time to make her own decision, and that night, she entered the center.

Father of the Bride

Father of the Bride, which starred Elizabeth Taylor as the bride and Spencer Tracy as the father, was a 1950 MGM comedy that has become a movie classic. Based on an amusing novel by Edward Streeter, the story is told from the point of view of the father of a young woman who grows up before his eyes, turning from a blue-jeaned teenager into a radiant bride. The comedy aspect comes from the plans for the wedding itself, and the contrast between the father's "sensible" attitudes and the women's world of elaborate and expensive preparations. The script encapsulates the 1950s view of the differences between the sexes, poking fun without agitating for change. Robert Hatch, writing in *The New Republic*, suggested that the family represented "the perfect flowering of the American dream."

The supporting cast of *Father of the Bride* included Joan Bennett as Elizabeth Taylor's mother, Don Taylor as the young man she marries, Billie Burke as his mother, and Russ Tamblyn as the bride's bratty younger brother. Spencer Tracy stole every scene in which he appeared, and received a nomination for Best Actor, although he didn't win the Oscar. Interestingly, MGM execs had originally wanted Jack Benny to play the role, but agreed with director Vincente Minnelli that it would be a casting mistake after they saw Benny's screen test.

It was, of course, Elizabeth Taylor who got the most publicity from the MGM machine. At the time the movie was released, she became a bride in real life, marrying first husband Nicky Hilton. Articles about her own wedding, written before the fact, were illustrated with stills from the movie, and the parallel was heightened by the fact that Helen Rose designed similar dresses for her screen and real-life weddings. The windfall publicity helped to draw audiences to the box office, but it is the quality of the movie that makes it still popular on TV and in videocassette.

Most reviewers referred to Elizabeth Taylor as "perfectly cast," presumably a reference to her own concurrent nuptials. *The New York Herald Tribune* added, "Elizabeth Taylor's good looks aid her in creating the illusion that in each succeeding scene the audience, like father, is seeing her for the first time." Alton Cook said, "Miss Taylor demonstrates that she is still in the promising-young-actress stage of her career."

Father's Little Dividend

In 1951, MGM followed up the enormous box-office success of *Father of the Bride* by releasing a sequel, *Father's Little Dividend*, again costarring Elizabeth Taylor as the recent bride, now a mother-to-be, and Spencer Tracy as her father. When Taylor reported to the set to start filming, she was herself a young married woman, but her marriage to Nicky Hilton was already falling apart. Producer Pandro Berman recalled, "That girl looked so weary and forlorn. I remembered her as having a keen sense of humor, but she no longer thought anything was funny. She didn't laugh. She had lost twenty pounds and had become a chain smoker. She complained of pains, and doctors diagnosed colitis and an incipient ulcer."

The sequel moved the plot of the wedding-oriented original along to its natural conclusion, as the young couple have their first baby. As in the initial film, the real focus of the movie was on the character of the father, as he adjusted to becoming a grandfather and seeing his own "little girl" turn into a lovely young mother. And once again, Spencer Tracy walked off with every scene in which he appeared.

Although sequels tend to suffer by comparison with the original, contemporary reviews lauded the director (Vincente Minnelli) and his reassembled cast for a successful extension of the original premise. *Variety* said the movie did "what few sequels are able to manage—live up to the first," and *Newsweek* enthused that all the players were "just right in the roles to which they have become accustomed." *Variety* commented that "Elizabeth Taylor beautifies her scenes as the new mother."

When the original movie was released, MGM publicity was able to capitalize on the fact that Elizabeth Taylor, the film bride, was also a bride in real life. The studio may have hoped for a further parallel when they planned the sequel, but in fact, by the time *Father's Little Dividend* was released, Elizabeth Taylor was already divorced from first husband Nicky Hilton. Far from being distressed by the divergence between the actress and her screen character, audiences seemed to enjoy seeing Taylor enact on film the happy ending she had missed in real life.

A Female Elvis

During Elizabeth Taylor's 1988 stay at the Betty Ford Center (her second), one of the staffers commented, "With all the drugs she's absorbed, she's a female version of Elvis—and you know what happened to him." The parallels between these two prisoners of their own great fame are striking, especially in their similar problems with prescription drugs.

After Taylor emerged from her first stay at the Betty Ford Center, she talked frankly about some of her addictions. "For thirty-five years, I couldn't go to sleep without at least two sleeping pills. I'm a genuine insomniac. And I'd always taken a lot of medication for pain. I'd had nineteen major operations, and drugs had become a crutch. I wouldn't take them only when I was in pain. I was taking a lot of Percodan. I'd take Percodan and a couple of drinks before I would go out. I just felt I had to get stoned to get over my shyness. I needed oblivion, escape."

Waldo Fernandez

Waldo Fernandez is the interior designer responsible for the redecoration of Elizabeth Taylor's Bel Air house in 1988. Calling his client a "legend," Fernandez also said she was an easy client to work with. "We only disagreed on one thing," he explained. "I wanted pastel carpeting and she wanted white." Unsurprisingly, the carpeting is white.

In the course of the job, designer and client, who were introduced by Burt Bacharach and his wife Carol Bayer Sager, became good friends. In the summer of 1989, he and Elizabeth shared a rented beach house in Malibu—each, Fernandez reported, with their respective amours. "We're like a family." One reason they get along so well together may be their shared tastes. Fernandez reveals his own aesthetic when he says, "Who put the word 'vulgar' in the dictionary?"

A Filmography: Elizabeth Taylor's Theatrical Releases

There's One Born Every Minute. Universal, 1942. 59 minutes
Producer: Ken Goldsmith
Director: Harold Young
Screenwriters: Robert P. Hunt and Brenda Weisberg, based on a story by Robert P. Hunt
Cast: Hugh Herbert, Tom Brown, Peggy Moran, Guy Kibbee, Edgar Kennedy, Carl "Alfalfa" Switzer, Elizabeth Taylor

Lassie Come Home. Metro-Goldwyn-Mayer, 1943. 88 minutes
Producer: Samuel Marx
Director: Fred M. Wilcox
Screenwriter: Hugh Butler, based on the novel by Eric Knight
Cast: Roddy McDowall, Donald Crisp, Edmund Gwenn, Dame May Whitty, Nigel Bruce, Elsa Lanchester, Elizabeth Taylor

Jane Eyre. 20th Century-Fox, 1944. 96 minutes
Producer: William Goetz
Director: Robert Stevenson
Screenwriters: Aldous Huxley, Robert Stevenson, and John Houseman, based on the novel by Charlotte Brontë
Cast: Orson Welles, Joan Fontaine, Margaret O'Brien, Peggy Ann Garner, John Sutton, Sara Allgood, Henry Daniell, Agnes Moorehead, Mae Marsh, Elizabeth Taylor

The White Cliffs of Dover. Metro-Goldwyn-Mayer, 1944. 126 minutes
Producer: Sidney Franklin
Director: Clarence Brown
Screenwriters: Claudine West, Jan Lustig, and George Froeschel, based on the poem "The White Cliffs" by Alice Duer Miller
Cast: Irene Dunne, Alan Marshal, Frank Morgan, Roddy McDowall, Dame May Whitty, C. Aubrey Smith, Peter Lawford, Van Johnson, Elizabeth Taylor, June Lockhart.

National Velvet. Metro-Goldwyn-Mayer, 1944. 125 minutes
Producer: Pandro S. Berman
Director: Clarence Brown
Screenwriters: Theodore Reeves and Helen Deutsch, based on the novel by Enid Bagnold
Cast: Mickey Rooney, Donald Crisp, Elizabeth Taylor, Anne Revere, Angela Lansbury, Arthur Treacher

The Courage of Lassie. Metro-Goldwyn-Mayer, 1946. 93 minutes
Producer: Robert Sisk

Director: Fred M. Wilcox
Screenwriter: Lionel Hauser
Cast: Elizabeth Taylor, Frank Morgan, Tom Drake, Selena Royle, Carl "Alfalfa" Switzer

Cynthia. Metro-Goldwyn-Mayer, 1947. 98 minutes
Producer: Edwin H. Knopf
Director: Robert Z. Leonard
Screenwriters: Harold Buchman and Charles Kaufman, based on the play *The Rich Full Life* by Vina Delmar
Cast: Elizabeth Taylor, George Murphy, S.Z. Sakall, Mary Astor, Gene Lockhart, Spring Byington, Scotty Beckett, Anna Q. Nilsson

Life With Father. Warner Brothers, 1947. 118 minutes
Producer: Robert Buckner
Director: Michael Curtiz
Screenwriter: Donald Ogden Stewart, based on the play by Howard Lindsay and Russel Crouse, which was in turn based on the book by Clarence Day, Jr.
Cast: William Powell, Irene Dunne, Elizabeth Taylor, Edmund Gwenn, ZaSu Pitts, James Lydon, bit part for Arlene Dahl

A Date with Judy. Metro-Goldwyn-Mayer, 1948. 113 minutes
Producer: Joe Pasternak
Director: Richard Thorpe
Screenwriters: Dorothy Cooper and Dorothy Kingsley, based on the characters created by Aleen Leslie
Cast: Wallace Beery, Jane Powell, Elizabeth Taylor, Carmen Miranda, Xavier Cugat, Robert Stack, Selena Royle, Scotty Beckett, Leon Ames

Julia Misbehaves. Metro-Goldwyn-Mayer, 1948. 99 minutes
Producer: Everett Riskin
Director: Jack Conway
Screenwriters: William Ludwig, Harry Riskin, and Arthur Wimperis, adapted by Gina Kaus and Monckton Hoffe, based on the Margery Sharp novel, *The Nutmeg Tree*
Cast: Greer Garson, Walter Pidgeon, Peter Lawford, Cesar

Romero, Elizabeth Taylor, Lucile Watson, Nigel Bruce, Mary Boland

Little Women. Metro-Goldwyn-Mayer, 1949. 122 minutes
Producer: Mervyn LeRoy
Director: Mervyn LeRoy
Screenwriters: Andrew Solt, Sarah Y. Mason, and Victor Heerman, adapted by Sally Benson, based on the novel by Louisa May Alcott
Cast: June Allyson, Peter Lawford, Margaret O'Brien, Elizabeth Tayalor, Janet Leigh, Rossano Brazzi, Mary Astor, Lucile Watson, C. Aubrey Smith, Elizabeth Patterson, Leon Ames, Ellen Corby

Conspirator. Metro-Goldwyn-Mayer, 1950. 87 minutes
Producer: Arthur Hornblow Jr.
Director: Victor Saville
Screenwriter: Sally Benson, based on the novel by Humphrey Slater, adapted by Sally Benson and Gerard Fairlie
Cast: Robert Taylor, Elizabeth Taylor, Robert Flemyng, Harold Warrender, Honor Blackman, Marjorie Fielding, Wilfred Hyde-White

The Big Hangover. Metro-Goldwyn-Mayer, 1950. 82 minutes
Producer: Norman Krasna
Director: Norman Krasna
Screenwriter: Norman Krasna
Cast: Van Johnson, Elizabeth Taylor, Percy Waram, Fay Holden, Leon Ames, Edgar Buchanan, Selena Royle, Gene Lockhart, Rosemary DeCamp, Philip Ahn

Father of the Bride. Metro-Goldwyn-Mayer, 1950. 93 minutes
Producer: Pandro S. Berman
Director: Vincente Minnelli
Screenwriters: Frances Goodrich and Albert Hackett, based on the novel by Edward Streeter
Cast: Spencer Tracy, Elizabeth Taylor, Joan Bennett, Don Taylor, Billie Burke, Leo G. Carroll, Moroni Olsen, Melville Cooper, Rusty Tamblyn

Father's Little Dividend. Metro-Goldwyn-Mayer, 1951. 82 minutes
Producer: Pandro S. Berman
Director: Vincente Minnelli
Screenwriters: Frances Goodrich and Albert Hackett, based on characters created by Edward Streeter
Cast: Spencer Tracy, Joan Bennett, Elizabeth Taylor, Don Taylor, Billie Burke, Moroni Olsen, Marietta Canty, Russ Tamblyn

A Place in the Sun. Paramount, 1951. 122 minutes
Producer: George Stevens
Director: George Stevens
Screenwriters: Michael Wilson and Harry Brown, based on the novel *An American Tragedy* by Theodore Dreiser and the stage adaptation by Patrick Kearney
Cast: Montgomery Clift, Elizabeth Taylor, Shelley Winters, Anne Revere, Raymond Burr, Herbert Hayes, Keefe Brasselle, Shepperd Strudwick, Fred Clark

Callaway Went Thataway. Metro-Goldwyn-Mayer, 1951. 81 minutes
Producers: Norman Panama and Melvin Frank
Directors: Norman Panama and Melvin Frank
Screenwriters: Norman Panama and Melvin Frank
Cast: Fred MacMurray, Dorothy McGuire, Howard Keel, Jesse White. Guest stars: June Allyson, Clark Gable, Dick Powell, Elizabeth Taylor, Esther Williams

Love Is Better Than Ever. Metro-Goldwyn-Mayer, 1952. 81 minutes
Producer: William H. Wright
Director: Stanley Donen
Screenwriter: Ruth Brooks Flippen
Cast: Larry Parks, Elizabeth Taylor, Josephine Hutchinson, Tom Tully

Ivanhoe. Metro-Goldwyn-Mayer, 1952. 106 minutes
Producer: Pandro S. Berman
Director: Richard Thorpe
Screenwriter: Noel Langley, based on the novel by Sir Walter Scott, adaptation by Aeneas McKenzie

Cast: Robert Taylor, Elizabeth Taylor, Joan Fontaine, George Sanders, Emlyn Williams, Robert Douglas, Sebastian Cabot

The Girl Who Had Everything. Metro-Goldwyn-Mayer, 1953. 69 minutes
Producer: Armand Deutsch
Director: Richard Thorpe
Screenwriter: Art Cohn, based on the Adela Rogers St. John novel, *A Free Soul*
Cast: Elizabeth Taylor, Fernando Lamas, William Powell, Gig Young, James Whitmore

Rhapsody. Metro-Goldwyn-Mayer, 1954. 115 minutes
Producer: Lawrence Weingarten
Director: Charles Vidor
Screenwriters: Fay and Michael Kanin, based on the novel *Maurice Guest* by Henry Handel Richardson, adapted by Ruth and Augustus Goetz
Cast: Elizabeth Taylor, Vittorio Gassman, John Ericson, Louis Calhern, Stuart Whitman

Elephant Walk. Paramount, 1954. 103 minutes
Producer: Irving Asher
Director: William Dieterle
Screenwriter: John Lee Mahin, based on the novel by Robert Standish
Cast: Elizabeth Taylor, Dana Andrews, Peter Finch, Abraham Sofaer, Abner Biberman

Beau Brummel. Metro-Goldwyn-Mayer, 1954. 111 minutes
Producer: Sam Zimbalist
Director: Curtis Bernhardt
Screenwriter: Karl Tunberg, based on the play by Clyde Fitch
Cast: Stewart Granger, Elizabeth Taylor, Peter Ustinov, Robert Morley, James Donald, James Hayter, Rosemary Harris

The Last Time I Saw Paris. Metro-Goldwyn-Mayer, 1954. 116 minutes
Producer: Jack Cummings

Director: Richard Brooks
Screenwriters: Julius J. Epstein, Philip G. Epstein, and Richard Brooks, based on the F. Scott Fitzgerald story, "Babylon Revisited"
Cast: Elizabeth Taylor, Van Johnson, Walter Pidgeon, Donna Reed, Eva Gabor, Kurt Kaznar, George Dolenz, Roger Moore

Giant. Warner Brothers, 1956. 198 minutes
Producers: George Stevens and Henry Ginsberg
Director: George Stevens
Screenwriters: Fred Guiol and Ivan Moffat, based on the novel by Edna Ferber
Cast: Elizabeth Taylor, Rock Hudson, James Dean, Carroll Baker, Jane Withers, Chill Wills, Mercedes McCambridge, Sal Mineo, Dennis Hopper, Rod Taylor, Earl Holliman, Alexander Scourby, Elsa Cardenas, Barbara Barrie

Raintree County. Metro-Goldwyn-Mayer, 1957. 187 minutes
Producer: David Lewis
Director: Edward Dmytryk
Screenwriter: Millard Kaufman, based on the novel by Ross Lockridge, Jr.
Cast: Montgomery Clift, Elizabeth Taylor, Eva Marie Saint, Nigel Patrick, Lee Marvin, Rod Taylor, Agnes Moorehead, Rhys Williams, DeForrest Kelley, bit part for Gardner McKay

Cat on a Hot Tin Roof. Metro-Goldwyn-Mayer, 1958. 108 minutes
Producer: Lawrence Weingarten
Director: Richard Brooks
Screenwriters: Richard Brooks and James Poe, based on the play by Tennessee Williams
Cast: Elizabeth Taylor, Paul Newman, Burl Ives, Jack Carson, Judith Anderson

Suddenly Last Summer. Metro-Goldwyn-Mayer, 1959. 114 minutes
Producer: Sam Spiegel
Director: Joseph L. Mankiewicz

Screenwriters: Gore Vidal and Tennessee Williams, based on the play by Tennessee Williams
Cast: Elizabeth Taylor, Katharine Hepburn, Montgomery Clift, Albert Dekker, Mercedes McCambridge

Scent of Mystery. (Holiday in Spain) A Michael Todd, Jr. Release, in Smell-O-Vision, 1960. 125 minutes
Producer: Michael Todd, Jr.
Director: Jack Cardiff
Screenwriter: William Ross, based on an original story by Kelley Roos
Cast: Denholm Elliott, Peter Lorre, Beverly Bentley, Paul Lukas, Liam Redmond, Leo McKern, Diana Dors, cameo appearance by Elizabeth Taylor

Butterfield 8. Metro-Goldwyn-Mayer, 1960. 109 minutes
Producer: Pandro S. Berman
Director: Daniel Mann
Screenwriters: Charles Schnee and Michael Hayes, based on the novel by John O'Hara
Cast: Elizabeth Taylor, Laurence Harvey, Eddie Fisher, Dina Merrill, Mildred Dunnock, Betty Field, Jeffrey Lynn

Cleopatra. 20th Century-Fox, 1963. 243 minutes
Producer: Walter Wanger
Director: Joseph L. Mankiewicz
Screenwriters: Joseph L. Mankiewicz, Ranald MacDougall, and Sidney Buchman, based on the histories of Plutarch, Suetonius, and Appian, and *The Life and Times of Cleopatra* by C.M. Franzero
Cast: Elizabeth Taylor, Richard Burton, Rex Harrison, Pamela Brown, George Cole, Hume Cronyn, Cesare Danova, Roddy McDowall, Martin Landau, Francesca Annis, Michael Hordern, Carroll O'Connor, Jean Marsh

The V.I.P.s. Metro-Goldwyn-Mayer, 1963. 119 minutes
Producer: Anatole De Grunwald
Director: Anthony Asquith
Screenwriter: Terence Rattigan
Cast: Elizabeth Taylor, Richard Burton, Louis Jourdan,

Elsa Martinelli, Margaret Rutherford, Maggie Smith, Rod Taylor, Linda Christian, Orson Welles, Michael Hordern

The Sandpiper. A Filmways Picture, a Metro-Goldwyn-Mayer Release, 1965. 116 minutes
Producer: Martin Ransohoff
Director: Vincente Minnelli
Screenwriters: Dalton Trumbo and Michael Wilson, based on an original story by Martin Ransohoff, adaptation by Irene and Louis Kamp
Cast: Elizabeth Taylor, Richard Burton, Eva Marie Saint, Charles Bronson, the voice of Peter O'Toole

Who's Afraid of Virginia Woolf? An Ernest Lehman Production, a Warner Brothers Picture, 1966. 130 minutes
Producer: Ernest Lehman
Director: Mike Nichols
Screenwriter: Ernest Lehman, based on the play by Edward Albee
Cast: Elizabeth Taylor, Richard Burton, George Segal, Sandy Dennis

The Taming of the Shrew. A Co-Production of Royal Films International and F.A.I. Productions, a Columbia Pictures Release, 1967. 122 minutes
Executive Producer: Richard McWhorter
Producers: Richard Burton, Elizabeth Taylor, and Franco Zeffirelli
Director: Franco Zeffirelli
Screenwriters: Paul Dehn, Suso Cecchi D'Amico, and Franco Zeffirelli, based on the play by William Shakespeare
Cast: Elizabeth Taylor, Richard Burton, Cyril Cusack, Michael Hordern, Michael York

Doctor Faustus. An Oxford University Screen Production in Association with Nassau Films and Venfilms, a Columbia Pictures Release, 1967. 93 minutes
Producers: Richard Burton and Richard McWhorter
Directors: Richard Burton and Nevill Coghill

Screenwriter: Nevill Coghill, based on the play "The Tragicall History of Doctor Faustus" by Christopher Marlowe
Cast: Richard Burton, Elizabeth Taylor, Andreas Teuber, Elizabeth O'Donovan, Ian Marter

Reflections in a Golden Eye. A John Huston–Ray Stark Production, Released by Warner Brothers–Seven Arts, 1967. 109 minutes
Producer: Ray Stark
Director: John Huston
Screenwriters: Chapman Mortimer and Gladys Hill, based on the novel by Carson McCullers
Cast: Elizabeth Taylor, Marlon Brando, Brian Keith, Julie Harris, Zorro David, Robert Forster

The Comedians. A joint effort of Maximilian Productions (Bermuda) and Trianon Productions (Paris) for Metro-Goldwyn-Mayer, 1967. 160 minutes
Producer: Peter Glenville
Director: Peter Glenville
Screenwriter: Graham Greene, based on his novel
Cast: Richard Burton, Elizabeth Taylor, Alec Guiness, Peter Ustinov, Paul Ford, Lillian Gish, Raymond St. Jacques, Zaeks Mokae, Roscoe Lee Browne, Georg Stanford Brown, James Earl Jones, Cicely Tyson

Boom! A John Heyman Production for Universal Pictures, 1968. 110 minutes
Producer: John Heyman and Norman Priggen
Director: Joseph Losey
Screenwriter: Tennessee Williams, based on his short story, "Man Bring Up This Road" and his play *The Milk Train Doesn't Stop Here Anymore*
Cast: Elizabeth Taylor, Richard Burton, Noel Coward, Joanna Shimkus, Michael Dunn, Romolo Valli, Howard Taylor

Secret Ceremony. A Universal/World Film Services Ltd/Paul M. Heller Production, Released by Universal Pictures, 1968. 109 minutes
Producer: John Heyman and Norman Priggen
Director: Joseph Losey

Screenwriter: George Tabori, based on a short story by Marco Denevi
Cast: Elizabeth Taylor, Mia Farrow, Robert Mitchum, Pamela Brown, Peggy Ashcroft

The Only Game in Town. A George Stevens–Fred Kohlmar Production for 20th Century-Fox, 1970. 113 minutes
Producer: Fred Kohlmar
Director: George Stevens
Screenwriter: Frank D. Gilroy, based on his play
Cast: Elizabeth Taylor, Warren Beatty, Charles Braswell, Hank Henry

Under Milk Wood. A Timon Production, Released in the U.S. by Altura Films International, 1971. 90 minutes
Producers: Hugh French and Jules Buck
Director: Andrew Sinclair
Screenwriter: Andrew Sinclair, based on the radio play by Dylan Thomas
Cast: Richard Burton, Elizabeth Taylor, Peter O'Toole, Glynis Johns, Vivien Merchant, Sian Phillips, Ryan Davies, Angharad Rees

Zee & Co. (Also titled *X Y & Zee.*) A Zee Film, a Kastner–Ladd–Kanter Production, released by Columbia Pictures, 1972. 110 minutes
Executive Producer: Elliott Kastner
Producers: Jay Kanter and Alan Ladd, Jr.
Director: Brian G. Hutton
Screenwriter: Edna O'Brien
Cast: Elizabeth Taylor, Michael Caine, Susannah York, Margaret Leighton, John Standing

Hammersmith Is Out, A J. Cornelius Crean Films Inc. Production, distributed by Cinerama Releasing Corporation, 1972. 108 minutes
Producer: Alex Lucas
Director: Peter Ustinov
Screenwriter: Stanford Whitmore
Cast: Elizabeth Taylor, Richard Burton, Beau Bridges, Peter Ustinov, Leon Ames, George Raft

Night Watch. A Joseph E. Levine and Burt Productions Presentation, an Avco Embassy Release, 1973. 99 minutes
Producers: Martin Poll, George W. George, and Bernard S. Straus
Director: Brian G. Hutton
Screenwriter: Tony Williamson, based on the play by Lucille Fletcher
Cast: Elizabeth Taylor, Laurence Harvey, Billie Whitelaw, Robert Lang, Tony Britton, Bill Dean

Ash Wednesday. A Sagittarius Production, A Paramount Pictures Release, 1973. 99 minutes
Producer: Dominick Dunne
Director: Larry Peerce
Screenwriter: Jean-Claude Tramont
Cast: Elizabeth Taylor, Henry Fonda, Helmut Berger, Keith Baxter, Monique Van Vooren

That's Entertainment. A Metro-Goldwyn-Mayer Picture, a United Artists Release, 1974. 132 minutes
Executive Producer: Daniel Melnick
Producer: Jack Haley, Jr.
Director: Jack Haley, Jr.
Screenwriter: Jack Haley, Jr.
Cast of narrators: Fred Astaire, Bing Crosby, Gene Kelly, Peter Lawford, Liza Minnelli, Donald O'Connor, Debbie Reynolds, Mickey Rooney, Frank Sinatra, James Stewart, Elizabeth Taylor

Identikit (Also titled *The Driver's Seat*.) A Rizzoli Film, an Avco Embassy Pictures Corporation Release, 1974. 105 minutes
Producer: Franco Rossellini
Director: Giuseppe Patroni Griffi
Screenwriters: Raffaele La Capria and Giuseppe Patroni Griffi, based on the Muriel Spark novella
Cast: Elizabeth Taylor, Ian Bannon, Guido Mannari, Mona Washbourne, Maxence Mailfort

The Blue Bird. 20th Century-Fox, 1976. 99 minutes
Executive Producer: Edward Lewis
Producer: Paul Maslansky
Director: George Cukor
Screenwriters: Hugh Whitmore and Alfred Hayes, based on the play by Maurice Maeterlinck
Cast: Elizabeth Taylor, Ava Gardner, Jane Fonda, George Rose, Cicely Tyson, Will Geer, Mona Washbourne, Robert Morley, James Coco

Victory at Entebbe. David L. Wolper Production, 1976. 150 minutes
Executive Producer: David L. Wolper
Producer: Robert Guenette
Director: Marvin J. Chomsky
Screenwriter: Ernest Kinoy
Cast: Helmut Berger, Theodore Bikel, Linda Blair, Kirk Douglas, Richard Dreyfuss, David Groh, Helen Hayes, cameos by Burt Lancaster and Elizabeth Taylor.

A Little Night Music. New World Picture, 1977. 124 minutes
Executive Producer: Heinz Lazek
Producer: Elliott Kastner
Director: Harold Prince
Screenwriter: Hugh Wheeler, based on the theatrical musical with music and lyrics by Stephen Sondheim and book by Hugh Wheeler, suggested by *Smiles of a Summer Night* by Ingmar Bergman
Cast: Elizabeth Taylor, Diana Rigg, Len Cariou, Lesley-Anne Down, Hermione Gingold

Winter Kills. Avco Embassy, 1979. 97 minutes
Executive Producers: Leonard J. Goldberg and Robert Sterling
Producer: Fred Caruso
Director: William Richert
Screenwriter: William Richert, based on a book by Richard Condon
Cast: Jeff Bridges, John Huston, Anthony Perkins, Eli Wallach, Sterling Hayden, Ralph Meeker, Toshiro Mifune, Richard Boone, cameo by Elizabeth Taylor

The First Aids Benefit

APLA, or AIDS Project Los Angeles, sponsored the first AIDS benefit ever, on the night of September 19, 1985. The event raised more than $1 million for victims of the disease that had previously been spoken of only in whispers, thanks in large part to the generous support of Elizabeth Taylor, who was radiant in black lace and emeralds given her by Richard Burton. Committee members included Shirley MacLaine, Yoko Ono, Roddy McDowall, Richard Pryor, and Brooke Shields. Among the performers were Carol Burnett, Sammy Davis, Jr., Diahann Carroll, Cyndi Lauper, Rod Stewart, and Bette Midler.

The event was held just a few weeks before the death of Taylor's good friend Rock Hudson. Burt Lancaster read a statement from the ailing star, saying, "Please be sure that I am with you in thought and spirit. I am particularly proud to learn that there is such a significant turnout of people from my industry present and extremely proud of my good friend, Elizabeth Taylor, who organized this event." Although there were later allegations that Hudson had known nothing of the statement issued in his name, the benefit undoubtedly helped ameliorate public attitudes toward victims of AIDS.

The First Divorce

Elizabeth Taylor has often talked about the pain she felt during her first divorce. "When I was first divorced, I was eighteen and I had only been married nine months. I was very naive and really totally crushed. It was the first divorce in my family." It was a period of great disillusionment in her life.

First Earnings

Universal Studios signed Elizabeth Taylor to her first movie contract in 1942, paying her $200 a week. She made only one movie for them, *There's One Born Every Minute*, before they dropped her, but she earned a total of $8,000 during the life of the contract. As required by the law passed to protect Hollywood's child stars from greedy or incompetent parents, half of the money was put away in Elizabeth's name, to be held until she came of age. The other half could be spent as the Taylors saw fit.

First Home of Her Own

Although Elizabeth Taylor had lived in a cozy Hollywood apartment after her separation from Nicky Hilton, she did not buy a home of her own there until her marriage to Michael Wilding. At the time she signed a new contract with MGM, an event nearly simultaneous with her 1952 wedding, she also borrowed $50,000 from the studio to help pay for a comfortable $75,000 house. The house was really a two-bedroom cottage, but it had been remodeled by previous owners to create more rooms. There was also a small guest house on the property. With the birth of the Wildings' second child, they realized they had outgrown their first home, and bought a second on Summit Drive.

First Memory

Elizabeth Taylor told journalist Liz Smith that her earliest memory was of pain—when as a little girl she burned her finger on an electric heater in the family's London house.

First Oscar

Elizabeth Taylor had been nominated for an Oscar for three previous roles, but her first win came with her role of Gloria Wandrous in MGM's *Butterfield 8*. Taylor had not wanted to do the film at all, publicly calling it "a piece of shit." But MGM insisted, announcing that they would not allow her to work for 20th Century-Fox in the glamourous starring role of *Cleopatra* until she honored her expiring MGM contract and agreed to make *Butterfield 8*. Taylor was surprised to receive an Academy Award nomination—and even more surprised to win the Academy Award for her performance as a call girl destroyed by her love for one of her clients. Fellow nominee Deborah Kerr said graciously, "The Oscar should go to Elizabeth. Not because of her grave illness but because her performance in *Butterfield 8* is superb." But another nominated actress, Shirley MacLaine, said flatly, "I was beaten by a tracheotomy." Taylor was as quick as everyone else in Hollywood to make the connection between her win and her near-fatal bout of pneumonia while she was in London to start production on *Cleopatra*. She later explained, "The reason I got the Oscar was that I had come within a breath of dying of pneumonia a few months before."

Whatever the reason, the night she accepted the Oscar left the American public with an indelible image of the beautiful young star, so pale and weak, with the scar of a tracheotomy still livid on her slender throat. Taylor said, "I was filled with gratitude when I got it, for it meant being considered an actress and not a movie star. My eyes were wet and my throat awfully tight." Her husband Eddie Fisher offered to carry the award for her if it was getting too heavy. "It isn't," Elizabeth answered. "I'll carry it until it's too much. I waited a long time." She later commented, "Any of my three previous nominations was more deserving. I knew it was a sympathy award, but I was still proud to get it."

First Screen Kiss

Elizabeth Taylor's first screen kiss came from actor James Lydon, in the movie *Cynthia*—not, as often reported, Robert Stack in *A Date with Judy*. *Cynthia*, released in 1947, was the story of a sickly young girl who fights her way to a normal life and thereby regains good health. The climax of the plot is her desire to attend the prom, escorted by Lydon, a goal she finally achieves. On that wonderful night, with her hair up in a sophisticated style and a locket on a black velvet ribbon emphasizing the off-the-shoulder cut of her dress, she turns into the belle of the ball. Of course, her admiring and devoted escort just *has* to give her a kiss! The moment was shy and tender, with none of the sensual passion Taylor would later learn to capture on the screen.

Taylor's first screen kiss was a momentous publicity event. It made front-page headlines in many newspapers, and movie theaters all over the country held "Why I Deserve To Be Kissed by Liz" contests.

First Wedding Ring

Elizabeth Taylor's first wedding ring, from Nicky Hilton in 1950, was a $10,000 diamond-studded platinum band. It went with a five-carat engagement ring.

Carrie Fisher

Carrie Francis Fisher is the daughter of Elizabeth Taylor's fourth husband, Eddie Fisher, and his first wife, Debbie Reynolds. Carrie, born on October 21, 1956, was a much-photographed toddler when her father left her mother to marry Elizabeth Taylor. She later became an actress, appearing with her mother in her nightclub act as well as on Broadway in *Irene*, and then winning the role of the sexually precocious teenager who seduces Warren Beatty in *Shampoo*. Her big break came with the role of Princess Leia in George Lucas's *Star Wars* films. Carrie married and divorced singer Paul Simon. Her autobiographical novel, *Postcards from the Edge*, hit the best-seller list and was released in 1990 as a movie, starring Meryl Streep and Shirley MacLaine. Her second novel, *Surrender the Pink*, was also a best seller.

Eddie Fisher

Eddie Fisher was a very close friend of Mike Todd, Elizabeth Taylor's third husband. The two men met through Fisher's agent, who often supplied talent for Mike Todd's shows. Friends noticed how Eddie quickly tried to model himself after Mike, even ordering the same food in restaurants. Eddie later commented defensively, "Maybe I had adopted some of Mike's superficial characteristics, but I wasn't trying to step into his shoes. I was still me."

Eddie and his wife Debbie Reynolds attended Todd's wedding to Elizabeth Taylor, for which Eddie was Mike's best man and Debbie acted as Elizabeth's bridesmaid. The two couples remained close friends until Todd was killed in a plane crash in March 1958. Eddie, himself devastated with grief, assumed the role of comforter to the bereaved widow. He was for a time a tower of strength in her life, caring for her and helping her through a very dark and depressing period.

By late summer of that year, Taylor had apparently decided she wanted to marry Fisher. The couple spent a weekend together at Grossinger's, the Catskills resort where Eddie was performing, and then extended their togetherness in a New York hotel, when Eddie was scheduled to be at home in Hollywood celebrating his third wedding anniversary with Debbie. In what amounted to a national scandal, Elizabeth and Eddie announced they intended to wed as soon as he could be divorced from his wife. Debbie greeted photographers at the front door of the couple's Hollywood home, wearing pigtails and carrying baby son Todd's (named after you-know-who) inexpensive vinyl bottle bag, the kind instantly recognized by every mother in America. She told reporters she still loved Eddie and hoped he would come back home. Taylor was promptly denounced as a home-wrecker.

In the course of an appearance at a Las Vegas hotel, Fisher established Nevada residence and obtained an immediate divorce decree. His marriage to Elizabeth Taylor took place in Las Vegas, on May 12, 1959, in a ceremony at a Jewish temple. The following year, Elizabeth and Eddie adopted a young crippled German girl named Maria.

Fisher, the fourth child of a Jewish street peddler from South Philadelphia, was born Edwin Jack Fisher on August 10, 1928. A beautiful baby, he was called "Sonny Boy" by the nurses at the hospital; the name was later shortened to "Sonny," a favorite nickname used by all his friends. He struggled up the ladder, starting with occasional jobs at Grossinger's. His career really got off the ground when he was taken on as a client by Milton Blackstone, who introduced him to Eddie Cantor, a career mentor. Fisher spent two years in the army in the early 1950s, making records on every leave, and he came out a teen idol. In 1953, every record he made hit the charts—often with both the A and the B side. His biggest hit was "Oh My Papa"; others were "I'm Yours," "Lady of Spain," and "Any Time." Fisher was also the host of a hit TV musical variety show called *Coke Time*.

In September 1955, he married Debbie Reynolds in a ceremony at Grossinger's, and the couple was promptly labeled by the press "America's Sweethearts." They had two children, Carrie Francis (1956) and Todd Emmanuel (1958). In 1959, Eddie divorced Reynolds and married Taylor. Divorce came again on March 6, 1964, when Taylor wanted to be free to marry Richard Burton. Fisher next married singer Connie Stevens in February 1968, several months after the couple's first child, Joely, was born. Their second daughter, Tricia, was born in December of that year. They were divorced in 1969. His fourth wife was Terry Richard, a Louisiana beauty queen, whom he married on October 29, 1975. The marriage lasted only four months.

The negative publicity surrounding his marriage to Taylor, coupled with changes in American musical tastes due to the popularity of rock and roll, very nearly ended Fisher's career. His TV show was canceled in 1959, and he never had another record on the charts. In 1970, Eddie was forced to declare bankruptcy, and shortly thereafter, he sought help in freeing himself from an addiction to amphetamines and cocaine. Further bad publicity came when police questioned him in regard to the 1976 murder of a private detective linked to Eddie's drug purchases. In 1981, Fisher wrote a kiss-and-tell autobiography, *Eddie: My Life, My Loves*.

Liz watchers agree that the problems in her relationship with Eddie came when she began to recover her own strength, and then to look for the kind of male toughness she had found in Mike Todd—and was later to find again in Richard Burton. "I let myself go into marriage with Eddie because I felt so sick and dead and cold after Mike's death," she later confessed. "I really thought for some idiotic reason that Eddie needed me, and I should make *somebody* happy. It turned out that all we had in common was Mike."

The breakdown in the marriage was accelerated when Elizabeth met Richard Burton on the set of *Cleopatra*. Although Eddie accompanied her on location in Rome, she treated him with a mixture of contempt and hostility. According to one published report, when she came home from the set to find her husband—proud possessor of many gold records—singing in the bedroom, she shouted, "For Christ's sake, Eddie, knock it off!"

Maria Flynn

Maria Flynn was a child actress in the early 1940s, best known for her role in *Intermezzo* with Ingrid Bergman. Maria was cast as the Duke's granddaughter in *Lassie Come Home*, but when producer Sam Marx looked at the first rushes, he saw that she had grown nearly a head taller than Roddy McDowall, the star of the film. Maria had to go, and the replacement Marx found was young Elizabeth Taylor. The movie got her a contract with MGM and launched her career. Marx later said he never heard of Maria Flynn again.

Food Binges

According to 1989 reports from various sources, Elizabeth Taylor sometimes binges on junk food—perhaps in reaction to her attempts at remaining on her diet. Although in public she is generally restrained in her eating habits, she overeats in private, concentrating on such foods as fried chicken and mashed potatoes with gravy. There are also reports that she sends her chauffeur into convenience stores to purchase ice cream bars, potato chips, and candy, then sits in the back of her limo and consumes them all in one sitting.

The "Food Poisoning" Episode

While Elizabeth Taylor was in Rome shooting *Cleopatra*, she fell ill and was rushed to the hospital with what studio press releases described euphemistically as "food poisoning." Close media scrutiny revealed the fact that the star's illness was actually due to an overdose of sedatives. Richard Burton, alarmed by the scandal that their romance was causing, had left for Paris with his wife and two daughters, and Taylor was in despair because she believed their romance was over. Eddie Fisher took his wife home from the hospital and tried to repair their marriage with constant attention and the gift of a $250,000 emerald necklace. Within weeks, Taylor and Burton met again, and the romance continued.

Footprints at Grauman's Chinese Theatre

One of the most sought-after rituals of stardom in the 1940s and 1950s was being asked to put your footprints in the cement outside Grauman's Chinese Theater in Hollywood. In 1956, that honor was accorded Elizabeth Taylor. She and her *Giant* costar, Rock Hudson, left both foot- and handprints in Grauman's wet cement, while photographers snapped away.

Malcolm Forbes

Malcolm Forbes was one of Elizabeth Taylor's steadfast admirers. Forbes, born in New York City in 1919, attended Princeton, worked for a year as the publisher of a weekly newspaper in a small Ohio town, and then joined his father in 1946 at *Forbes*, the magazine of which he was chairman and CEO until his death in 1990. A true Renaissance man, Forbes wrote books, collected the Fabergé eggs that were once the favorite gifts of Russia's Romanov rulers, won awards for his sartorial elegance, and set many records in hot air ballooning. Divorced in 1985 from his wife of forty years, he began at about the same time to escort Elizabeth Taylor to a variety of highly publicized events, and rumors flew that the two would marry. Although the rumors conflicted with the concurrent speculation about Taylor and new beau Larry Fortensky, Forbes remained a close friend and admirer of Taylor and enjoyed creating little surprises to cheer her up. Among his gifts to Elizabeth were a motorcycle, in purple to match her eyes. In the summer of 1989, Elizabeth Taylor was Malcolm Forbes's official hostess for the fabulous party to celebrate his seventieth birthday with hundreds of his friends in Morocco.

Larry Lee Fortensky

In 1988, while a patient at the Betty Ford Center, Elizabeth Taylor met fellow patient Larry Lee Fortensky, with whom she became romantically involved. Larry, thirty-eight and divorced, is a former truck driver who was placed on probation after a drunk-driving conviction in 1987. After Taylor's release from the clinic, he was photographed escorting her to a Michael Jackson concert, and also reportedly accompanied her to meetings of Alcoholics Anonymous.

When press reports about Fortensky's past (cruelly labeling him a "jailbird") began to appear, the romance seemed to cool off. Then Taylor went to Paris to promote her Passion perfume in the European market, and apparently absence made the heart grow fonder. When she returned, she took Larry with her for a weekend in San Francisco, at the Fairmount, the model for the TV series *Hotel*. Taylor was in town to attend a celebrity bash, and according to one report, she decided at the last minute not to take Larry with her. She got out of the limo and told the chauffeur to drive Larry around until it was time to return for her.

Rumor has it that her closest advisers have been much opposed to her involvement with Fortensky. Her publicist was quoted as saying Fortensky doesn't even know which fork to use at the dinner table. Perhaps that is why the couple seems to have spent time in quiet settings. For example, in the summer of 1989, the couple spent a weekend in the mountains near Santa Barbara, at a small unpretentious lodge, and visited his relatives for an evening of barbecue, one of Larry's favorite foods.

It seems likely that the bond between Taylor and Fortensky is based on their shared experience of fighting addictive behavior. Friends report that Liz feels free to "be herself" with the supportive and uncritical Larry, and that comfort is important to her long-term recovery.

As is always the case with the men in Taylor's life, there have been rumors of an impending marriage, which Fortensky has denied. He did, however, move into her Bel Air mansion, and she gave him a Pontiac Sunbird. In the late summer of 1989, gossips claimed that Liz had accepted Larry's proposal and would wed him in a simple ceremony at her home. Then she appeared at Malcolm Forbes's birthday party in Morocco, and suddenly the tabloid headlines blared that her relationship with Fortensky was over. Yet a trip with Fortensky to Thailand the following month seemed to contradict the rumors.

According to an article in the tabloid *Globe*, Elizabeth has offered Larry a million dollars to marry her, but he has refused to become another "Mr. Liz Taylor"; in the fat-obsessed *National Enquirer's* version of the story, Larry turned her down because she had gained too much weight. The *Globe* article quotes friend Roddy McDowall as telling Taylor that "you can't buy happiness—or a husband." It goes on to quote Taylor telling Larry, "All I want to do now is please you, sweetheart."

Pleasing her is exactly what he seems to be doing. Just before Christmas, 1990, he shaved off his mustache, presumably for her. He continued to be her cool and nonobstructive escort for events ranging from AIDS fund-raisers to department store appearances for "Passion." *People* reporter Landon Y. Jones may have provided an important insight into what makes their relationship solid. It's Fortensky's wry sense of humor.

At one point when she was in Marina del Rey Hospital, he smuggled in a tiny miniature goat in a cardboard box. "I thought it was cake!" Liz told Jones. She named the goat Marina.

Responding to snipes about Fortensky being a "poor boy," she said, "No boy is poor if he's rich at heart."

Marriage, though, is out, she insisted. "In today's society, you don't need to be married . . . not at my age, anyway."

Time, of course, will tell.

Fortieth Birthday Party

Elizabeth Taylor celebrated her fortieth birthday on February 27, 1972, with a party for 200 in Budapest, where her husband Richard Burton was on location for the movie *Bluebeard*. Guests at the party thrown by Burton, which went on for three days, included Princess Grace of Monaco, Beatle Ringo Starr, Michael Caine, David Niven, French hairdresser Alexandre, and Italian jeweler Gianni Bulgari. Taylor's son Michael Wilding, Jr., then living in a commune in Wales, pointedly refused to attend, criticizing his mother for such ostentation. Alan Williams, the son of Richard Burton's old friend Emlyn, was also in a critical mood; he called Taylor "a beautiful doughnut covered in diamonds and paint."

Burton's gift to Taylor was a twenty-five–carat yellow heart-shaped diamond set as a pendant, surrounded by rubies and white diamonds. The cost was $50,000. A previous owner of the ancient stone (the Indian ruler who built the Taj Mahal) had commissioned a carving into the back of the diamond, visible only when it is held up to the light: "Words of love."

Publicity surrounding the entire birthday celebration was surprisingly negative (perhaps because the press had been barred), with Burton and Taylor being criticized for their capitalistic extravagance in Eastern Europe. To mollify the critics, Taylor donated a sum equal to the cost of the birthday party to UNICEF. A check for $45,000 was presented to that organization's representative, Peter Ustinov.

Freak Accident on the set of Elephant Walk

While Elizabeth Taylor was shooting publicity stills for *Elephant Walk* on a Hollywood set, a freak accident drove a metal splinter into her eye. The scene took place in a hurricane, with powerful wind machines simulating the power of nature. For the photograph, Taylor was required to throw back her head, and at that moment, the splinter entered her eye. At first the studio physician thought that the star's eye was just irritated; it was not until several weeks later that the presence of the splinter was discovered. Delicate eye surgery was required to remove it, and for some weeks there was a fear that Taylor might lose the sight in the eye. Happily, she made a full recovery.

Hugh French

Hugh French was an Englishman residing in Hollywood who became Richard Burton's agent in the late 1950s. After Elizabeth Taylor's marriage to Burton, Hugh French became her agent as well, replacing Kurt Frings. One of Hugh French's professional associates was Michael Wilding, which is how Taylor's second husband ended up representing her fifth husband as an agent.

The Friar's Club Award

In 1983, Elizabeth Taylor was honored as Woman of the Year by the Friar's Club, an exclusive group of show-biz celebrities. Dressed all in white and wearing the tiara Mike Todd had given her, Taylor received tributes from Frank Sinatra, Dinah Shore, Ella Fitzgerald, and Brooke Shields.

Fried Chicken

Elizabeth Taylor has always freely admitted that she doesn't do much of her own housework. Husband Michael Wilding claimed she burned the toast when she tried to fix breakfast, and years of living in hotel suites didn't do anything to improve her domestic skills. But she says one thing she did learn how to cook well (while married to John Warner) is fried chicken. She calls her specialty "English-Virginia fried chicken." It happens to be one of her favorite dishes.

Kurt Frings

In 1958, Elizabeth Taylor signed a contract with European agent Kurt Frings. He represented Audrey Hepburn, as well as Lucille Ball and Brigitte Bardot. Frings was the one who negotiated Taylor's $1 million contract with 20th Century-Fox, making her the highest-paid actress in the world. He later recalled, "I didn't use a gun . . . The thing was that until that time none of her pictures had lost any money. Without a sure drawing card, Fox could not have considered the investment. It was a matter of whether they wanted to do the project or not. It is up to the agent to know what a studio wants badly and to hold out for it. When we had to start again in Rome, we charged them a second million."

Kurt and his wife Ketti—like Kurt, Austrian-born—were included in Taylor's intimate circle. They attended her weddings, comforted her when Mike Todd died, gave her emotional support when she was the subject of vicious criticism in the press. Kurt also helped her adopt a German orphan, her daughter Maria. After Taylor's marriage to Richard Burton, she switched agents and was thereafter represented by Burton's agent, Hugh French.

Aaron R. Frosch

Attorney Aaron R. Frosch represented Elizabeth Taylor in her divorce action against Eddie Fisher. Like many people involved in a professional capacity with the Burtons, Frosch became a good friend of both Elizabeth and Richard. He lent the couple his house in Quogue, Long Island, for one of their attempts at a reconciliation before their first divorce, and then represented Taylor in the second divorce. Frosch, a graduate of Brooklyn Law School with an office in Manhattan, also represented Taylor when she adopted her daughter Maria, and he successfully handled the negotiations that kept Maria in the Burton family when her parents later reappeared and threatened to file suit for the return of the child they had put up for adoption because of her badly crippled hip. Frosch wrote Marilyn Monroe's will and was an executor of her estate. He continued to represent Burton in a number of legal matters until the actor's 1976 marriage to Suzy Hunt. Frosch died in 1989.

Fund for Children of the Negev

In 1982, Elizabeth Taylor, acting through the Ben Gurion University in Israel, initiated the Fund for the Children of the Negev, an international charitable fund benefitting poor children of the Negev Desert, both Israelis and Palestinians.

Funeral of Mike Todd

Elizabeth Taylor had become hysterical when she was told of the death of her husband, Mike Todd, in a plane crash in the early-morning hours of Sunday, March 23, 1958. She had to be heavily sedated, and when she left for the funeral, she was still unable to stand on her own. She flew to Chicago, Todd's family home, in a plane provided by Howard Hughes. Her companions included her physician, Dr. Rex Kennamer; her brother Howard; designer Helen Rose, who had made the dress Elizabeth wore when she married Todd; AP reporter Jim Bacon, who was to have flown on *The Lucky Liz* with Todd but canceled at the last minute for fear of the weather; and Todd's close friend Eddie Fisher. Fisher's wife, Debbie Reynolds, had volunteered to stay at Elizabeth's home to look after her three children.

Todd's bronze coffin was buried at the foot of the grave of his father, Rabbi Hyman Goldbogen, in the Waldheim Cemetery, a Jewish cemetery in a Chicago suburb. Hundreds of curious spectators thronged the cemetery just to get a look at the celebrities who attended the famous showman's funeral, and to stare at his grief-stricken widow, wearing a black suit and diamond earrings. Her dear friend Montgomery Clift, who had flown out from New York to be with her, remembered, "It was noisy, vengeful. I saw envy in their faces, envy and hatred and bleakness." The crowds pressed around the widow and tore off her veil; it took her a terrifying ten minutes to make her way back to her waiting car. Later she and Monty talked about an odd detail they had both noticed. Many of the curiosity seekers were munching potato chips, as if they were at a movie. For weeks after the funeral, Elizabeth received an average of 2,000 letters of condolence a day. One was from Mamie Eisenhower, saying, "The President and I extend our deepest sympathy."

A macabre footnote: In 1978, grave robbers stole the body of Mike Todd, in an apparent search for a diamond ring. The remains were recovered and reinterred.

-G-

Tony Geary

Tony Geary was the heartthrob with a leading role in *General Hospital*, the TV daytime soap. Taylor was a fan of the program and arranged to appear on it briefly as a lark. After meeting on the set, she and Geary became involved in a short-lived but passionate romance.

General Hospital

In the spring of 1982, the ratings of the daytime TV soap, *General Hospital*, shot up when Elizabeth Taylor appeared in several episodes as the mysterious Mrs. Considine, playing opposite the show's leading man, romantic idol Tony Geary. Taylor was a fan of the soap and approached the producer with a request to do a guest shot. Her appearance sparked rumors of a romance with Tony Geary, given additional fuel when she announced she was filing for a divorce from John Warner.

Genocide

In 1982, Elizabeth Taylor served as the narrator of a documentary film about the treatment of Jews by the Nazis during World War II, prepared by the Simon Wiesenthal Center for Holocaust Studies.

Giant

Giant is unquestionably one of the highlights of Elizabeth Taylor's film career. In the 1956 movie, directed by George Stevens, she played the role of Leslie Lynnton Benedict, wife of a Texas rancher (Rock Hudson). The audience watches her age from a young bride to a middle-aged matron, coping along the way with the attentions of ranchhand Jett Rink (James Dean in his last movie role before his untimely death in a car crash) and with a myriad of family problems ranging from unwelcoming in-laws to interracial marriage.

Based on the best-selling novel by Edna Ferber, *Giant* was a good story to start with, and director George Stevens did an excellent job of bringing it to the screen. He had worked with Taylor once before, in *A Place in the Sun*, and based on the performance he coaxed out of her in that 1951 movie, his expectations were higher this time around. Stevens could on occasion be a source of gentle encouragement to his stars, but he was also known to be ruthless about getting what he wanted on the screen. According to one report from the set, when Stevens was unable to get Taylor to render the correct degree of anguish in one scene, he surreptitiously told the wardrobe girl to give her shoes that were several sizes too small. The pain in her feet was reflected in her face!

Critical response to Elizabeth Taylor's performance was warm. One reviewer said her portrayal of Leslie was "compounded of equal parts of fervor and Ferber"; another commented that "she displays new artistry in meeting the sterner demands of parenthood and grandparenthood."

Variety said, "Miss Taylor . . . turns in a surprisingly clever performance that registers up and down the line. She is tender and yet stubborn. Curiously enough, she's far better in the second half of the film when her hair begins to show some gray."

Giant produced a number of Academy Award nominations, but as was the case with many of her best movies in the 1950s, Elizabeth Taylor was not among those nominated. Rock Hudson, James Dean, and Mercedes McCambridge (as Taylor's jealous sister-in-law) were nominated for their performances; the screenplay, score, and movie itself were also nominated. Out of ten nominations, there was only one winner: George Stevens for Best Director.

Gee Gee

Gee Gee was a white poodle that was a companion to Elizabeth Taylor and the two little Wilding boys in the 1950s. Her husband Michael thought she was too lenient with Gee Gee, allowing her and her daughter Mugwumps the run of the house without any discipline. Taylor's previous husband, Nicky Hilton, had made the same complaint several years earlier.

The Girl Who Had Everything

The Girl Who Had Everything, with Elizabeth Taylor starring in the title role, was shot in the early months of the star's first pregnancy, not long after her marriage to British actor Michael Wilding. The plot of this 1953 MGM release was a melodrama, with Taylor cast as the daughter of a wealthy criminal lawyer (played by William Powell, with whom she had previously appeared in *Life with Father*). She falls in love with an obvious Mr. Wrong (Fernando Lamas), a handsome but shady character who is one of her father's clients. Naturally, she disregards her father's attempts to discourage the romance, but after her boyfriend assaults her father and then is knocked off by his criminal associates, she returns to the family home a chastened young woman, ready to marry her faithful—and eminently suitable—beau, played by Gig Young.

The Girl Who Had Everything was actually a remake of the 1931 movie, *A Free Soul*, which made Clark Gable a star in the role of the gangster boyfriend; Norma Shearer played the heroine in that version, and won an Oscar nomination for her performance. The remake couldn't hold a candle to the original. Critics found the script of *The Girl Who Had Everything* implausible and complained that the movie wasted the talents of Powell and Taylor. It was one more in the series of films that depended primarily on the breathtaking beauty of Elizabeth Taylor to carry an entire production; as one reviewer put it, "Miss Taylor is her usual beautiful self, gracing the screen in formals, bathing suits and sports clothes."

Jules Goldstone

Jules Goldstone became Elizabeth Taylor's agent at the time she was cast in *National Velvet*, and he continued to represent her throughout her entire career at MGM. When Taylor divorced first husband Nicky Hilton, she stayed for a period with Goldstone and his wife, and it was Goldstone who recommended to her the secretary who then became her roommate, Peggy Rutledge.

Goldstone sometimes found his famous client irritating to deal with. After he no longer represented her, he complained that she had often undermined his negotiations. While he was trying to win a large salary from MGM for Elizabeth, she would go behind his back to talk to studio execs and settle for getting all the clothes from her next picture instead. Goldstone also commented, "I felt very paternal and very protective toward Liz. I used to tell her she was the nearest thing to royalty we had in this country, that she had the adulation of the world, but I don't think she took it in, in spite of all the fan mail."

In 1958, Elizabeth Taylor ended her professional relationship with Jules Goldstone, signing instead with Kurt Frings. Yet she continued to acknowledge the role of Goldstone's guidance in shaping her career.

Gone with the Wind

Hollywood in 1939 was totally absorbed in the question of the casting of the movie version of Margaret Mitchell's bestselling novel, *Gone with the Wind*. After Clark Gable was selected to play the dashing Rhett Butler, the search for the perfect Scarlett became a national mania, and every dramatic actress, from Bette Davis to Katharine Hepburn, tested for the part. Once producer David O. Selznick had chosen Vivien Leigh as his Scarlett, competition shifted to smaller roles in the film. Among the actresses who hoped to be in *Gone with the Wind* was the seven-year-old Elizabeth Taylor. She and her mother both thought she was ideal for the part of Bonnie, the daughter of Scarlett and Rhett, especially since she bore a strong resemblance to Vivien Leigh. Unfortunately, Elizabeth's father refused to let her test for the role. Her first screen test did not come until several years later, at Universal Pictures.

Nearly two decades later, Elizabeth Taylor replaced Vivien Leigh as the star of *Elephant Walk* after Leigh suffered a nervous breakdown on location in Ceylon. The clothes made for Vivien Leigh had to be let out slightly to fit Taylor, but the two were such a close match that it was possible to use background footage shot of Leigh on location in the movie starring Taylor.

Goodbye, David Janssen

The producer of *Butterfield 8*, Pandro Berman, had cast David Janssen as the piano player who is a platonic friend of call girl Gloria Wandrous (Elizabeth Taylor). But when production began, Taylor said she wanted her husband Eddie Fisher to play the part. He had turned down a nightclub tour to stay with her, as they had agreed when they were wed, and she felt he should have some compensation. MGM execs, concerned about Taylor's threats to stall the production of the movie they had forced her to appear in, felt that giving Fisher the role was a small price to pay for peace. So Berman was told to let Janssen go and use Fisher instead. Berman, no fan of Elizabeth Taylor, later said, "I hated doing it, but I had no choice. Fisher was a bum. He was a drug addict and on top of that he was a lousy actor." Taylor subsequently came up with many pages of additional dialogue to expand her husband's role, but on that point Berman stood firm.

Gossip Columnists

For decades, Elizabeth Taylor has been a boon to writers of gossip columns. From the time of her first screen kiss in 1948 to the present-day covers of the tabloids, reports true and false about the life and especially the loves of Liz Taylor have sold millions of newspapers and magazines. Living amid the constant swirl of rumors has been difficult for the star, who has resented the intrusion into her privacy and the generally unflattering nature of much of the reportage. She once characterized gossip columnists as "bitches." In a 1987 press conference to announce the licensing agreement for her Passion fragrance, Taylor was teasingly asked by veteran gossiper Liz Smith whether she still held the same opinion. Taylor shot back, "I'll tell you tomorrow, Liz."

Grace Notes

Director George Stevens's first choice for the role of Rock Hudson's wife in *Giant* was Grace Kelly, who turned it down. Rumor has it that Grace Kelly was also Stevens's choice for the role of Angela in *A Place in the Sun*.

Granny Hot Pants

In the summer of 1971, Elizabeth Taylor became a grandmother for the first time when her son Michael Wilding and his wife Beth had their first child, a daughter named Laele. Taylor was photographed returning from a visit to meet the new baby, wearing the scantiest hot pants outfit, daisy trimmed go-go boots, and the gleaming Krupp diamond. She told reporters, "You know, everybody assumes that this whole thing would upset me. That's silly. If you want to be honest, I feared turning thirty more than I fear being called Grandma."

"Grapple-Snapping"

"Grapple-snapping" is a word Elizabeth Taylor's brother made up when they were children. It means snacking—grabbing something to eat and gulping it down. In her book *Elizabeth Takes Off*, the star revealed that part of her weight problem was due to lifelong habit of grapple-snapping that became especially serious when she was on the campaign trail with then-husband John Warner.

Sidney Guilaroff

For many years, Elizabeth Taylor's favorite hairdresser has been Sidney Guilaroff. He first became her ally on the set of *National Velvet*. Director Clarence Brown told Taylor she must cut her own hair to do the scene in which Velvet cuts her hair to impersonate a boy. Taylor was distressed by the order and worried about the length of time it would take for her own hair to grow back. So she went to Guilaroff, the movie's hairdresser, and he created a wig for her which he then cut to look like it had just been chopped off. It was such a success that even the director was fooled for a time.

After Taylor grew up and became a star of the first magnitude, she got into the habit of demanding in her movie contracts a guarantee that Guilaroff would do her hair. This caused great labor troubles on the set of *Cleopatra*, because he did not belong to the Italian labor union that controlled labor relations in Rome. He became a member of Taylor's inner circle, often traveling with her, attending her parties, and lending her emotional support. In the grief-stricken days after Mike Todd was killed, Guilaroff even slept on a sofa in Elizabeth's bedroom, so she would always have someone near her.

Gun Control

After the 1968 assassination of Senator Robert F. Kennedy, Elizabeth Taylor took out a full-page advertisement in *The New York Times* in support of gun control. A lifelong Democrat, she had gotten to know the Kennedys through her friendship with Peter Lawford, whose first wife was Kennedy's sister Pat. Taylor and husband Richard Burton had become good friends of Bobby and Ethel, and the two men often competed to see who could recite the largest number of Shakespearean sonnets from memory. (Burton once won by reciting one of the sonnets backward.) The senator's death was a personal loss to Taylor, one that she blamed in part on the lack of gun control laws in the United States.

-ℋ-

Philippe Halsman

Elizabeth Taylor has said that she first learned to view herself as a woman when she had a photographic sitting with famed camera portraitist Philippe Halsman. He taught the sixteen-year-old how to make herself look older. "You have bosoms," Taylor quotes him as saying, "so stick them out!" As the cheesecake photos taken in her teen years demonstrate, she learned to comply.

Halston

After Elizabeth Taylor's second divorce from Richard Burton, fashion designer Halston joined her inner circle of friends. "We giggle and laugh and talk ten times a day," he told a reporter in 1976. He also helped her choose her clothes, guiding her toward a sleeker, more sophisticated image. She confided that the designer was also extremely tactful as she gained weight in the late 1970s. "Dear Halston kept me in pantsuits all the way up that ladder of fat." The designer died in 1990.

George Hamilton

Throughout 1986 and 1987, Liz watchers were interested to observe what appeared to be a romance between the star and her suntanned escort, George Hamilton. Hamilton, who has a reputation as a ladies' man, squired Taylor to many social events during those years, and they seemed to be enjoying one another's company. They costarred in a made-for-TV movie in 1987, called *Poker Alice*. But by early 1988, Taylor and Hamilton were no longer an item. There were rumors that the problem was George's eye for other women, including Catherine Oxenberg, whom he had met on the set of *Dynasty*. Other rumors suggested it was Liz who had found someone else, when she began dating Malcolm Forbes. One unidentified source said the real trouble was the clash of egos of two beautiful people: The *Star* quoted a "friend" as saying, "Elizabeth is an excessively vain person. But although you might not think it possible, George is even more vain. He spends as much time looking in the mirror as he did looking at Elizabeth, and that must have galled her."

Hamlet

In 1964, Richard Burton appeared in a stage production of *Hamlet*—in the title role, of course. It previewed in Toronto in the spring, and then went to Broadway. Normally, Shakespeare does not draw record crowds, but the scandal of the Burton–Taylor relationship, capped by their marriage while Burton was working in Toronto, made *Hamlet* a huge success. Every performance was sold out, and in all the production grossed over $6 million. Burton's reviews were for the most part highly laudatory.

Hammersmith Is Out

Hammersmith Is Out (1972) was the last theatrical movie in which Elizabeth Taylor and Richard Burton appeared together. Burton played Hammersmith, a criminal mastermind who is a Mephisthophelean figure. Taylor was Jimmie Jean Jackson, a buxom Southern waitress, a good old girl, latching on to love interest (and Faustian stand-in) Beau Bridges, playing a character named Billy Breedlove who is promised wealth and power by Hammersmith. The movie was directed by the Burtons' good friend Peter Ustinov, who saw it as a lighthearted spoof.

Elizabeth Taylor stole the show. She clearly had a good time camping it up in a strawberry-blonde wig and some exceptionally cheesy costumes, cleverly designed by Edith Head. "Gee, we could even have things we don't want," she says, as she hastens to enjoy the good life she has suddenly fallen into (and spoofs the publicity surrounding the big-spending Burtons in real life). Richard Burton seemed less comfortable, underplaying his part with the grim stare of the drugged. The movie was one more failure at the box office for the Burtons, but Taylor's own reviews were good. The *Spectator* said, "There is nothing to do except watch Elizabeth Taylor as a dumb redhead act everyone else out of the picture."

Hand Signals

When young Elizabeth Taylor first appeared in movies, her mother was always present on the set, and acted as her coach. Sara Taylor developed a set of hand signals to communicate with her daughter, letting her know when she should modulate her voice, or smile more, or restrain her performance.

Dick Hanley

Dick Hanley, once Louis B. Mayer's secretary, was Mike Todd's assistant at the time the producer was married to Elizabeth Taylor. When Todd was killed in a plane crash, Hanley stayed by Taylor's side, helping her through the difficult early days of her widowhood. He then became her executive assistant, a post he retained for the rest of his life. Hanley even had his own assistant, John Lee, to help him carry out his duties. When Dick Hanley died in 1970, Taylor (then married to Richard Burton, who also used Hanley's services) was saddened by the loss of someone who had been close to her for so many years. She paid for a lavish funeral.

Happy Birthday to Louis B. Mayer

While Elizabeth Taylor was a young starlet at MGM, she participated in the annual birthday parties for studio head Louis B. Mayer. Every year, all the young stars would gather on a huge sound stage and sing "Happy Birthday" to the Hollywood mogul. He generally responded with a speech about the MGM "family." "You must think of me as your father," he would tell them. "You are all my children." His annual bout of fatherly feelings lasted only until one of his "children" refused to do as he instructed.

Harlech Television

In 1969, Richard Burton helped finance a venture called Harlech Television, in partnership with Lord Harlech, once a friend of President John F. Kennedy and later an escort of his widow Jacqueline. Burton's financial investment was limited by law to about $250,000. The concept behind the company, which broadcast to Wales, was for Richard and his wife Elizabeth Taylor to put their time and talent to work elevating the standards of commercial television. But little came of the venture. The couple did appear for the opening of Harlech TV, but the media concentrated entirely on Taylor's acquisition of the Krupp diamond, which she had purchased just days earlier.

Four years later, Burton was criticizing Harlech TV for sending him bad scripts, and Lord Harlech was complaining that Burton hadn't attended a single program meeting and confined his activities to writing occasional letters of suggestion. Then Harlech TV found an investment partner in ABC-TV in America, and subsequently made a deal to act as production company for the TV movie, *Divorce:His/Divorce: Hers*, starring Taylor and Burton. Although the movie was a critical flop, and those present remember its production as a terrible trial, it did make money for Harlech TV stockholders. Shortly thereafter, Richard Burton was asked to resign from the Harlech board.

Rex Harrison Sues

Rex Harrison, costar of *Cleopatra*, feared that 20th Century-Fox would try to publicize the movie by exploiting the romance between Elizabeth Taylor and Richard Burton. Of course, he was right. He had negotiated a clause in his contract that stipulated that his name and picture had to appear beside Burton's, and be the same size, in all the advertisements. But Fox ignored the clause and put up a huge billboard on Broadway that showed Anthony and Cleopatra with no Caesar in sight. Harrison's lawyers promptly sued the studio. Her tells about the amusing result in his autobiography, *Rex*. "I was told that a very strange thing had occurred on Broadway. Men had been seen climbing up the scaffolding and sticking up a minute picture of Caesar in one corner of this gigantic poster, so that it now looked like a postcard with a stamp in the corner." It took more legal threats before a new poster, showing all three stars in equal size, was created.

Laurence Harvey

Elizabeth Taylor made two movies with Laurence Harvey, who became one of her close friends. They had another, more personal connection: Harvey's first wife was Margaret Leighton, who later became Elizabeth Taylor's ex-husband Michael Wilding's fourth, and last, wife.

Laurence Harvey (his professional name) was born in 1928 in Lithuania of Jewish parents, who emigrated to South Africa before World War II. He saw wartime service with the Allies and after the war went to England, where he was accepted as a student in the prestigious Royal Academy of Dramatic Art. He played Shakespeare at the Old Vic and later scored a huge success in the movie *Room at the Top*.

Elizabeth Taylor and Laurence Harvey costarred in *Butterfield 8*, for which she won an Academy Award in 1961. Harvey had requested her as his costar in *Of Human Bondage*, but she turned the role down and the studio signed Kim Novak instead. Taylor and Harvey didn't work together again until 1973, when they made *Night Watch*, Harvey's last major film. At that time he was battling cancer, and during the production he was hospitalized for surgery to remove part of his colon; he joked that he should thereafter be called "Semicolon."

Shortly after the film was finished, Harvey's condition deteriorated. Taylor flew to London to be with him and his wife in the last days of his life. He died on November 25, 1973, at the age of forty-five. Taylor, then a patient at UCLA Medical Center, collaborated with Peter Lawford to arrange a memorial service for her friend at St. Alban's Church in Westwood. Accompanied by Lawford and Henry Wynberg, she was allowed to leave the hospital long enough to attend. During the eulogy, delivered by John Ireland, Taylor wept, and later she told reporters, "I still can't believe I'll never see him again. He was a part of the sun."

Harvey seemed to bring his costars good luck. Taylor's first Oscar came for a movie in which she played opposite him; and the year before, the Best Actress statuette went to Simone Signoret, for *Room at the Top*, costarring Laurence Harvey. One of the losers was Elizabeth Taylor, for *Suddenly Last Summer*.

Hasty Pudding Woman of the Year

In 1978, Elizabeth Taylor won the Woman of the Year award from Harvard's prestigious Hasty Pudding Club.

Hawthorne Grammar School

Hawthorne School, located in Beverly Hills, was the public school for Grades One through Eight where young Elizabeth Taylor was enrolled when the Taylor family moved to Pacific Palisades, not long after their arrival in Los Angeles on the eve of World War II. Her brother Howard also attended Hawthorne.

Sally Hay

Richard Burton's fourth—and last—wife was Sally Hay. He met her in 1982 when she was a production assistant to director Tony Palmer (later to direct the film portrait called *Richard Burton: In from the Cold*) on the set of *Wagner*, in which Burton starred. She was then thirty-four, and had worked in various production jobs at the BBC since leaving high school. Richard first asked Palmer if he had any objections—"It was so sweet, and kind of old-fashioned, and rather formal"—and then asked Sally out to dinner. Thereafter he pursued her diligently, and soon she agreed to live with him. An excellent cook, she gave small dinner parties for his friends, and tactfully often included Elizabeth Taylor in the group. The following year, Burton obtained a Haitian divorce from third wife Suzy Hunt, and he and Sally Hay were married in Las Vegas on July 3, 1983, during the run of *Private Lives*, in which Burton was costarring with Elizabeth Taylor. When the newlyweds returned, Burton's ex-wife threw them a small party in her dressing room.

After the show closed in late 1983, Richard and Sally spent time in their new home in Haiti and then went to Burton's villa in Celigny. He told a reporter, "Sally's been renovating me like an old house. She's doing a wonderful job." Sally was at her husband's side when he died on August 5, 1984.

Sally Burton returned to television in 1986, appearing as an interviewer for BBC documentary called *Women in Hollywood*.

Edith Head

Edith Head was one of the best-known Hollywood costume designers; she won eight Oscars for her work. The stars she dressed ranged form Mae West in *She Done Him Wrong* to Audrey Hepburn in *Roman Holiday* and *Sabrina*—and back to Mae West again in *Myra Breckinridge*. Head first worked with Elizabeth Taylor on *A Place in the Sun*, creating the costumes that turned Taylor into the very embodiment of every red-blooded man's dream of the rich and beautiful girl in the convertible. Head, who won an Academy Award for her work on that 1951 film, always remembered the white formal she designed for Taylor: "When Elizabeth moved, she looked like sunlight moving over water." In her autobiography, *Dress Doctor*, she analyzed the details behind the effect: "For the debut gown, I relied on flowers, little violets, to accent the bodice, and I sprinkled them on the skirt. It's very difficult to look dated with flowers. The dress became especially dramatic because I made the skirt exceedingly full, with yards and yards of tulle over a pastel underskirt, and the flowers made the bust look fuller. The combination of the full bust and wide skirt accented the waist, making it appear even smaller than it was. Elizabeth prided herself on her tiny waist and was always willing to wear her gowns very tight to achieve a waspish look. I can still hear her telling me, 'Tighter, Miss Head, tighter.'"

Head also remembered the fun of working with the beautiful young star. "Elizabeth would always bring her pets with her, even to a fitting, which was sometimes a little upsetting to the fitter. She would bring dogs, cats, parakeets, squirrels—whatever her latest fancy was. What a picture! Here's this beautiful, exotic and very sexy girl listening to a schoolteacher tell her about the Seven Wonders of the World or whatever, with all the animals around and the fitter being very cautious because one of the dogs was cavorting about. It was like a three-ring circus; it was lovely."

Years later, Head also designed Taylor's wardrobe for such films as *Hammersmith Is Out* (1972) and *Ash Wednesday* (1973). Her last film with Taylor was The *Blue Bird*, (1976). Edith Head commented on the pleasures of dressing the star, saying, "When Elizabeth Taylor is elegant, there is nobody who can be so elegant. She moves so beautifully." Head added, "She has aged gracefully, despite what her detractors have said. She is beautiful when she is plump and she is lovely when she trims down."

Edith Head, born in Searchlight, Nevada, became a close friend of Elizabeth Taylor. During the star's separations from Richard Burton in 1973, she and daughter Maria stayed in Head's guest house. The designer warned the press not to conclude that the marriage was finished: "I've been with Elizabeth and Richard all over Europe, and I can tell you I have never seen two people who are so compatible . . . I know that Elizabeth is so much in love with Richard, and I know from the way she talks that she is looking at this as only a temporary separation." Following Head's death, October 24, 1981, her memorial service was attended by many stars, including Bette Davis, who gave the eulogy, and Elizabeth Taylor.

The Health and Beauty Connection

Elizabeth Taylor once told her MGM stand-in, Marjorie Dillon, "If I don't feel I look really good, I feel just awful physically."

Here's Lucy

Elizabeth Taylor and husband Richard Burton made a guest appearance, playing themselves on *Here's Lucy* in the season opener for 1970. The plot starts with Lucy's mistaking Richard Burton for a plumber and goes on to a hilarious scene in which Lucy meets Taylor, bowing and calling her "Your Majesty," and then begs to try on her fabulous Krupp diamond. Of course Lucy gets it stuck on her finger! The show earned the highest ratings of any series during the fall premiere week that year.

Her Own Harshest Critic

Elizabeth Taylor has frequently said that she thinks she falls short of real beauty. Her complaints about her own looks are primarily related to her body rather than her face. In a 1964 interview published in *Life*, she said, "I'm too short of leg, too big in the arms, one too many chins, big feet, big hands, too fat." In 1989, she told TV interviewer Leonard Maltin, "I don't like my voice, I don't like the way I look, I don't like the way I move, I don't like the way I act. I mean period." She then drew the obvious and sad conclusion: "So you know I don't like myself."

C. David Heymann

Carol Communications has announced that best-selling biographer C. David Heymann's next subject will be Elizabeth Taylor. Author of the blockbuster *A Woman Named Jackie* about Jacqueline Kennedy Onassis, Heymann said he was going to try to obtain his new subject's cooperation.

Noting that Kitty Kelley, who preceded him with her book on Jackie, had also written a best-selling bio of Taylor, Heymann said, "That was eight or nine years ago, and it contained inaccuracies, same as her book on Jackie."

The High Cost of Pregnancy

Elizabeth Taylor's first two pregnancies, with her sons by Michael Wilding, proved to be expensive ones. Under contract to MGM for $5,000 a week, Taylor was paid only for the weeks she actually worked. The months when she was unable to appear in front of the cameras because of her pregnant condition were also months that brought in no salary, for a total loss that probably reached at least $100,000 per pregnancy. As Taylor later explained bitterly, "Every time I got pregnant, kindhearted old MGM would put me on suspension."

High School Graduation

Elizabeth Taylor earned her high school credits by studying at MGM's schoolhouse on the lot. But when it was time to graduate, Taylor, like many other young stars, attended a graduation ceremony at an ordinary public high school. Hers took place at the University High School in Los Angeles. She wore a fetching white cap and gown, and posed for pictures with her proud parents. Four months later, the girl graduate became a bride.

Conrad Nicholson "Nicky" Hilton

Elizabeth Taylor's first husband was Conrad Nicholson "Nicky" Hilton, to whom she was introduced early in 1950 by her friend and fellow actor at MGM, Peter Lawford. Nicky was the son of hotel magnate Conrad Hilton, the Donald Trump of his day, whose fortune was then estimated at more than $100 million. Self-made Conrad approved of his son's choice of a wife, saying, "They've got everything, haven't they? Youth, looks, position, no need to worry about where their next meal is coming from."

Nicky Hilton, twenty-three at the time of the marriage, was nominally employed by his father. He had briefly attended college at Loyola (the Hiltons were Catholics), served in the Navy, and enrolled in the famed Ecole Hoteliere in Switzerland. When he proposed to Elizabeth Taylor, he was on the Hilton payroll, but he had no real career and hoped it would stay that way. Nicky Hilton was in fact the stereotypical second generation of a rich family, overindulged and without ambition. A genuine playboy, he was interested primarily in drinking and gambling with his cronies. Handsome, charming, and understandably impressed by the teenaged Taylor's stardom and glamour, he courted her with expensive presents and visits (with her parents) to the Hilton Family mansion in Bel Air. Elizabeth Taylor, sheltered by her parents and MGM, probably had no idea what Nicky did with his time when he was not in her company.

In the spring of 1950, Nicky gave the seventeen-year-old Elizabeth a five-carat diamond, and their engagement was officially announced. At the time, Taylor told the press, "I knew from the beginning Nicky was a person I could love and trust." When reporters asked Taylor what she and her fiancé had in common, she answered quickly, "We both love hamburgers with onions, oversized sweaters, and Ezio Pinza." As things turned out, that was not enough to base a marriage on.

Elizabeth and Nicky were married on May 6, 1950, in a Catholic ceremony that was exploited by MGM for publicity of Taylor's just released film, *Father of the Bride*. The honeymoon began in Carmel, California. Then the newlyweds flew to New York and boarded the *Queen Mary* (although they were not able to book the bridal suite, occupied by the Duke and Duchess of Windsor, later to become friends of Taylor and her fifth husband, Richard Burton). Once in Europe, the newlywed Hiltons traveled to London, Paris, Rome, and Monte Carlo.

While still on the honeymoon, their relationship took an immediate nosedive. Nicky was enraged by the adulation showered on Elizabeth everywhere by her fans. He later told a reporter, "It was life in a goldfish bowl. One time a battery of reporters and photographers invaded our suite—it happened all the time—and one of the photographers said to me, 'Hey, Mac, get out of the way, I want to snap a picture!'" Nicky seemed to prefer to drink and gamble rather than spend time with his bride. He went to the casinos while she remained in their luxury accommodations crying her eyes out every night. On the return trip aboard the *Queen Elizabeth*, it was noticeable that Nicky ignored Elizabeth, but she seemed intent on having a good time and stayed up dancing without him.

When the fourteen-week honeymoon ended and the couple returned to California, the relationship was no better. Elizabeth miscarried early in a pregnancy, while Nicky went through with a planned fishing trip. He hated being Mr. Elizabeth Taylor, and she—very much in love—could not cope with her husband's resulting hostility. On December 5, seven months after her wedding, Elizabeth Taylor left Nicky Hilton. MGM released her tactfully worded statement about the separation: "I am sorry that Nick and I are unable to adjust our differences, and that we have come to a final parting of the ways. We both regret this decision, but after personal discussion, we realize there is no possibility of a reconciliation." Taylor tried to carry on, filming *Love Is Better Than Ever*. Everyone who knew her agreed that she was devastated by the failure of her marriage, and she became so overwrought she had to spend a week in the Cedars of Lebanon hospital.

In February 1951, Elizabeth Taylor appeared in a Santa Monica courtroom and obtained her first divorce. She asked for no alimony, but was allowed to keep her $50,000 diamond ring and her 100 shares of Hilton Hotel stock, a wedding present from her former father-in-law. The actress then threw herself into a romance with director Stanley Donen, and Hilton subsequently announced his engagement to actress Betsy von Furstenburg. Yet there were rumors—some of them with confirming evidence—that Elizabeth and Nicky saw each other again secretly on several occasions after the divorce.

Nicky Hilton married two more times, once to von Furstenburg and then again to Patricia Maclintock, with whom he had two sons. They were separated at the time of his death of a massive heart attack in 1969, at the age of forty-two.

His 'n' Liz Rolls

Mike Todd, Elizabeth Taylor's third husband, bought a Rolls-Royce Silver Cloud as "the family car." It had two phones, and the bar had two different trays, one marked "His" and the other "Liz."

Home in Bel Air

After Elizabeth Taylor separated from John Warner, she bought herself a home in Bel Air, a luxurious area of Los Angeles. The former home of Frank Sinatra's ex-wife Nancy, the hilltop house cost $2 million and has a fabulous view of the twinkling lights of Los Angeles. She decorated the first-floor rooms in white, enlivened only by her art collection—Renoirs, Rouaults, and Modiglianis—and scores of huge orchid plants (to match her eyes) in full bloom. Her two Oscars sit on a shelf in the dining room. One wall contains her favorite photographs: the Helmut Newton shot used to promote Passion perfume, a huge portrait of Rock Hudson, pictures of Taylor and Burton with their friends the Duke and Duchess of Windsor. Outside, a large heated pool awaits Taylor and her guests.

Honey

Honey was a golden retriever, named for her color, that was a beloved member of the Wilding household for many years.

The Hope Award

Elizabeth Taylor was the winner of the second annual Hope Award (named after the comedian) for her many contributions to the world of entertainment. The presentation was made at a 1989 gala in Hollywood, with tickets priced at $2,500 apiece, that was taped for later broadcast on ABC-TV. Those who spoke or performed in tribute to Elizabeth included longtime friend Roddy McDowall, June Allyson, Mickey Rooney, Cyd Charisse, Carol Burnett, Dudley Moore, Robert Stack, Ann Miller, Margaret O'Brien, and Charles Bronson. Guests included Taylor's ninety-two-year-old mother and her sons Michael and Chris Wilding. The event was the first major public appearance for Liz, who had emerged only weeks earlier from the hospital where she was treated for back pain and related drug dependency. She was radiant in a black chiffon dress covered by a mink-trimmed sequinned coat, wearing a fortune in emeralds and diamonds from Harry Winston at her ears and throat. After the gala, Taylor was the guest of honor at a party for 450 people. In an interview that night, the star commented on the criticism she has sometimes faced: "What I do on the screen is my responsibility to the public. I have to be true to myself and live according to my standards. If they don't meet everybody's approval, that's too bad. It's my approval—and that of those close to me—that matters."

Hedda Hopper

Hedda Hopper was a powerful Hollywood gossip columnist who liked to joke that her lavish estate was "the house that fear built." Born in 1890, she married actor DeWolf Hopper and moved to Hollywood, where she appeared in more than fifty movies in small parts. She started a radio show in 1938 and quickly moved on to a nationally syndicated column.

Elizabeth Taylor first met the columnist even before she started to work in the movies; family friend Victor Cazalet had given the Taylors an introduction to Hopper, an art collector, when they moved from London to California. Hopper was one of Francis Taylor's first customers in his gallery in Beverly Hills. Like most people in the movie business, young Elizabeth courted Hopper's good opinion. She invited Hedda to her first wedding, and kept her informed about her second. But Hopper's power waned, and Taylor became angry over some of the stories the columnist published. "When I confided in her as a friend, she blabbed the whole story in her column about my romance with Eddie Fisher. She even made up quotes."

Later Hopper was openly critical of Taylor's decision to live with Richard Burton. "In the old days, the scandal would have killed her professionally," Hopper mused. "In these changed times, it seems only to help her reputation." The columnist lost a $100,000 libel suit to Taylor's ex-husband Michael Wilding when she alleged that he was homosexual.

Hedda Hopper died in 1966. Her son, William Hopper, achieved enduring fame for his role as Paul Drake in the TV series *Perry Mason*.

Sheran Cazalet Hornby

One of Elizabeth Taylor's closest friends is Sheran Cazalet Hornby. The two met in childhood, as Sheran was the niece of Victor Cazalet, a friend and patron of the Taylor family. Sheran married a newsagent and lives in London. She still sees Taylor regularly, during the star's frequent trips to London.

How Tall Is Elizabeth Taylor?

Press releases from MGM in the 1950s described their star Elizabeth Taylor as being five feet, four inches tall. Although her screen presence could certainly make her look at least that height, she is actually two inches shorter, a petite five-foot-two in her stocking feet.

Rock Hudson

During the filming of *Giant*, there was much speculation that Elizabeth Taylor (then married to Michael Wilding) and costar Rock Hudson had fallen in love. No amount of denial quelled the rumors, which only died down when Hudson married Phyllis Gates, his agent's secretary.

Rock Hudson was born in Winnetka, Illinois, in 1925. Although he began his movie career as an acting novice, he learned on the job and quickly found himself cast as a leading man. One of his best performances came in *Magnificent Obsession* (1954); other memorable movies were *A Farewell to Arms, Pillow Talk, Lover Come Back, Send Me No Flowers, Tobruk,* and *Ice Station Zebra*.

Taylor and Hudson remained friends until Hudson's

death from AIDS in 1985. Taylor planned the memorial service held for her old friend at his home on October 19, 1985. She greeted the guests and later spoke briefly of her cherished memories of Hudson.

Howard Hughes

In 1949, billionaire Howard Hughes became interested in Elizabeth Taylor. In hot pursuit, Hughes bought expensive paintings from her father's Hollywood gallery, and he also flew the entire family to Reno for a holiday weekend. But Taylor remained unimpressed and soon became engaged to Floridian William Pawley.

Several years later, after Elizabeth had divorced first husband Nicky Hilton, Hughes tried again. Always attracted to beautiful and successful stars, Hughes was rumored to want to marry Taylor, and even to have offered the star $1 million if she would agree to become his wife. As an added inducement, he attempted to set up a movie studio geared solely toward making Elizabeth Taylor films. Obviously, it wasn't enough to tempt Liz. She complained about his low standard of personal hygiene and his shabby style of dress. She signed another contract with MGM, and soon thereafter married Michael Wilding.

The Humanitarian Award

In 1981, Elizabeth Taylor was the recipient of the Damon Runyon/Walter Winchell Humanitarian Award, in recognition of her generous contributions of both money and time to a variety of charitable causes all over the world.

Suzy Hunt

Susan Miller Hunt, called "Suzy," met Richard Burton at the ski lift in Gstaad, over the Christmas holidays of 1975, after his October remarriage to Elizabeth Taylor. The statuesque blond, then twenty-seven and a model, was the estranged wife of English racing-car driver James "The Shunt" Hunt. In January, when Burton went to New York to begin rehearsals for *Equus*, he called Suzy Hunt and invited her to join him. Shortly thereafter, he asked Taylor for a second divorce. Burton and Hunt were married in Arlington, Virginia, since blood tests there took less than a day, on August 21, 1976—as soon as his divorce from Taylor was obtained. They immediately flew back to New York for a wedding supper for ten guests at Laurent, a chic Manhattan restaurant.

The five-foot-ten Suzy, convent-educated in England, had lived in Spain and was comfortable being a part of international society. Yet she was quiet and self-effacing, content to be Richard's audience. He told the press, 'Without Susan, I think, without any exaggeration whatsoever, I might very easily be dead. When I played *Equus*, it was the first time in my life I'd been on stage without a drink, and I shook and shivered."

The couple separated in August 1981, although an official announcement was not made until the following February. Burton told reporters, "I'm a very difficult and dangerous man to live with, you know," and the rumor was that he had started drinking again. They were divorced in Haiti in September 1982.

"I Love You" in Welsh

In February 1982, when Elizabeth Taylor celebrated her fiftieth birthday, she was in London with the traveling company of *The Little Foxes*. Her former husband, Richard Burton, was also appearing on the London stage, and he came to her birthday party. The two danced, kissed, and cuddled in public. Several days later, Elizabeth surprised Burton, and the theater audience, by strolling out on the stage during his performance and telling him, in Welsh, that she loved him.

Shortly thereafter, it was announced that Taylor and Burton would costar in *Private Lives*. Many people believed that another reconciliation of the famous couple was in the making—and perhaps Elizabeth herself was hopeful. But the pressures of working together created new rifts, and during the run of the play, Burton married Sally Hay. Taylor learned of the marriage from the press (Burton said he had tried to call her but had been unable to get through) and three days later she fell ill.

Identikit

Identikit is perhaps the least recognized of Elizabeth Taylor's great performances. In this 1974 movie, she plays a woman going mad, who is searching for someone to kill her before she descends into total lunacy. The movie was based on a Muriel Spark novella called *The Driver's Seat*, the title given the film for proposed U.S. distribution. The picture was filmed in Rome, backed by Italian money, and produced and directed by Italians. Many viewers found the subject matter profoundly uncomfortable—a discomfort that was increased by the skill of Taylor's performance. Rex Reed, who saw the movie in Europe, said, "Taylor allows the camera to search out her daring flight into insanity with penetrating self-assurance." But few critics ever reviewed *Identikit*, which was never distributed in the United States.

One reason the film never found U.S. distribution may have been the flap it caused at the time of the 1974 Cannes film festival. Taylor's film had its gala premiere in Monte Carlo, as a benefit for the Red Cross in Monaco, at the time of the French festival. Since Taylor made a personal appearance and Princess Grace and Prince Rainier were the hosts, *Identikit* completely upstaged the movies that were being shown at Cannes, much to the irritation of the powers that be in the world of commercial movies.

Impressing the Russians

Early in 1958, Elizabeth Taylor went to Russia with husband Mike Todd, to help him sell *Around the World in 80 Days* to the Russians. "What impressed the Russians most was that a bum like me could grow up in America and become Elizabeth Taylor's husband, which is a helluva better job than being President of the United States!"

In Love with Burton's Socks

Elizabeth Taylor was initially so much in love with Richard Burton she couldn't bear to be separated from him. According to a story that made the rounds in Hollywood, she once confessed that during a particular absence, she wandered into the bedroom, found a pair of his socks that the dog had been chewing on, and "mooned" over them for hours. The flattered Burton liked to tell people that when he was away from home, Taylor made love to his socks.

Insuring the Jewels

Richard Burton took out insurance on the jewelry he had given Elizabeth Taylor with famed Lloyd's of London. Never a one to store her diamonds in a dusty bank vault, Taylor asked for a policy that covered daily wear of all the gems in her collection—the most expensive type of coverage. The policy did contain a clause that promised Burton a large refund if certain of the most valuable pieces, such as the sixty-nine–carat Cartier diamond ring, were kept in a bank vault for six months of the year, but he never was able to collect.

Interplanetary Productions

In the 1960s, when Elizabeth Taylor was receiving salaries in excess of $1 million for a movie, plus a percentage of gross receipts, she incorporated herself in order to provide some tax relief. The name of the corporation was Interplanetary Productions. Richard Burton, making about the same amount in salaries, formed his own separate corporation, called Atlantic Programmes Limited.

During the filming of *Butterfield 8*, the star frequently expressed her low opinion of the movie and her role in it. But, as she once commented in another context, "Success is a great deodorant," and winning the Oscar for her portrayal of Gloria Wandrous helped reconcile her to the film's flaws. (NEAL PETERS COLLECTION)

Elizabeth Taylor's first screen appearance came in the 1942 movie *There's One Born Every Minute,* in which she and costar Alfalfa Switzer played bratty children. (NEAL PETERS COLLECTION)

Frank Sinatra paid a surprise visit to the 20th Century Fox set of *Jane Eyre* (1944) starring Peggy Ann Garner (left) as the young Jane and featuring Margaret O'Brien (far right) as Mr. Rochester's ward, Adele, and Elizabeth Taylor as the doomed Helen, her third film role. (NEAL PETERS COLLECTION)

The MGM publicity machine made the most of Elizabeth Taylor's first grown-up role, in *Cynthia*. According to the grooming tips released with this photo, "To keep her hair neatly in place and add extra sheen, Elizabeth Taylor uses a hair pomade—she also likes it on her eyebrows." (NEAL PETERS COLLECTION)

Elizabeth Taylor and Montgomery Clift (seen here in a publicity photo for *A Place in the Sun*) not only looked alike, they sometimes seemed to be twin halves of a single soul. (LESTER GLASSNER COLLECTION/NEAL PETERS)

After Mike Todd's death, Elizabeth Taylor poured her emotions into her role as Maggie the Cat in *Cat on a Hot Tin Roof*, surprising her costar Paul Newman with her wonderful performance. (NEAL PETERS COLLECTION)

A memorable moment from a memorable movie: Elizabeth Taylor on the Moroccan beach in *Suddenly Last Summer*. (NEAL PETERS COLLECTION)

Elizabeth Taylor and husband Michael Wilding go out for a night on the town with their friends Jean Simmons and Stewart Granger. English actors Wilding and Granger were longtime friends, and Taylor became friendly with the dashing star of swashbucklers when they costarred in *Beau Brummell*. (NEAL PETERS COLLECTION)

Elizabeth Taylor was always at her happiest—and most beautiful—when she became a mother. The birth of Liza Todd was a golden moment in the star's life. The photographer has encircled the sizable diamond that was her engagement ring from Mike Todd, just in case we might have missed it. (NEAL PETERS COLLECTION)

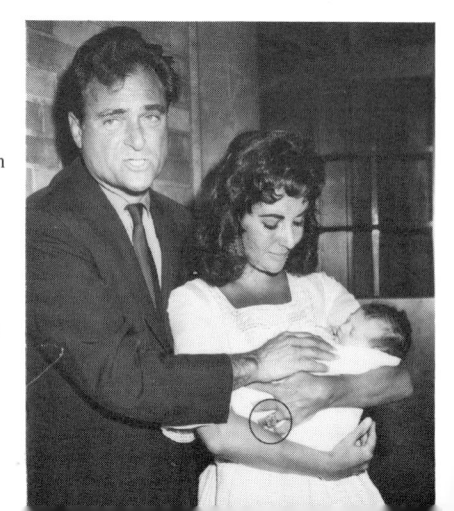

The calm before the storm: Liz, Eddie, and Debbie, sometime after the death of Mike Todd and before Debbie found out . . . (NEAL PETERS COLLECTION)

Elizabeth Taylor wore moss-green chiffon when she married Eddie Fisher in a Jewish cermony in Las Vegas. (LESTER GLASSNER COLLECTION/NEAL PETERS)

With her hair in curlers, Liz relaxes with new husband Eddie Fisher and son Michael Wilding, Jr. (foreground) at Grossinger's resort. (NEAL PETERS COLLECTION)

In 1959, Elizabeth Taylor attended husband Eddie Fisher's opening at the Tropicana Hotel, with her parents Francis and Sarah Taylor. (NEAL PETERS COLLECTION)

A woman beautiful enough to break your heart—a 1974 portrait.
(NEAL PETERS COLLECTION)

A jubilant Taylor clutches her Oscar for *Butterfield 8* —thankful to be alive and a winner at last.
(NEAL PETERS COLLECTION)

This is the famous billboard advertising *Cleopatra* that initially appeared with all three stars and was later cropped to exclude Rex Harrison. (LESTER GLASSNER COLLECTION/NEAL PETERS)

Elizabeth Taylor and Richard Burton made headlines for their extravagant lifestyle. Attending a party on the Grand Canal in Venice in 1967, Taylor wears not only what the press nicknamed the "Cigarette Headdress" but also the fabulous emerald necklace that was a gift from Burton. (NEAL PETERS COLLECTION)

Elizabeth Taylor has always enjoyed being a mother. Here in a hotel room while on location for a movie in 1976, she spends time with daughters Maria (left) and Liza. (NEAL PETERS COLLECTION)

Taylor with her son Michael Wilding in the late 1970s—not a good period for either one of them. (BOB SCOTT/NEAL PETERS)

Even Elizabeth Taylor had to admit that there was something faintly comic about the length of her engagement to Victor Luna. He gave her a beautiful sapphire ring, rather like Princess Diana's . . . but larger. (BOB SCOTT/NEAL PETERS)

One of Elizabeth Taylor's greatest fans is Michael Jackson, who has devoted an entire room in his house to his collection of Taylor memorabilia. Note the Krupp diamond on Liz's finger. (BOB SCOTT/NEAL PETERS)

Elizabeth Taylor is known for her long friendships and strong loyalties. A case in point is her relationship with Roddy McDowall, which began when they were child costars in *Lassie Come Home* and continues to the present day. (BOB SCOTT/NEAL PETERS)

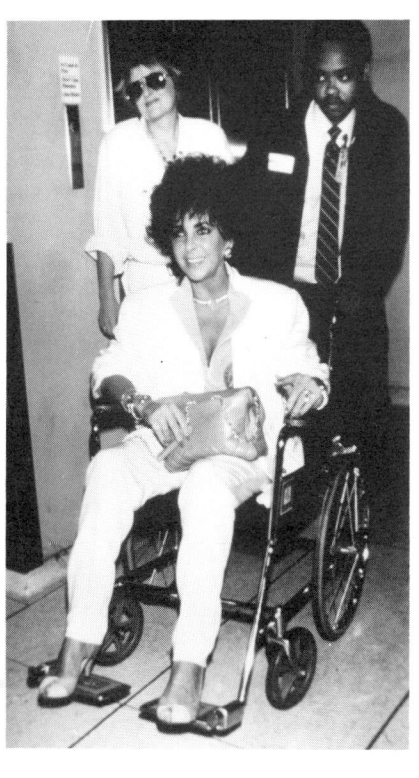

Because of her bad back, a wheelchair is often provided for Elizabeth Taylor when she travels. Here Liz is at Los Angeles Airport in 1986.
(BOB SCOTT/NEAL PETERS)

Holding a 1989 press conference in Los Angeles, Liz announced her support of a national fund-raising drive for AIDS research. The death of her good friend Rock Hudson is one reason for her continued, intense efforts.
(BOB SCOTT/NEAL PETERS)

Billionaire publisher Malcolm Forbes celebrated his 70th birthday in 1989 with Liz at his Palais Mendoub in Tangier, Morocco. They are flanked by native costumed guards. A couple of Malcolm's motorcycles are parked in view. (RON GALELLA)

"Intimate Little Party for a Few Chums"

On October 17, 1957, Mike Todd and his wife Elizabeth Taylor gave a party at New York's Madison Square Garden for 18,000 people, to celebrate the first anniversary of the release of his hugely successful film, *Around the World in 80 Days*. There was a 17-foot cake that weighed 1,000 pounds, door prizes that included an airplane and four Oldsmobiles, circus animals performing for the guests' entertainment, and plenty of champagne and food: 15,000 hot dogs, 10,000 egg rolls, 15,000 donuts, and 10,000 slices of pizza. Todd had previously persuaded CBS to pay him $300,000 to buy the rights to televise the party live, with comedian George Jessel as the master of ceremonies and Elizabeth Taylor, in a black strapless gown and eye-popping jewels, cutting the cake.

The party turned out to be a giant fiasco, with mobs of people shouting and fighting to get to the food and drink. Afterward, Mike and Elizabeth swore they would never again give a party for more than eight guests.

Ivanhoe

Ivanhoe was one of MGM's most successful big-budget epics. Based on the novel by Sir Walter Scott, the movie starred Robert Taylor in the title role, Elizabeth Taylor as the ill-fated Rebecca, and Joan Fontaine as her Anglo-Saxon rival in love, Rowena. George Sanders was the villain who condemned Rebecca to the stake for witchcraft (a situation from which Ivanhoe of course rescues her), and Emlyn Williams played a Saxon serf. The movie was shot at studios outside London and released in late 1952.

At the time that production of *Ivanhoe* was slated to begin, Elizabeth Taylor was involved in a romance with Hollywood director Stanley Donen. She was therefore reluctant to leave California to begin work in England. Perhaps to put pressure on her, MGM announced that the role of Rebecca would be played by Deborah Kerr. In the end, Elizabeth acquiesced, although she always underrated the movie as a "medieval Western." In fact, the sets, costumes, and cinematography of *Ivanhoe* were superb, and the adaptation of Scott's novel was sensitively handled, especially in regard to the anti-Semitic aspects of the plot. The movie was a success at the box office; and if critics were not as warm as audiences, they were at least accepting. "Elizabeth Taylor gives a sincere, if unrelieved, study of Rowena's rival in love," said *Variety*. Bosley Crowther said, "Both of these able performers [Taylor and the actor who played her father, Felix Aylmer] handle with grace and eloquence the frank and faceted characters of the rejected Jews." The *Saturday Review* gave the actress a dismissive compliment: "Elizabeth Taylor is beautiful enough as Rebecca."

Elizabeth Taylor's willingness to accept her assignment in England was rewarded by her introduction while there to British actor Michael Wilding. A few months after she had returned to California, she made a public announcement that she planned to marry Wilding and flew to the surprised man's side.

—J—

Michael Jackson

One of Elizabeth Taylor's greatest admirers is pop star Michael Jackson. One room of his California home is a virtual shrine to Liz, full of her photos and memorabilia. And he managed to obtain the lifesize photo of the young Elizabeth that was part of the decor at her fifty-fifth birthday party, given in her honor by friends Burt Bacharach and Carole Bayer Sager. It now stands in Michael's driveway.

Cecilia "Cissie" Jenkins James

Cecilia Jenkins, always called Cissie, was one of Richard Burton's older sisters, the seventh child and oldest girl. She was married to coal miner Elvid James and had a home of her own when her father, an alcoholic Welsh coal miner, decided he was unable to raise the younger children after the death of their mother. Richard was sent to Port Talbot, seven miles away from his birthplace, to live with Cissie, who in many respects took the place of his mother. Richard later wrote about her, "She was more mother to me than any mother could ever have been. I was immensely proud of her. I shone in the reflection of her green-eyed black-haired gypsy beauty." Photos of Cissie in her youth show a marked resemblance to Elizabeth Taylor.

During Richard's marriage to Taylor, the star took great care to establish a good relationship with her husband's sister. It required all her warmth and charm, because Cissie disapproved of Richard's divorce from Welsh actress Sybil Williams. Unsurprisingly, Elizabeth triumphed over family disapproval and was accepted by Cissie and all the rest of the Jenkins family.

Jane Eyre

The 1944 screen version of Charlotte Bronte's romantic novel, *Jane Eyre*, featured Elizabeth Taylor in the small role of Helen, young Jane's friend during her dismal days at Lowood Institution for orphans. The early part of the film, in which Taylor appears, is often heavily edited to shorten televised versions, sometimes omitting Taylor entirely. Her character, Helen, is a beautiful and sweet-natured little girl who befriends Jane Eyre at the brutal institution in which they are trapped. The sanctimonious head of Lowood accuses Helen of vanity because he cannot believe her gorgeous curly hair is natural; he cuts her hair and then makes her parade in the rain wearing a sign that labels her "Vain." Jane (played as a girl by Peggy Ann Garner) learns that Helen is seriously ill and creeps into her sick friend's bed to comfort her. In the morning, Jane awakes to find Helen dead. Elizabeth Taylor's unusual beauty gave the deathbed scene a special pathos.

This was the fifth version of *Jane Eyre* to be filmed. It starred Orson Welles as the enigmatic Mr. Rochester and Joan Fontaine as the prim but spirited Jane, who is governess to his little ward, played by Margaret O'Brien. Script credits mention both Aldous Huxley and John Houseman, but the most effective dialogue is the lines that come from the powerful and mysterious novel. Director Robert Stevenson emphasized the wildly romantic aspect of the original work in the Gothic settings and deeply shadowed black-and-white cinematography.

Once again, Taylor's part was too small for review attention. The movie itself, and the performances by the leading actors, were well received.

Jeepers Creepers

In 1945, MGM released publicity photos of its new young star, fresh from her triumph in *National Velvet*, at home with her black cat named Jeepers Creepers.

Ivor Jenkins

Ivor Jenkins was an older brother of Richard Burton, to whom the star always remained close. Ivor sometimes stayed with the Burtons in Switzerland, and also lived in Richard's house in Celigny as a caretaker when Richard was away. The local pub in Celigny put up a dart board for his use, honoring the wishes of a regular customer. In 1969, Ivor was left completely paralyzed after a freak accident in Switzerland; opening the house for the rest of the family late at night, he tripped over a doorway and broke his neck. He died two years later.

Jewels Love Liz

In 1987, an interviewer commented to Elizabeth Taylor, "Miss Taylor, you seem to love jewels so much." Liz shot back, "No, they love me!"

Jocko

Jocko was a chimpanzee that lived in the Regents Park zoo in London during the 1930s. Young Elizabeth Taylor often visited Jocko and once posed for a picture with his arm around her. According to one report, the chimp sometimes had to be subdued by zoo guards when he got too affectionate with the little girl.

Ingemar Johanssen

Ingemar Johanssen was a Swedish boxer who once held the World Heavyweight title. He met Elizabeth Taylor at Grossinger's, when she was there with Eddie Fisher before their 1959 marriage. Johanssen and Taylor became friends, and Taylor attended both his fights with Floyd Patterson. Max Lerner, with whom Taylor was having an affair during her marriage to Fisher, alleges that Taylor was also having an affair with Johanssen.

Julia Misbehaves

Julia Misbehaves was a 1948 vehicle designed to showcase MGM star Greer Garson, in which Elizabeth Taylor played the supporting role of Garson's eighteen-year-old daughter. In the movie, the young woman hasn't seen her mother since she left her husband (Walter Pidgeon) when their child was young. Garson returns at the time of the daughter's engagement to a proper young man and intervenes to pair the young woman off with the man she really loves, an impecunious artist (played by the then-elegant Peter Lawford).

The movie was an attempt to give a boost to Garson's sagging career by pairing her again with her *Mrs. Miniver* costar and displaying her comedic abilities, but as several critics have pointed out, MGM did not put enough money or creative resources behind the venture for it to succeed. Reviews were lukewarm, and so were the box-office receipts. *Time*, calling Taylor "one of the loveliest girls in the movies," complained that "here she is made-up and hair-done and directed into tired, tiresome conventional prettiness." On a more positive note, Otis L. Guernsey, Jr. said, "The picture receives a most valuable decoration in the presence of Elizabeth Taylor, former child star, who has developed into one of the cinema's reigning queens of beauty and talent. She plays Julia's daughter with both sincerity and charm."

In *Julia Misbehaves*, Elizabeth Taylor received her second screen kiss (the first was in *Cynthia*, released the previous year). The kisser in question was juvenile lead Peter Lawford, about whom Taylor later said, "Peter to me was the last word in sophistication. He was terribly handsome, and I had a tremendous crush on him." Elizabeth and Peter were to become very good friends in real life, although never romantically linked.

-K-

Pauline Kael on Elizabeth Taylor

Pauline Kael reviewed many of the movies starring Elizabeth Taylor, and in the course of her comments, frequently reflected on the nature of Taylor's public appeal. Kael thought Taylor had a talent for "comic toughness" and admired the way she was able, by sheer force of her personality, to steal not just scenes but whole movies from more skillful actors. In 1972, reviewing *X Y and Zee*, Kael suggested, "When she goes too far, she's like the blowziest scarlet woman in a Mexican movie, but she's still funny . . . The weight she has put on in these last years has not made her gracefully voluptuous; she's too hard-boiled to be Rubensesque. The weight seems to have brought out this coarseness and now she basks in it."

In that same review, Kael also ruminated on the changes in Taylor over the years. "Elizabeth Taylor has changed before our eyes from the fragile child with a woman's face to the fabled beauty to this great bawd. Maybe child actresses don't quite grow up if they stay in the movies; maybe that's why, from ingenue-goddess, she went right over the hill."

Kalizma

Kalizma is the name of the yacht owned by Elizabeth Taylor and Richard Burton. Burton bought the 110-foot ship, then called the *Odysseia*, for just under $200,000 in 1967, when he and Taylor were on the island of Sardinia for the shooting of *Boom!* The ship had been built in 1906 for an eccentric Englishman, who had installed an organ so he could listen to concerts at sea; during both world wars, it had been used as a patrol boat. Burton spent at least another $200,000 in decorating it to his wife's taste. He gave designer Arthur Barbosa the stipulation that the main cabin and the drawing room had to be ready almost immediately, so Taylor and Burton could live on the ship while they were on location. It was named after their three daughters: *Ka*te Burton, *Li*za Todd, and *Ma*ria Burton. There were seven staterooms, provided with all the comforts of home, including antique furniture and a bootblack to polish guests' shoes. In 1989, the ship was again on the market, with an asking price of $2,500,000.

Kitty Kelley

Kitty Kelley wrote a best-selling biography of Elizabeth Taylor that remains one of the most complete examinations of the star's life and work. Kelley interviewed more than 400 people for *Elizabeth Taylor: The Last Star*, published in 1981. Kelley subsequently used the same gossipy, behind-the-scenes approach to good effect in her best-selling bios of Frank Sinatra and Nancy Reagan.

Dr. Rex Kennamer

Dr. Rexford "Rex" Kennamer was for many years Elizabeth Taylor's physician, and also a close personal friend. It was Kennamer who broke the news to her of Mike Todd's death in a plane crash. In the 1960s, when Kennamer repeatedly treated Taylor for severe back pain, rumors began to circulate that she was suffering from cancer of the spine. The rumors eventually reached the ears of the patient herself, who feared there might be some truth that was being withheld from her. Kennamer was the only person able to reassure her that she was not dying.

Kennamer also treated Taylor's friends Montgomery Clift and Rock Hudson. He was, in fact, widely associated with Hollywood stars. As Clift's biographer Robert LaGuardia put it, "*Everyone* went to him, not only because he was an excellent doctor, but because he was also a trusted confidant. With his easy Southern charm, he mingled well at parties, and was able to help the most disparate personalities find friendship." Kennamer remains loyal to his famous patient, Elizabeth Taylor. "If you ever get into Elizabeth's small circle of friends, you stay there," he commented.

Evelyn Keyes

In the summer of 1956, when Mike Todd first met Elizabeth Taylor (and her then-husband Michael Wilding) the producer was living with actress Evelyn Keyes. Keyes, in her autobiography *Scarlett O'Hara's Younger Sister*, wrote about her own first glimpse of Mike Todd: "He had on yesterday's pin-striped gangster suit. Shoes with perforated toes. And if that wasn't bad enough, he had long slicked-down patent-leather style hair that even George Raft had stopped affecting years before. And a perfectly monstrous cigar in his mouth."

Despite this unpromising beginning, the two fell in love, and Evelyn moved into Mike's Park Avenue apartment in New York. She traveled with him to Venice, London, Mexico City, Havana, and many other cities, as he planned the elaborate production of *Around the World in 80 Days*; it was Keyes who introduced Todd to Cantinflas, who played the role of Passepartout. As Keyes recalled that period, "He thrived, he bloomed, he was doing what he was born for. Dealing, plotting, hiring; the writer of the screenplay had to be found, the director, cameraman, stars, assistants, crew, and, above all, money had to be got hold of, large sums, *millions*." After a trip to Russia, Mike gave Evelyn a fifteen-carat emerald-cut diamond engagement ring.

At about the same time, Mike Todd chartered a boat for a relaxing weekend cruise and invited a number of guests to join them, including Elizabeth Taylor and husband Michael Wilding. Keyes says she noticed nothing between Todd and Taylor, and adds that she would never have suspected an attraction. "Elizabeth was everything Mike professed not to care for; she was the epitome of movie star in dress, attitudes and behavior. And she never stopped drinking champagne from the moment she stepped on the boat until she got off two days later. Besides actresses, Mike didn't like women who drank a great deal."

Then Taylor and Wilding separated. Todd became interested in Taylor despite her actresslike attitude and behavior, and Keyes learned through the press that her own engagement had been terminated. Todd's gentlemanly goodbye gesture was to give her five percent of the stock in his corporation, Michael Todd Company. (After his death, she got $100,000 for her shares.) Keyes, whose first big part, in *Gone with the Wind*, gave her the title for her autobiography, has been married to King Vidor, John Huston, and Artie Shaw.

About Elizabeth Taylor, Keyes's comments are generous. "What she is, she is without pretense. That she happens to be beautiful, that she is successful at what she does, that she has been a movie star all her life and knows no other kind of existence—are the ingredients that make her what she is . . . But the same ingredients also give Elizabeth a sense of self that makes her comfortable to be around. It also gives her the courage to fight for what she wants, and against things she doesn't like." Evelyn Keyes revealed that she and Elizabeth spent an evening together, when Keyes lived in Spain with Artie Shaw and Taylor was there shooting scenes for *Suddenly Last Summer*. The two women shared their memories of Mike Todd, and Taylor concluded sadly that she thought Keyes had shared the best years of the showman's life.

Adnan Khashoggi

An example of Elizabeth Taylor's legendary loyalty to her intimates is her continuing friendship with Adnan Khashoggi. Once thought to be the richest man in the world, Khashoggi formerly wined and dined Liz in the fashion she is accustomed to. Then the Arab's empire began to fall apart. He lost much of his money and hit bottom when he was indicted for allegedly helping Ferdinand and Imelda Marcos bilk the Philippine treasury. Out on $10 million bail and awaiting trial, Khashoggi was the escort Taylor chose in the fall of 1989 for the launching of her Passion for Men cologne. Wearing a fabulous silk dress with furs cuffs, she swept into the reception on Khashoggi's arm and pointedly took no notice of the electronic bracelet he wore to insure that he did not try to leave the country before his trial.

Adnan Khashoggi was born in Mecca in 1935, a son of King Ibn Saud's personal physician. Educated in Egypt and California, he began building his empire in the 1960s and was reportedly worth more than $1 billion within a decade. He owned lavish homes in London, Paris, Rome, and Riyahd, in addition to a huge two-story apartment in Manhattan's Olympic Towers and an estate in Marbella, Spain, where he several times entertained Elizabeth Taylor. He also owned the luxury yacht *Nabilia* (later sold to Donald Trump, who himself was forced to sell it in 1991.)

Khashoggi's business dealings began to come under U.S. government investigation in the late 1970s. Amid rumors of his covert role in the Iran-Contra affair, he was indicted for his dealing on behalf of the Marcoses. The negative publicity, coupled with government pressure, caused his business empire to collapse.

Ralph Kiner

Baseball player Ralph Kiner, an outfielder for the Pittsburgh Pirates and later a broadcaster for the New York Mets, dated Elizabeth Taylor in 1949, shortly before she met her first husband, Nicky Hilton.

King Charles

In the 1944 movie *National Velvet*, Elizabeth Taylor played a young girl who wins a horse in a raffle, trains the horse in secret, and rides it to a win in England's prestigious Grand National. The name of the horse in the movie, a dark chestnut with a white blaze on its face, was "The Pi" (short for Pirate), but the real horse used for the shooting was King Charles, a grandson of famed race horse Man O'War. Costar Mickey Rooney recalled that the horse was downright mean. "I advised Elizabeth to steer clear of him when the trainer wasn't around. But what I said went in one ear and out the other. Even when the cameras weren't rolling, she'd ride the Pi bareback. And he'd do things for her that he wouldn't even do for the trainer."

When the movie was finished, MGM gave King Charles, then figured to be worth $500, to thirteen-year-old Elizabeth Taylor in recognition of the contribution her outstanding performance made to the success of the movie. She boarded the horse at the Egon Marz stables in Malibu, and shortly thereafter King Charles went lame.

The producer of *National Velvet*, Pandro Berman, has revealed a sequel to the story of MGM's gift of the horse to the picture's young star. Years later, Berman met Taylor again when he produced *Butterfield 8*. She approached him on the set, asking, "Say, aren't you the guy that gave me that horse after *National Velvet*?" Berman, braced for a torrent of thanks, admitted that he was. "You son of a bitch!" exclaimed Taylor. "I'm still paying for feed for that goddam horse!"

Knitting

Richard Burton jokingly told reporters before his marriage to Elizabeth Taylor how their relationship as husband and wife would work: "You may be quite certain that I shall be in the center of the stage. Elizabeth will be in the wings—knitting."

The Krupp Diamond

One of Richard Burton's gifts to Elizabeth Taylor was the flawless thirty-three-carat diamond that had once belonged to Vera Krupp, the wife of German munitions tycoon Alfred Krupp. At the time of Burton's purchase, the Krupp diamond was valued at more than $300,000. According to the story told by Elizabeth, the gift was the result of a bet she and her husband made about a game of Ping-Pong. Richard, an expert player, challenged her to a match, and to overcome her reluctance to play against him, promised to buy her a perfect gem if she could score ten points against him. "He was so cocky that I got him sloshed and beat him," Taylor explained.

The Krupp diamond is about the size of a peach pit. Taylor liked to joke about the strange coincidence that caused the stone once owned by a Nazi sympathizer to end up on the finger of "a little Jewish girl like me." The Krupp remains Taylor's favorite piece of jewelry, and she wears it not only for formal dress occasions but also while lounging around the house. Visitors to Taylor's home have described seeing it casually left on her bathroom sink, like a piece of costume jewelry—a perfect example of true chic!

— L —

Lalique Crystal

One of Elizabeth Taylor's enthusiasms is Lalique crystal. She has a valuable collection of beautiful Lalique *objets*.

Lancaster Hotel

When Elizabeth Taylor travels to Paris, she likes to stay in the Lancaster Hotel, a chic little establishment just off the Champs-Elysées. During her marriage to Richard Burton, they often stayed on the two top floors of the hotel, occupying twenty-one rooms with their four children and large entourage. The bill (in 1960s dollars) came to $10,000 a week.

Lassie Come Home

Elizabeth Taylor appeared in the first Lassie vehicle, *Lassie Come Home*, which was also Taylor's first movie for MGM after the studio signed the young actress in 1943. This was the movie that really started Taylor's long career as an actress (although it was *National Velvet* that made her a star). The star of the movie was of course Lassie, the canine heroine created by Eric Knight in a 1938 story for *The Sat-*

urday Evening Post, which he subsequently expanded into the novel, *Lassie Come Home*. Over the years, there were seven more Lassie movies made, and then the stories about the intelligent collie were adapted—and Americanized—for the television series that ran for many years.

The sentimental plot of *Lassie Come Home* told of the great love between a poor farmboy in Scotland and the family's beautiful collie, which must be sold to a wealthy nobleman to solve some pressing financial problems. The dog keeps running away from her gilded kennel to rejoin the boy, a habit that culminates in a thrilling 1,000-mile journey. Eventually, the kindly nobleman creates a happy ending by offering the boy a job as Lassie's keeper.

The real stars of the first Lassie movie were Pal, the collie (male) who played Lassie, and Roddy McDowall, fresh from his enormous success in *How Green Was My Valley*, as the boy Lassie loves. Elizabeth Taylor played the granddaughter of the nobleman, who cajoles the elderly gent into recognizing the bond between the boy and the dog. According to producer Sam Marx, Taylor got the part only because the child actor originally cast to play opposite McDowall had grown too tall by the time the shooting started. The producer always remembered his first sight of Elizabeth, when she came in to read for the part. "I didn't expect much from Elizabeth," he later recalled. "We had five other girls whom we were considering. We practically had selected one. But the moment Elizabeth entered, there was a complete eclipse of all the others. She was stunning, dazzling. Her voice was charming, and she had no self-consciousness whatsoever."

Other members of the very talented supporting cast were Donald Crisp and Elsa Lanchester as the boy's parents, Nigel Bruce as the duke, and Dame May Whitty and Edmund Gwenn as a couple who help Lassie as she makes her way back home. The director of the picture was Fred Wilcox, whose sister had married the president of Loew's, the company that owned MGM. This connection by marriage probably explained how a B picture, referred to on the lot as "the dog movie," was made in color and boasted such a good supporting cast.

Most of the reviews omitted mention of the young actress who played the duke's granddaughter, but the critic of *The*

New York Sun called her "vivid," and *Variety* said she was a "pretty moppet" who "shows up to good advantage." *The Chicago Tribune* was prophetic: "A lovely-looking youngster named Elizabeth Taylor is a refreshing newcomer to films. Her eyes show glowingly in Technicolor sparkle. She makes a delightful companion for Lassie. Both are slated for a glorious future."

One story from the set of *Lassie Come Home* has entered the Elizabeth Taylor mythology. The cinematographer, Leonard Smith, was disconcerted by his first close-up of the ten-year-old girl and ordered her to remove all the false eyelashes and eye makeup—only to learn that he was seeing the natural Elizabeth Taylor.

The Last Time I Saw Paris

Based on F. Scott Fitzgerald's poignant short story, "Babylon Revisited," *The Last Time I Saw Paris* costarred Elizabeth Taylor and Van Johnson as characters modeled after the legend of Scott and his wife Zelda. It was the kind of role that Elizabeth Taylor played best: impetuous, emotional, hedonistic, used to getting her own way. Although the plot and dialogue of this 1954 movie were far inferior to the short story on which it was based, there was enough left of the characteristic Fitzgerald world of frenetic gaiety giving way to disillusionment and defeat to provide a charged atmosphere.

According to gossip that leaked out from the set, director Richard Brooks fell in love with Elizabeth Taylor (then married to Michael Wilding) during the filming. He understood her deep need for emotional support and approval, and did his best to provide it. He wanted to help her accomplish the most professional work she could. And the result was one of her best performances in the 1950s.

Although critics had many reservations about the script and the awkward and disjointed flashbacks through which the story is told, for the most part they commended Taylor's work in the film. *The Film Daily* called this "the best work of her career," and *Variety* called it "her best work to date and shows a thorough grasp of the character, which she makes warm and real, not just beautiful." Otis L. Guernsey, Jr. commented, "She is not only a stunning creature but a vibrant one as she flings herself into the role of an impetuous, alluring, pleasure-loving beauty. She wears yellow and red—the colors of gaiety—but her performance is such that disillusionment is never out of sight."

The Lavender Scrapbooks

One of Eddie Fisher's most imaginative gifts to Elizabeth Taylor was his first wedding anniversary present of a complete set of all her movie scripts specially bound in lavender leather. Each script also contained still photographs, which Fisher had laboriously collected. The end papers were lavender paisley, and the titles were stamped in 14-carat gold. Fisher said, "She nearly fainted with pleasure when she saw all those books." When Richard Burton first noticed them, he commented that he thought it was the most overwhelmingly generous gesture he'd ever known.

Peter Lawford

Actor Peter Lawford was born on September 7, 1923 in London, the child of a career Army officer, a general who was later knighted. Beginning his movie career at the tender age of eight, Peter was under contract to MGM at the same time as Elizabeth Taylor. Although he was nine years older than Elizabeth, they were cast as romantic leads in two movies. In *Julia Misbehaves*, Lawford played the artist Taylor really loved, in preference to her fiancé, and much of the plot was devoted to her mother's attempts—finally successful—to pair them off. In *Little Women*, Peter Lawford played Laurie Laurence, the young man who first courts Jo March (June Allyson) and then is snatched up by Amy (Elizabeth Taylor), whom he promptly marries. In a third

MGM movie, *The White Cliffs of Dover*, they played another romantic couple, but not opposite one another: the young sweethearts were played by Roddy McDowall and Elizabeth Taylor, and their more mature counterparts by Peter Lawford and June Lockhart.

The two stars, rather similar in their romantic good looks and their slight English accents, became friends in real life. Taylor has confessed that she was initially awed by the older Lawford's suave sophistication, and claimed she once had a tremendous crush on him. Perhaps because he was nearly ten years older, her girlish crush went no further. It was Lawford who introduced Elizabeth Taylor to Nicky Hilton, her first husband.

Lawford himself married in 1954. His first wife was Patricia Kennedy, the sister of the future president, with whom he had four children. They were divorced in 1966, and five years later Lawford married Mary Rowan, daughter of comedian Dan Rowan. As that marriage deteriorated, he was once again linked with Elizabeth Taylor, often acting as her escort as well as being a close friend. Although gossip had it that they were involved in a romance, Lawford said they only talked about old times. Gossips also hinted that Taylor was interested in Lawford's son Christopher!

In 1983, by an ironic coincidence, the two old friends entered the Betty Ford Center at the same time, for treatment of their drug dependency problems. "Who would have thought it forty years ago?" mused Lawford, about himself and Taylor. "But we're both going to make it." Lawford, by then married to his fourth wife, Pat Seaton, died the following year.

Lawsuit Against Lloyd's of London

At the end of 1960, insurers Lloyd's of London told producer Walter Wanger that he must remove Elizabeth Taylor from the screen version of *Cleopatra*. Lloyd's felt that her illnesses had already cost too much money and insisted she be replaced by Shirley MacLaine, Kim Novak, or Marilyn Monroe. Wanger replied that Elizabeth remained 20th Century-Fox's choice for the lead role. Lloyd's responded by refusing to pay the claim Wanger submitted for the money lost for a production that was costing about $40,000 a day. Wanger promptly took Lloyd's to court, asking for $3 million. He finally settled for $2 million—and he still had Elizabeth Taylor as the Queen of the Nile.

Lawsuit by 20th Century-Fox

When 20th Century-Fox began to comprehend the scope of the financial disaster created for the studio by *Cleopatra*, they looked around for a scapegoat. They found Elizabeth Taylor, then under attack in the worldwide media for her love affair with Richard Burton, which reinforced her "homewrecker" image. Fox instructed its lawyers to sue both Taylor and Burton, on the grounds that their off-camera antics had damaged *Cleopatra*'s box-office receipts. Taylor eventually settled with the studio for about $2 million. Anyone who has ever watched the three-plus–hour film knows its failure didn't need any help from Elizabeth Taylor, but the suit made her virtually unemployable in Hollywood for two years. It was MGM that finally got up the courage to offer her work, in *Sandpiper*, at a price of $1 million plus 10 percent of the gross.

"Le Scandale"

Richard Burton referred to the worldwide media coverage of his romance with Elizabeth Taylor as "Le Scandale." It probably began early in 1962, on the day that Taylor was taken to the hospital with what was officially called food poisoning but really was an overdose taken when she thought Burton was ending their affair. "Le Scandale" officially ended with their marriage in the spring of 1964. Thereafter, they were merely one of the most famous couples in the world, but no longer the most scandalous.

Learning to Drive

Elizabeth Taylor was in her mid-fifties before she learned to drive. When she turned sixteen, she was already leading the sheltered life of a great star, chauffeured everywhere she wanted to go, so learning to drive seemed irrelevant. It was not until 1989 that she decided she would like to be able to get around Hollywood on her own; she finally got her first driver's license that summer. Her reward to herself for passing the test was a brand-new bright red Aston-Martin. Several months later, while backing the sporty Aston-Martin out of the driveway, she hit her beige Rolls-Royce. The damage? About $6,000.

Leaving Now

According to a story told by Eddie Fisher in his 1981 autobiography, *Eddie: My Life, My Loves*, his wife Elizabeth Taylor once tried to commit suicide during their marriage. He said she always hated to be alone, and they had made an agreement when they wed that they would never be apart for more than one night. After a particularly bitter quarrel, Eddie told her he was leaving the next day. "You're leaving in the morning?" she asked angrily. "Well, I'm leaving now." Taylor promptly took an overdose of Seconal and Miltown. Fisher called the doctor, had his wife's stomach pumped, and hushed the whole thing up.

The Legendary Taylor–Todd Fights

Everyone who knew Elizabeth Taylor and Mike Todd agreed that they were a couple who loved to fight. They shouted insults at one another, and even occasionally indulged in physical violence; it all served to electrify their passion. Todd told a reporter, "We fight because we love it. When she's mad she looks so beautiful that I want to take her in my arms and smother her with kisses. But I control myself—I fight—because it's so much fun to make up again."

Debbie Reynolds described one of the Todds' epic confrontations in her autobiography, *Debbie: My Life*. Reynolds says that during a heated argument at the Fishers' home, Mike hit Elizabeth so hard he knocked her to the floor. She screamed and hit him back, and he retaliated by dragging her across the room by her hair. Debbie was so upset by all the violence that she tried to jump on Mike to make him stop. The next thing she knew, Elizabeth and Mike were lying on the floor kissing and making up, and everyone was angry at Debbie for interfering. Mike shouted at Debbie to knock it off, and Elizabeth said, "Don't be such a Girl Scout." Eddie later told her, "They were just having a good time. Why couldn't you leave them alone?"

Max Lerner

Political columnist Max Lerner wrote a sympathetic article about Elizabeth Taylor at the time of her marriage to Eddie Fisher, when so many writers criticized her heavily. She was touched by his support and asked to meet him. According to Taylor biographer Kitty Kelley, they soon thereafter began an affair that went on intermittently for several years.

Lerner, born in 1902 in Russia to Jewish parents, has been called one of the outstanding political thinkers and journalists of the left wing of American democracy. Educated at Yale and the prestigious Brookings Institute Graduate School in Washington, he taught at Sarah Lawrence, Harvard, and Williams colleges. His writings for *The Nation* and *The New Republic* were well known and influential. At the time Lerner, then almost sixty years old, met Elizabeth Taylor, he was a Brandeis University professor with impeccable intellectual credentials. He later said that Taylor considered him her "intellectual Mike Todd."

Lerner, a married man, agreed to work with Taylor on an autobiography tentatively titled *Elizabeth Taylor: Between Life and Death*. She told him she would do the recalling and he could do "the heavy thinking." Then Eddie Fisher found out about their romantic involvement, which led to Mrs. Lerner's finding out as well. The affair came to an abrupt end, as did the book project.

Life Covers

The actress who has been on the cover of *Life* most frequently is Elizabeth Taylor, with thirteen covers to her credit—the first in 1947, when she starred in *Cynthia*. Her closest challenger is Marilyn Monroe, with a mere six appearances on the magazine's cover.

Life With Father

Life with Father was a book of humorous reminiscences written by Clarence Day, Jr. about his father, a successful late-nineteenth-century broker with an irascible temper that camouflaged an enormous devotion to his wife and children. Playwrights Howard Lindsay and Russel Crouse turned the warmly funny book into a very successful play, which ran on Broadway for nearly eight years. In 1947, MGM made a movie version, starring William Powell as Father. Powell turned in a splendid performance in a role that was a complete departure from the urbane sophisticates he usually portrayed, and he was ably supported by Irene Dunne, playing the wife who kindly allows her husband to suppose himself the head of the household.

At the request of the author's widow, Elizabeth Taylor was loaned to Warner Brothers for this 1947 picture, to take the role of Mary Skinner, a visitor to the Day household who sparks a romance with Clarence Junior. Her costar was James Lydon, who had also played her boyfriend in *Cynthia*, released earlier the same year. Taylor's was a minor role, but she looked appropriately charming and girlish in her period costumes and held her own with the talented ensemble cast. *The New York Times* called her "very appealing," and *Variety* said she was "sweetly feminine." The reviewer for *The Film Daily* said, "Elizabeth Taylor is alternately kittenish, silly and coquettish, as she is romantically involved with Clarence, Jr."

The Little Foxes

In 1981, Elizabeth Taylor appeared on stage in a production of *The Little Foxes*. The starring role of the greedy Regina Giddens had been played by Tallulah Bankhead when the play originally opened on Broadway in 1939. Bankhead was praised by reviewers for her "superb command of the entire character," her "gothic force," and her awareness of the "poisonous spirit within." The role of Regina was called the finest performance of Bankhead's career.

Playwright Lillian Hellman thought Bankhead was so good in the role that she had never again agreed to another stage production, with the exception of a short revival at Lincoln Center in 1967, starring Colleen Dewhurst and directed by Mike Nichols. There had been a movie version in 1941, starring Bette Davis, about whom one reviewer said, "This is one of those terrifyingly cruel, calculating, sinister roles which have made Bette famous and she plays it with masterful insight and persuasion." When Hellman heard that Elizabeth Taylor wanted to play Regina on Broadway, the playwright agreed to the new production immediately. "Elizabeth is the right person at the right age at the right time." Taylor's costars were Maureen Stapleton and Anthony Zerbe, and the production was directed by Austin Pendleton (who played the role of Regina's nephew Leo in the 1967 production). The play opened in Florida on Taylor's birthday in February, then traveled to Washington, and finally opened on Broadway at the Martin Beck Theater.

Before the Broadway opening, Taylor came down with a throat infection and a high fever. "I'm using all my willpower to get over this," she vowed. "No matter how sick I am, I will go on for the opening. I won't cancel it, even if I am croaking." She kept her promise. Large crowds came to see the movie queen in person, and most of her reviews were wonderful. *Newsweek* called her "a gutsy broad who's been through it all, taking her shot on hard-nosed Broadway." *Time*'s critic said, "In air and bearing, she possesses regal command. Her arrant good looks, particularly those thrush-startled eyes, fix all other eyes upon her." *The New York Times* enthused, "It may have taken her a long time to get to Broadway, but she has arrived in high style . . . She rewards the role of Regina, that malignant Southern bitch-goddess, with a performance that begins gingerly, soon gathers steam and then explodes into a black and thunderous storm that may just knock you out of your seat." Edwin Wilson in *The Wall Street Journal* said, "From the moment she sweeps on stage in the wine-colored full-length dress designed by Florence Klotz, she captures the audience's attention." Frank Rich wrote, "No doubt it's superfluous to point out that Miss Taylor has charm, grandeur and sex appeal. The news here is that she has the killer instinct too—and the skill to project it from a stage." One of the best reviews came from the critic at *The New Yorker*, known for its fastidiousness. "She seems perfectly at ease on the stage of the Martin Beck and readily holds her own in the presence of such seasoned troupers and scene stealers as Maureen Stapleton and Tom Aldredge. The fact that she is what is commonly called a superstar casts no taint upon the nature of her performance, which is well thought out and skillfully modulated. Tallulah Bankhead, who first played Regina (it was the finest role of her career) cannot have spoken the tremendous last lines of the second act any more effectively than Miss Taylor does. They are like repeated blows in the face, and the audience gasps at them, in mingled astonishment and pain."

Her performance was nominated for a Tony, but Elizabeth Taylor lost to Jane Lapotaire, for her portrayal of French singer Edith Piaf.

A Little Night Music

In 1977, Elizabeth Taylor appeared in the screen version of *A Little Night Music*, the Stephen Sondheim hit musical. She played the part of Desiree, an aging actress; her costars were Diana Rigg, Len Cariou, Lesley-Anne Down, and Hermione Gingold. The film was shot on location in Vienna.

The costume designers searched much of Europe for the right jewelry for Taylor to wear in the period film, and reported that they were stumped when it came to locating a suitably massive fake of good quality to go with a gorgeous beaded gown the star was slated to wear in one scene. Finally, someone had the bright idea of asking Taylor herself to help—which she did by walking to her own jewelry box and pulling out the historic Peregrina pearl that had been a gift from Richard Burton.

Director Harold Prince was full of praise for his star. "Taylor has the unique willingness to try anything and not worry, like so many other stars, about her public image. She's the least vain person I've ever met. Not once did I catch her looking into a mirror, except when she checked her makeup before a scene. She's able to be herself. She's willing to be vulgar if called for, or cruel, or impulsive. She's just not the kind of actress who's concerned about the effect every little thing might have on the audience."

Since the movie was a musical, Taylor was called upon to sing several numbers, including the well-known "Send In the Clowns." One reviewer said she had "a pleasant, if not totally secure, singing voice." Taylor said singing made her nervous and petrified. *A Little Night Music* was poorly received by critics, many of whom focused on Taylor's weight rather than her performance. "All calories, cleavage and camp," sniped one, as another asked rhetorically why she couldn't go on a liquid protein diet. Another critic looked for a kinder explanation: "Elizabeth Taylor seems miscast, or at least, badly misdirected. She gives a sincere and very believable performance of a woman who is quickly becoming a matron and who desperately wants to settle down with a husband and father for her young daughter."

Taylor said she enjoyed making this movie more than most. Touchingly, she told an interviewer, "There is one particular line in the film that sounds like a cry from my heart—and the line is to my daughter: 'How would you feel about having a home of our very own and my acting when I really felt like it?'"

Little Swallows

In the late 1930s, the Taylor family spent many country weekends at Little Swallows, the name they gave a cottage on the Kent estate of their friend Victor Cazalet. He lent it to them to use as they wished, and they installed water and electricity and spruced it up. "Cottage" was a typical English understatement, as the sixteenth-century house had fourteen rooms and charming architectural details such as leaded casement windows. Every weekend little Elizabeth rode her pony (a gift from Cazalet) over the green Kentish countryside.

Little Women

In 1949, MGM released its remake of *Little Women*. Based on the classic novel written by Louisa May Alcott, it told the story of four girls growing up in Massachusetts at the time of the Civil War. Inevitably, this version invited comparison with the critically acclaimed 1933 RKO movie by David Selznick (who incidentally was the son-in-law of MGM's head, Louis B. Mayer). Most reviewers felt that despite its Technicolor lushness, the new version came in a distant second.

In MGM's production, Elizabeth Taylor played the role of Amy, the beautiful but spoiled and selfish sister. Jo, the tomboy who is the family's natural leader, was played by June Allyson; Janet Leigh was saucy Meg; and little Beth, whose death is the sentimental climax of the plot, was played by Margaret O'Brien. In a blonde wig and a succession of becoming period costumes designed by Walter Plunkett (also responsible for costumes in the RKO version), Elizabeth Taylor gave a good performance in a role similar to the one she had played in *A Date with Judy*—and would play again in *A Place in the Sun*. She steals her sister Jo's boyfriend (played by Peter Lawford) with conscienceless ease; in fact she displays no qualms about appropriating whatever she wants. But the keynote of Taylor's performance is its comedic overtone: She makes the brainless and high-spirited Amy funny and therefore likeable.

Mary Astor recalled that the set of *Little Women* was a happy one. At the time the movie was made, sixteen-year-old Elizabeth Taylor was "pre-engaged" to Glenn Davis and, according to Astor, "in love and talking on the telephone all the time." Taylor enjoyed working again with Peter Lawford, and their sense of fun spread to the rest of the cast. Astor wrote in her memoirs about one particular day when Peter Lawford, after discovering that Jo/June Allyson had cut her hair short, was supposed to say, "What have you done! You look like a porcupine!" But for some reason, Peter kept mispronouncing it "porkypine," making everyone on the set break out in laughter. Recalled Astor, "The scene would begin, with Peter insisting, 'I've got it! I've got it now!' and then, nearly at the end of the scene, he would burst in the door and say, 'What have you done! You look like a porkypine!' And everybody went to pieces."

Although reviewers were generally unkind in their comparison of June Allyson with Katharine Hepburn, her predecessor in the part of Jo, most agreed that Elizabeth Taylor was well cast as Amy, the role played by Joan Bennett in the Selznick version. Critic Howard Barnes said Taylor was "lovely and properly spoiled in the part of Amy," and *Newsweek* called her "appropriately trivial and attractive."

Liz Bashing

During their marriage, Richard Burton made a virtual career out of denigrating his wife's spectacular looks. He once described Elizabeth Taylor this way: "I can hardly say she's the most beautiful creature I've ever seen. She's a pretty girl and has wonderful eyes. But she has a double chin, an overdeveloped chest, and she's rather short in the leg." He concluded with apparent sympathy, "There isn't an inch of her body that isn't covered with scars. She's had more operations than a charwoman, and she's always talking about them, too."

Liz's Illnesses: Monty's view

Elizabeth Taylor's friend Montgomery Clift shared her tendency to express emotional problems through physical illnesses, a tendency that was exacerbated by his injuries in a 1956 car crash. He commented of Taylor, "Bessie Mae is the only person I know who has more wrong with her than I have."

Lizzie the Lizard

When Elizabeth Taylor was a little girl, her older brother Howard teased her by calling her "Lizzie the Lizard." Perhaps that is why she has never liked to be called Liz.

Arthur Loew, Jr.

The first man Elizabeth Taylor dated after the death of Mike Todd was Arthur Loew, Jr., heir to the Loew theater chain fortune. Their relationship was cut short by Liz's involvement with Eddie Fisher.

Lonely in Washington

Some years after her divorce from John Warner, Elizabeth Taylor revealed that the years her husband was in the U.S. Senate were the loneliest of her life. She had enjoyed the togetherness of the campaign, and the pleasure of being able to help her husband by her own appearances. But like many other Senate wives, she found that once he was elected, she was expected to stay in the background. They saw less and less of one another, and he became increasingly intolerant of the gaudy, excessive side of her personality. Even their sexual life disappeared. Elizabeth finally decided to return to work herself, signing on to appear on Broadway, playing the role of Regina in *The Little Foxes*. Her return to an independent life of her own, outside Washington, marked the effective end of the marriage.

Sophia Loren

Italian actress Sophia Loren and her producer husband Carlo Ponti were good friends of Richard Burton, and it was to their villa in Merino, outside Rome, that he fled when the first Taylor-Burton separation was officially announced. While he was their guest, Burton stopped drinking, went for daily swims, and played Scrabble with Sophia (she won). About a month later, Taylor flew to Rome to join him. After a brief tearful reconciliation, the relationship deteriorated and Burton began drinking again. Taylor left, and Burton immediately started production of *The Journey*, a movie in which he costarred with Sophia Loren. There were persistent rumors from the set of an affair between Burton and his leading lady, but insiders say she was not in love with Burton but was often angered by his difficult behavior. She later commented, "During the period I knew him, he was a tragic figure, the way kings in Shakespeare, once grand, are broken upon the wheel of preordained tragedy."

Love is Better Than Ever

Love is Better Than Ever, released in 1952, was apparently the best vehicle MGM could come up with for Elizabeth Taylor after her acting triumph in *A Place in the Sun*. Taylor played a small-town dancing teacher who attends a convention in New York and meets a slick talent agent (Larry Parks) who feigns an interest in her career merely to persuade her into one of his brief affairs. Since this *is* a fifties movie, the story ends with Taylor outsmarting her would-be seducer and in the end getting the wedding she had hoped for. Another sign of the fifties was MGM's uneasiness about releasing the movie after star Larry Parks had been blacklisted for his alleged membership in the Communist Party. The studio waited nearly eighteen months after the picture was finished before they deemed it safe to release, and even then their promotion of the movie was what you might call "'low-key."

Reviews were mixed, but *Cue* commented that Taylor displayed "a nice talent for underplayed comedy." Although the movie is rarely seen today, it has several positive attributes. One is the attractiveness of the twenty-year-old Elizabeth Taylor running around in short dance costumes. Another is the direction of Stanley Donen, who made the most of the slight material. Donen and Taylor were apparently involved in a romance at the time of the movie's production, but shortly thereafter Elizabeth Taylor went to England to shoot her next movie, *Ivanhoe*, and there she met and soon married her second husband, actor Michael Wilding.

Victor Luna

Victor Gonzalez Luna is a Mexican lawyer from Guadalajara who was for a time engaged to Elizabeth Taylor. Their relationship began when they met at a party in California not long after her divorce from John Warner in late 1982. Luna and Taylor became officially engaged in August 1983, when he presented her with a 16.5-carat cabochon sapphire ring; the announcement was made less than a month after Taylor's *Private Lives* costar and former husband Richard Burton married his fourth wife, Sally Hay. Taylor was still seeing Luna when she went for treatment at the Betty Ford Center. When she emerged, in the spring of 1984, she jokingly called her relationship with the divorced father of four "the longest engagement in the history of the world."

Within weeks, the engagement was over. Although the announcement was made in the fall, just after Richard Burton's death, both Taylor and Luna said the breakup had come months earlier. He told the press that the reason the engagement was off was that they could never manage to be in the same place. "Elizabeth works in Los Angeles or other parts of the world and I have to be here in Mexico. There was no use to keep an engagement when we could not live together. Things were always marvelous for us. We traveled the world together having a truly marvelous time. She has had a wonderful time and I have wonderful memories."

Lux Soap

In 1945, after Elizabeth Taylor's success in *National Velvet*, she was besieged with offers of commercial tie-ins of various sorts. The first the thirteen-year-old star accepted was a $3,000 fee for the use of her photograph in a print ad for Lux soap.

-M-

Mabel

Richard Burton often called his wife Elizabeth Taylor "Mabel." It was his way of saying that to him she was just an ordinary woman, not a superstar.

Madame Vacani's Dancing School

In 1934, when Elizabeth Taylor was just past her second birthday, she was enrolled in Madame Vacani's Dancing School, in London. Two other pupils of the school, who started the same year, were the daughters of the Duke and Duchess of York, Princess Elizabeth and Princess Margaret Rose. Some months later, at the tender age of three, a poised Elizabeth Taylor appeared in a short dance program performed for the royal family. According to one of the teachers at the school, the main point of the dancing lessons was to teach deportment and the social graces.

Made-for-TV Movies

Divorce: His/Divorce: Hers. ABC-TV, 1973. Starring Richard Burton and Elizabeth Taylor, with Carrie Nye and Barry Foster. Directed by Waris Hussein, produced by Terence Baker and Gareth Wigan, executive producer John Heyman. 144 minutes.

Return Engagement. NBC-TV, 1978. Starring Elizabeth Taylor and Joseph Bottoms. Directed by Joseph Hardy, produced by Mike Wise and Franklin R. Levy. Screenplay by James Prideaux.

The Mirror Crack'd. EMI Films Ltd., 1980. Starring Elizabeth Taylor, Angela Lansbury, Kim Novak, Rock Hudson, Tony Curtis, Edward Fox, and Geraldine Chaplin. Directed by Guy Hamilton, produced by John Brabourne and Richard Goodwin. 105 minutes.

Between Friends. HBO, 1983. Starring Elizabeth Taylor and Carol Burnett. Screenplay by Shelley List and Jonathan Estrin, based on the novel *Nobody Makes Me Cry* by Shelley List.

Malice in Wonderland. CBS-TV, 1985. Starring Elizabeth Taylor as Louella Parsons and Jane Alexander as Hedda Hopper. Directed by Gus Trikonis, screenplay by David Seidler and Jacqueline Feather. 105 minutes.

Poker Alice. 1987. Starring Elizabeth Taylor, Tom Skerritt, George Hamilton. 120 minutes.

Sweet Bird of Youth. NBC-TV, 1989. Starring Elizabeth Taylor, Mark Harmon, Rip Torn, and Valerie Perrine. Directed by Nicolas Roeg, based on the play by Tennessee Williams. 120 minutes.

Malcolm Arrives Bearing Gifts

In the summer of 1989, Malcolm Forbes flew to Los Angeles on his private plane, *The Capitalist Tool*, to attend the wedding of his niece. Since he was in the vicinity, he paid a visit to his on-again off-again companion, Elizabeth Taylor. Malcolm arrived bearing gifts that included a watercolor by contemporary artist Bill Stone, a cake decorated to resemble one of the gem-studded Fabergé eggs he collected, and a fabulous pair of ruby and diamond earrings rumored to have cost $250,000. As Liz donned its earrings for the photographer who happened to be on hand, Forbes gallantly told her, "They're not nearly as beautiful as you are." Forbes was later asked what occasioned such a gift. He replied, "It's always an occasion to be with Elizabeth."

Malcolm's Birthday Party

On August 19, 1989, Malcolm Forbes celebrated his seventieth birthday with a party for 1,000 people at his chateau in Tangier, Morocco. His hostess for the event was Elizabeth Taylor, who was at his side the entire evening helping him greet the guests at the $3 million bash.

Many of the guests had arrived on the three jets Forbes had chartered, including a supersonic Concorde. They drew lots to see which of the six tents erected on the grounds they would sit in. The feast included 100 sheep, 600 chickens, and 1,500 eggs; afterward musicians and belly-dancers entertained the crowd and fireworks lit up the night sky. Only three guests were not seated at random: the two royal princes representing King Hassan, and Elizabeth Taylor. Wearing diamond pendant earrings and a caftan she had bought on a shopping expedition with Malcolm the day before, she sat next to the birthday boy as he chatted with his friends—a list that included former president Jimmy Carter, Donald and Ivana Trump, Barbara Walters, and

Henry and Nancy Kissinger. Forbes told reporters that his birthday wish was simply to live long enough to enjoy everything he got from Liz: "The greatest of those is her passion for men," he added provocatively.

Malice in Wonderland

In 1985, Elizabeth Taylor starred in a TV movie called *Malice in Wonderland*, in which she played the part of Hollywood gossip columnist Louella Parsons. Based on the book *Hedda and Louella*, the film was the "hiss and tell" story of rival gossip columnists Parsons and Hedda Hopper (played by Jane Alexander). The film was made after Taylor emerged from the Betty Ford Center looking thin and very beautiful, and she joked, "I should have been playing [Parsons] a year ago when I was fat and frumpy—like she was." Herself antagonistic toward gossip columnists in general, and Parsons in particular, Taylor sank her teeth into the part and delivered a fine performance. The only flaw was that she did indeed look too attractive to be convincing as Parsons, especially in her Nolan Miller wardrobe. But most reviewers agreed that she acquitted herself well.

Joseph L. Mankiewicz

Joseph L. Mankiewicz directed Elizabeth Taylor in two movies. The first was *Suddenly Last Summer*, followed by 20th Century-Fox's *Cleopatra*. Taylor recalls that at her first meeting with Mankiewicz, the director told her, "Elizabeth, you have to lose some weight. And for God's sake, tighten up those muscles. It looks like you've got bags of dead mice under your arms." That was in 1959, when the star was young and svelte, but she seems to have taken his complaint in good part.

Mankiewicz was the winner of two Oscars for direction: *A Letter to Three Wives* in 1949 and *All about Eve* in 1950;

both times, he also won the Academy Award for his screenplay. He became interested in the subject of Caesar, Antony, and Cleopatra when he adapted Shakespeare's *Julius Caesar* for the screen in 1953. *Cleopatra* was a movie he seemed destined to direct, but it proved to be a frustration to Mankiewicz from beginning to end. As he later commented, "Every aspect of Cleopatra has been written, gossiped, lectured, and talked about—except the film." The romance between Taylor and Burton so overshadowed the movie itself that Mankiewicz felt, he explained, like "whoever directed *Our American Cousins* at Ford's Theater on the night Lincoln was shot."

When shooting began on location in Rome, rumors began to fly that the star of the film, then married to Eddie Fisher, was romantically involved with its director. Joe Mankiewicz, born in 1909, bore a physical resemblance to Mike Todd. At that time he was a widower, with a charming and forceful personality. Observers noted the way he dominated Elizabeth Taylor on the set, and her apparent delight in taking his orders. But if there was a romance, its duration was brief, for soon Taylor met costar Richard Burton, and their grand passion began.

It is also difficult to believe that Mankiewicz could have found the time or energy for an affair, because all observers, including his son, who was also working on the production, agree that the director was stretched to the breaking point by the rigors of making *Cleopatra*. The movie was already over budget and behind schedule when he took the helm, after Rouben Mamoulian was fired. Mankiewicz would stay up all night rewriting the script and then shoot the scenes the next day. There was friction with Italian trade unions, which led to strikes. Every move the director made cost more than anyone anticipated. The elephants imported for the film went on the rampage, and so did the executives at 20th Century-Fox, who sent harassing telegrams every day. (The owner of the elephants later sued Fox for publicly commenting that his elephants were "wild.") It's a wonder that Joe Mankiewicz lived through the production; that he found time to romance his high-strung leading lady is unlikely.

Cleopatra proved disastrous to Mankiewicz's career. His subsequent directorial credits are scant.

Louis B. Mayer

Louis B. Mayer was the autocratic head of Metro-Goldwyn-Mayer in the 1940s, when Elizabeth Taylor was a young star signed to a contract at the studio. Although he encouraged his actors to "think of me as a father" and told them to "come to me with any of your problems, no matter how slight they seem to you," his record of responsiveness was not impressive. Usually, he simply lost his temper and told the actor to follow his orders with no further questions.

Louis Burt Mayer was born in Minsk, Russia, in 1885 and emigrated with his parents to Canada when he was three years old. After working briefly in the scrap metal business with his father, he moved to Boston and purchased several motion picture theaters. That led to his formation of a distribution company and then his own production company in Hollywood. In 1924, he was one of the partners who formed Metro-Goldwyn-Mayer, and he became the vice president in charge of production.

The period when Taylor started to work at MGM was the zenith of Mayer's power at the studio, when he was routinely paid nearly $1,000,000 a year and reigned like a tyrant over all those on the payroll, no matter how famous. Elizabeth Taylor, who called Mayer a dwarf with a big nose, had an unpleasant encounter with him in 1946, when she and her mother went to his office to protest her casting in a movie called *Sally in Her Alley*. According to Taylor, Mayer screamed at her mother, "You're so goddam stupid you wouldn't know what day of the week it is. Don't meddle in my affairs! Don't tell me how to make motion pictures! I took you out of the gutter!" Elizabeth, then fourteen, resented the insults to her mother, and ran out of Mayer's office, vowing never to set foot in it again. She kept her promise.

Mayer, married to Margaret Shenberg, had two daughters. The elder one, Edith, eventually became a good friend of Elizabeth Taylor. In 1951, Mayer lost a political struggle for full control of the studio and was ousted. He died of leukemia in 1957, leaving a large fortune to a charitable foundation.

Roddy McDowall

Elizabeth Taylor and actor Roddy McDowall became friends when they were both youngsters under contract at MGM. As children (Roddy was four years older than Elizabeth), they costarred in several movies. The first was *Lassie Come Home*, in which Roddy played the working-class lad who is Lassie's best friend and Elizabeth the granddaughter of a duke who reunites boy and dog. Taylor later commented, "The film is notable to me mainly because I met its star, a little boy named Roddy McDowall, who is now just about my oldest friend—and really the perfect friend. He makes you feel that you're terribly dear to him and even that maybe you're a dear person." In his turn, McDowall later told Taylor what he remembered about their first meeting: "You were perfect, an exquisite little doll, your features, the coloring, the shape of your face, you were the most perfectly beautiful little creature I ever saw and I began laughing because you . . . you were so totally unaware." You can see why Taylor considers him the perfect friend. Taylor and McDowall also appeared together in *The White Cliffs of Dover*, which featured them as childhood sweethearts. Years later, McDowall had a supporting role in *Cleopatra*.

The friendship that began in MGM's schoolhouse continued over many decades. For example, Roddy was there for Elizabeth after her divorce from Nicky Hilton, taking her ice skating at Rockefeller Center and out to dinner in Manhattan restaurants. And Roddy was among the first to know about Elizabeth's love for Richard Burton. He was sharing a villa in Rome with Richard (with whom he had appeared on Broadway in *Camelot*), his wife, and daughters during the shooting of *Cleopatra*. He was a sympathetic listener to all involved parties, and it says something for his admirable tact that he remained on good terms with everyone.

Roddy McDowall was born in London in 1928. A child star in English films in the 1930s, he (like Elizabeth Taylor) went to Hollywood on the eve of World War II. His first American success was in *How Green Was My Valley*, in 1942. Other vehicles included *My Friend Flicka* and *Kidnapped*. As an adult, he had supporting roles in *Midnight*

Lace, The Longest Day, Planet of the Apes, and *Funny Lady*. McDowall is reputed to possess one of the finest collections of old movies in the world. He is also a gifted photographer, who has often taken pictures of his friend Elizabeth. For example, he took the photos that were used on the cover and in the article about her in *Life* in 1964; he also took nude photos of Taylor on the set of *Cleopatra* that were published in *Playboy*.

MCL Films

When Elizabeth Taylor's agent, Kurt Frings, negotiated with MGM for her *Cleopatra* contract in 1960, he asked for and won for Taylor a share of ownership of the film itself. The actress set up a company to receive her 35 percent share of the film, calling it MCL Films, after her children Michael, Christopher, and Liza. Frings and Taylor's then husband, Eddie Fisher, also owned shares in MCL Films.

Measles

Elizabeth Taylor caught measles while she was in Italy in 1973 making *Ash Wednesday*. It took her several weeks to recover.

Measurements

In the 1950s, when Elizabeth Taylor was one of the biggest stars at MGM, it was customary for studios to release the measurements of their actresses. According to the publicity about Elizabeth Taylor, her measurements were 37-19-36.

The Medicine Chest: What's Inside?

According to reports released in late 1988, when several physicians treating Elizabeth Taylor for back pain were investigated for overprescribing drugs for the star and other patients, the actress was regularly taking an amazing variety of medication. It included:

- *Percodan*, an addictive pain killer related to morphine; Taylor was taking as many as 20 a day
- *Percocet*, a combination of Percodan and Tylenol, used to treat moderate pain, considered only slightly less addictive than Percodan
- *Demerol*, a highly addictive narcotic derived from morphine, with which Taylor was injected at least once a week
- *Darvon*, an addictive painkiller used for mild pain
- *Talacen*, a narcotic painkiller
- *Tylenol with codeine*, an analgesic combined with a narcotic that is known to be quickly addictive
- *Valium*, a tranquilizer known to be highly addictive
- *Centrax*, a tranquilizer used to treat anxiety and thought to be addictive
- *Xanax*, an addictive tranquilizer often prescribed for panic or anxiety, which Taylor was taking at the rate of twelve per day
- *Soma compound*, aspirin combined with a muscle relaxant, used to treat painful muscle spasms
- *Flexeril*, a muscle relaxant
- *Inderol*, for high blood pressure and headaches
- *Klorvess*, a source of potassium
- *Placidyl*, a sleeping pill that also acts to relax muscles

The Meeting of Two Queens

During the run of *The Little Foxes* (1981), Elizabeth Taylor was presented to Queen Elizabeth. Pictures of the two Elizabeths show that the Queen of the Screen looked prettier, but the Queen of Great Britain had more diamonds. The two women had previously met in Washington, at a bicentennial dinner party in 1976.

The Meeting on her Wedding Day

On the day that Elizabeth Taylor was to be married to her first husband, Nicky Hilton, an unexpected visitor turned up at the door of the Taylor home. It was Bill Pawley, to whom Elizabeth had been engaged before she met Nicky. Her plans to marry Pawley hit a snag when he insisted she give up her career and become plain Mrs. Pawley; in theory she was willing but in fact she was not ready to retire from the movies. Only the two principals know what was said during that meeting on the morning of her wedding day, but Pawley emerged in an angry mood and immediately flew back to Florida, while Elizabeth was seen to be crying. However, she pulled herself together and a few hours later was a radiant bride.

Memorial Service for Richard Burton

Several weeks after Richard Burton's death in August, 1984, a memorial service was held in London in the Church of St. Martin-in-the-Fields. Among the 1,300 mourners was former wife Elizabeth Taylor. She had not attended the small funeral in Switzerland, reportedly out of respect for Burton's widow Sally. But she was moved to tears and laughter by the service for her one-time love. Burton's elderly friend, Welshman Emlyn Williams, spoke about the romance that began on the set of *Cleopatra*. "Cupid's dart had hit both targets and set the Nile on fire. And the Tiber. Even the Thames sizzled a bit."

Men Elizabeth Taylor Admires

In response to a question in a 1973 interview by journalist Liz Smith, Elizabeth Taylor listed the men she most admired. They were: Richard Burton (to whom she was married at the time), the poet Stephen Spender, Pablo Picasso, Tennessee Williams, Marlon Brando, Leonard Bernstein, Mike Nichols, directors Brian Hutton and Joseph Losey, Michael Caine, Laurence Harvey, and Peter Ustinov.

The Men in Her Life

Glenn Davis
Bill Pawley
Vic Damone
Ralph Kiner
Howard Hughes
Montgomery Clift
Nicky Hilton
Stanley Donen
Michael Wilding
Mike Todd
Arthur Loew, Jr.
Eddie Fisher

Max Lerner
Ingemar Johanssen
Richard Burton
Henry Wynberg
Peter Darmanin
Ardeshir Zahedi
John Warner
Tony Geary
Victor Luna
Dennis Stein
Malcolm Forbes
Larry Fortensky

Richard Meryman, Jr.

Richard Meryman, Jr. was an associate editor at *Life* in 1964 when he conducted one of the most candid interviews ever given by Elizabeth Taylor. He had practiced for the Taylor assignment through previous articles about Marilyn Monroe and Sir Laurence Oliver. His interview with Elizabeth was actually a series of meetings that began in New York, was continued in Mexico, and ended in Paris. At the end, the star told Meryman, "You did good," to which he responded with a hug. He said he heard her back go SNAP!, but Taylor calmly said, "That's all right, luv. It felt good." The interview was published in the December 18, 1964, issue of the magazine.

Metro-Goldwyn-Mayer

Elizabeth Taylor was signed to a movie contract by Metro-Goldwyn-Mayer in 1943. That was after she had appeared in one film for Universal, *There's One Born Every Minute*, and then been dropped by that studio. Legend has it that Elizabeth got the opportunity to test for MGM when her father, then a Civil Defense air-raid warden, struck up a conversation with fellow warden and MGM exec Sam Marx, talking about his beautiful daughter. Taylor's first film for MGM was *Lassie Come Home*, in 1943; thereafter, she was signed to a long-term contract and became part of the studio system that groomed young people for stardom. She is often called the last true star to emerge from the system.

At the time Elizabeth Taylor started to work at MGM, the studio had the boastful motto, "More stars than there are in the heavens." The stars included Clark Gable, Greer Garson, and Katharine Hepburn. Younger stars such as Judy Garland, Jane Powell, Mickey Rooney, and Peter Lawford were starring in lighthearted musicals.

The MGM Contract

Metro-Goldwyn-Mayer originally signed Elizabeth Taylor as a member of the supporting cast of *Lassie Come Home*, paying her $100 for the short time she worked. After that trial period, she was offered a long-term contract, with a starting salary of $75 a week. Her salary stayed at that level until she appeared in *National Velvet*, the movie that made her a star. Then she got a raise to $750 a week.

Her next raise came in 1953, when her contract expired and MGM signed her to a new one for a term of seven years. Thereafter, her weekly salary was $5,000—and her mother was still on MGM's payroll as well. Taylor found herself in the 90 percent tax bracket, and when she had to take two maternity leaves (without pay) she was for a time in genuine financial difficulties.

The last picture Elizabeth Taylor made under contract to MGM was *Butterfield 8*, for which she won her first Oscar. Thereafter, she was a free agent, never again signing a contract for more than one movie at a time.

MGM Signs Michael Wilding

In 1952, Michael Wilding, the English actor who became Elizabeth Taylor's second husband early that year, signed a three-year contract with MGM. His salary was $3,000 a week. According to Hollywood gossip, his contract was part of MGM's effort to keep Elizabeth Taylor happy and induce her to sign a new contract that year with the studio.

Middle East Peace Mission

In December 1982, immediately after her divorce from John Warner, Elizabeth Taylor announced that she planned to embark on a peace mission to the Middle East. "I want to bring a sense of sincere friendship between myself and the people of America to Israel. I've always loved going to Israel and I hope I can be of major assistance in revitalizing Israel's tourist industry and bringing its friends back to the country." She planned to visit both Israeli prime minister Menachem Begin and Lebanese president Amin Gemayel, and hoped she could talk them into meeting one another face to face. The state department withheld official comment, but one unidentified source there said, "There is nothing we can do about it. She has the right to travel and meet with whomever she wishes. Who knows—she may do some good."

But Taylor's shuttle diplomacy was cut short by a fall that caused her to leave Israel in a wheelchair, returning to the United States for medical treatment.

Henry Miller Talks about the Burtons

An outspoken fan of the Burtons in the 1960s was Henry Miller, the trailblazing erotic author. He once explained why he held the couple in such high esteem. "They were never afraid to act out their true feelings. If she wants to wiggle her ass, she wiggles her ass. If he wants a piece of tail, he's not afraid to get a piece of tail. If they want to be cantankerous, they are cantankerous. Too many people want to do something that the public may frown on, even in these days. So they draw back, afraid of what society will say. The Burtons and The Taylors are getting rarer and rarer. They don't whisper—they shout. I don't believe in discipline and neither do they. They feel that nature should point the way."

Nolan Miller Designs for Elizabeth Taylor

In the 1989 made-for-TV movie *Sweet Bird of Youth*, Elizabeth Taylor's wardrobe was designed for her by Nolan Miller, who rose to prominence for his design work on *Dynasty* and now manufactures his own line of clothing. Miller talked to the press about the creation of Taylor's eight changes of costume: "She looks wonderful. Her weight is a little bit of a problem, so we kept the clothes very simple and played up the necklines. She's very easy to work with because she wears things like she's six feet tall."

Miller also designed the clothes Taylor wore for her role as Louella Parsons, the Hollywood gossip columnist, in the 1985 TV movie *Malice in Wonderland*.

Millfield

Millfield was the school in England attended by Elizabeth Taylor's two sons, Christopher and Michael Wilding.

The Million-Dollar Joke

Elizabeth Taylor was the first star to be paid the milestone salary of $1 million for a film, and she says it all started out as a joke. Producer Walter Wanger called Taylor to ask her to play Cleopatra in the movie of the same name. She was at that time married to Eddie Fisher, enjoying domestic life, and not particularly anxious to work, especially in a film with a foreign location. So she said to Eddie, who had happened to answer the phone when the producer called, "Tell him I'll do it for a million dollars—ha ha." To her surprise, Wanger agreed.

The Mirror Crack'd

In 1980, Elizabeth Taylor was cast in a leading role—one that had previously been turned down by Natalie Wood—in a TV movie version of an Agatha Christie mystery, *The Mirror Crack'd*. Taylor played an aging and reclusive movie queen, vulgar and overdressed, trying for a comeback. Others in the all-star cast included Taylor's good friend Rock Hudson playing her husband, Kim Novak as a rival star, Tony Curtis as a Hollywood producer, and Angela Lansbury as Christie's detective, Miss Jane Marple. Edward Fox played Marple's helpful nephew and Geraldine Chaplin was the producer's secretary.

There is an interesting Hollywood sidelight about Agatha Christie's plot. The mystery writer got her idea from a story she had heard about Gene Tierney. The glamorous star of *Laura* and other unforgettable movies contracted German measles during a pregnancy, when she was married to designer Oleg Cassini, and as a consequence their daughter was born severely retarded. The child had to be institutionalized, and Tierney herself suffered for many months from a severe depression. Some years later, a woman walked up to the actress at a party and said, "I am such a fan of yours that I once came out to see you at a premiere, and had the thrill of talking to you in person—even though I had a bad case of measles at the time." In Christie's novel, that revelation sets the stage for murder.

The Mirror Crack'd provided a great opportunity for fans to see many of their favorite stars of the 1950s. Thus it garnered respectable ratings on its initial broadcast and has been aired several times since. Artistically, the vehicle had little to recommend it, as most reviewers took pleasure in pointing out; they generally skipped over the question of performance and concentrated on listing the stars and analyzing how well they had withstood the ravages of time. But it was something of a romp for Elizabeth Taylor, and she especially enjoyed the chance to work again with friend Rock Hudson.

"Miss Tits"

Before Richard Burton became acquainted with his *Cleopatra* leading lady, Elizabeth Taylor, he referred to her by the derogatory "Miss Tits." Once he got to know her, the name was never heard again.

The Mole

Elizabeth Taylor has a mole on her right cheek. When she was a teenager, MGM urged her to have the mole removed, but she refused. In her publicity photos, the mole is sometimes airbrushed away, but in real life, it remains where it has always been.

Marilyn Monroe

Few Hollywood observers have been able to resist making a comparison between the two most celebrated movie queens of the 1950s: Elizabeth Taylor and Marilyn Monroe. Both were the focus of legends, and both participated in their creation. Both seemed to have had difficulty finding ordinary domestic happiness, and both were often demeaned by the very people in Hollywood who were making money from their screen appearances. The chief difference is that Marilyn is dead, and Elizabeth has the strength of a survivor.

The two women were never friends, and also never admitted to feeling any sense of rivalry. But they were exquisitely *aware* of one another, and their paths crossed frequently. They were devoted to the same hairdresser, Sidney Guilaroff, shot by the same photographers, dressed by the same Hollywood designers. Monroe costarred in *The Misfits* with Taylor's close friend Monty Clift. Elizabeth Taylor and Richard Burton were on friendly terms with Ethel and

Bobby Kennedy; Monroe was rumored to be something more than a friend to Bobby.

An ironic example of the influence the two actresses seemed to exert upon one another from afar came in 1962, when 20th Century-Fox, desperately trying to conserve funds as huge sums drained away through Taylor's movie, *Cleopatra*, canceled Monroe's last film, ironically entitled *Something's Got to Give*. Monroe was dead within weeks.

Montgomery Clift Foundation

After Elizabeth Taylor's dear friend Montgomery Clift died of a heart attack in the summer of 1966, Taylor announced that she planned to establish the Montgomery Clift Foundation. The purpose would be for research into heart disease, and the work would be administered by the American Heart Association. Taylor would set up the foundation with a gift of $1 million, money she had previously pledged to insure the production of *Reflections in a Golden Eye*, in which she wanted Montgomery Clift to costar with her. But the American Heart Association never received the money, and Clift's biographer Patricia Bosworth concluded, "As far as I know, it was only an idea."

Monty's Accident

On Saturday night, May 12, 1956, Elizabeth Taylor and her then husband Michael Wilding invited a few people for dinner at their house high up in Bel Air's Coldwater Canyon. The guests were Eddie Dmytryk, the director of *Raintree County*, the movie Taylor was then filming, and his wife; Rock Hudson, costar of Taylor's previous movie, *Giant*, and his wife-to-be, Phyllis Gates; actor Kevin McCarthy; and Taylor's close friend and *Raintree Country* costar, Montgomery Clift.

According to Clift's biographer, Patricia Bosworth, the

atmosphere of the evening was not a pleasant one, due in large part to the tension between the host and hostess, whose marriage was deteriorating. Michael Wilding was lying on a sofa suffering from back pain, and Clift lounged unshaven on the floor. Monty and Elizabeth talked desultorily about the film they were working on, sharing their enthusiasm over the work of cameraman Bob Surtees. Monty helped pour the rosé wine the Wildings were serving that night, but observers agreed that he drank only one glass himself. Clift later admitted that he had also taken two barbiturates, in the hope of being able to sleep when he got back home.

At the end of the evening, Monty asked Kevin McCarthy to drive in front of him and lead the way back down the winding road. Halfway down, McCarthy saw Monty's car begin to weave and skid, then crash into a telephone pole. McCarthy ran back to the house for help, and Taylor immediately called her own physician, Dr. Rex Kennamer (who also treated Monty). She then walked to the wreck and crawled into the bent metal and broken glass to cradle Monty's badly damaged head in her lap. McCarthy told Patricia Bosworth, "Some of [Monty's] teeth had been knocked out and his two front teeth were lodged in his throat. I'll never forget what Liz did. She stuck her finger down his throat and she pulled those teeth. Otherwise he would have choked to death."

Taylor rode in the ambulance with Monty to the Cedars of Lebanon Hospital and stayed there until she was assured there was no brain damage. Later, she would have many nightmares about the evening, and her bloodstained dress. Not only did Taylor visit Monty at the hospital every day, she also talked MGM into closing down production of *Raintree County* until Monty recovered, rather than recasting his part. Monty, deeply grateful for Elizabeth's loyalty and devotion in this crisis, gave her a grisly souvenir of the occasion: one of the teeth that had been rammed down his throat in the crash.

Monty's Opinion of Elizabeth Taylor's Acting

Montgomery Clift told writer James Jones that Elizabeth Taylor was extraordinary in her ability to catch a mood instantly, without needing explanation. "I'd rather work with her than any actress in the world," he said. "It's all instinct with her."

Mother-Daughter Hospital Stay

In 1988, Elizabeth Taylor's dependency on prescription drugs to subdue severe back pain drove her into the Betty Ford Center for supervised withdrawal. Her mother, ninety-two-year-old Sara Taylor, was admitted next door, at the Eisenhower Medical Center, at the same time, suffering from bleeding ulcers. Elizabeth made a visit by wheelchair to see her mother every day, often leaving in tears because her mother's condition was so critical. Yet both women recovered, and only a few months later, Sara Taylor was an honored guest at the ceremonies in which her daughter received the Hope Award.

Motorcycle Ride to Raise Money

In 1987, Elizabeth Taylor took part in a 100-mile motorcycle ride held by the Blue Star Motorcycle Club of New Jersey to raise money for AIDS research. Taylor went along for the ride with beau Malcolm Forbes. "Malcolm is making me a biker," she told reporters, while praising the bikers club for "their deep sense of caring and loving." The most striking feature of her outfit for the occasion was a temporary tattoo—a long snake on her forearm.

The Movies That Might Have Been: Roles Elizabeth Taylor Turned Down

Elizabeth Taylor declined to appear as Rima, the shy "bird" girl who lived in the forest in *Green Mansions*. Audrey Hepburn was given the part. After the birth of her first child, Taylor turned down an MGM film called *All the Brothers Were Valiant*. The part went to Ann Blyth. In 1975, Taylor was slated to costar with Richard Burton in *Abakarov*, playing an aging movie queen, but an argument with director Wolf Vollmar put an end to that idea. Three roles that Elizabeth Taylor turned down went to Shirley MacLaine: Gittel in *Two for the Seesaw*; Irma in *Irma La Douce*; and the lead in *What A Way to Go*. Taylor had planned two projects in which she was to costar with Richard Burton, which fell by the wayside due to the couple's personal problems and ensuing divorce. She was to play Nancy in a film version of the musical *Oliver*, with Burton playing Bill Sykes, and the two were to play opposite one another in *Sands of the Kalahari*. Elizabeth Taylor turned down the leading role in *Myra Breckinridge*, which eventually went to Raquel Welch.

Mr. Sheehee's Dancing School

In 1940, young Elizabeth Taylor was enrolled in Mr. Sheehee's dancing school, a Hollywood institution located on La Cienega Boulevard. Many of her classmates were the children and grandchildren of Hollywood execs.

"My Little Heifer"

John Warner frequently referred to his wife Elizabeth Taylor as "my little heifer."

The Mystery of the Diamond Ring

In 1977, nearly twenty years after Mike Todd's death, grave robbers dug up his bronze coffin and broke into it. They were seeking a diamond ring rumored to have been buried with the showman. According to Todd's brother Frank, the ring was more than a rumor. "He had a huge diamond ring with him at the time of burial. He sure as hell did! I know because I was at the funeral—and Elizabeth Taylor insisted that he be buried with it. I estimate the ring's value at $100,000." A spokesman for Elizabeth Taylor, John Springer, told the press, "I have no specific information about a diamond ring. A very simple wedding band from Elizabeth was buried along with the remains—but it was of little economic value."

But wait! According to all reports, that wedding ring, melted and twisted in the plane crash that killed Todd, was returned to Taylor by authorities in New Mexico, and she wore it for years, even during the time she was married to Eddie Fisher, as a link with the husband she mourned. Just to make the whole question murkier, an ambulance driver who was one of the first to arrive at the scene of the crash told reporters in 1977, "He had a nice-looking diamond wedding ring on his left hand. He was identified by it at the plane crash site." On the other hand, a state policeman who assisted in investigating the crash, remembered no diamond ring. "It is possible that if Todd was wearing the ring, it was lost in the crash." The grave robbers, who anonymously contacted a private detective to let authorities know where to recover the remains, said they found no ring. Taylor has never made any further public comment on the mystery surrounding Mike Todd's diamond ring.

-N-

National Velvet

In 1944, Elizabeth Taylor became a full-fledged movie star when she appeared in the title role of Velvet Brown in *National Velvet*. The novel of the same name, written by Enid Bagnold in 1935, had been a best-seller for young adults (Taylor was one of the book's fans long before she was cast in the movie), telling the story of an English country girl and the horse she wins in a raffle and then trains and rides to a win in the prestigious Grand National steeplechase.

When it was announced that MGM had bought the rights to the novel and planned to create a film version, young Elizabeth desperately wanted to play the role of the heroine. The story often told by Taylor biographers is that producer Pandro Berman was dubious, because she seemed too small to portray a girl who can disguise herself as a grown-up jockey and then guide her horse to a win in the gruelling Grand National. (Apparently, youthfulness was not the first criterion for the part: MGM tested both Margaret Sullavan and Katharine Hepburn for Velvet.) According to Hollywood legend, eleven-year-old Elizabeth embarked on a program to stretch herself and gain weight; her will triumphed, and she got the part she wanted. According to producer Pandro Berman, however, the oft-told story is pure hogwash. He told an interviewer that MGM had already cast her in the part, knowing all they had to do was simply wait to start production until she had grown tall enough.

Although Taylor emerged as the star of the movie after

it was released, top billing was given to young Mickey Rooney, who played the role of the experienced stable boy who helps Velvet train her horse. Also billed above Taylor was Donald Crisp, in the role of her father. Anne Revere played her quietly encouraging mother, a role for which she won an Oscar, and a baby-faced Angela Lansbury played the role of Velvet's older sister (replacing Mona Freeman, originally cast in the part). The director was Clarence Brown, who said of his young star, "There's something behind her eyes that you can't quite fathom. Something Garbo had. I really hate to call her an actress. She's much too natural for that."

Reviews were unanimous in their praise for the young girl who played Velvet. Bosley Crowther, critic for *The New York Times*, said of Taylor, "Her face is alive with youthful spirit, her voice has the softness of sweet song, and her whole manner in this picture is one of refreshing grace." *The New York Post* critic called her "as natural and excellent a little actress as you would ever hope to see," and *Variety* labeled her "a new dramatic find" while predicting (correctly) that the movie would be one of the top box-office hits of the year. Kate Cameron said that Taylor was admirably suited to the role of Velvet and added, "She gives a glowing performance that actually overshadows her *vis-a-vis* Mickey Rooney, who is one of Hollywood's prime scene stealers." Critic Pauline Kael, writing many years later, gave it as her opinion that "the high point in Elizabeth Taylor's acting career came when she was twelve: under Clarence Brown's direction, she gave her best performance to date as Velvet Brown, the heroine of Enid Bagnold's account of a little girl's sublime folly." Taylor seems to agree with Kael, for she has called *National Velvet* "still the most exciting film I've ever done."

Many people who saw the film responded to the intensity of Elizabeth Taylor's passion for her horse. She also conveyed some of the ambiguity of that passion, a kind of pre-erotic love affair. The critic for the *New Republic* commented, "Not only does she make you wonder uncomfortably what her motives are when she says she wants to be 'the greatest rider in the world,' but her favorite pastime is galloping over the countryside as though she were riding a horse and doing some more galloping in bed before she goes to sleep."

The movie was a huge success at the box office, grossing more than $4 million in the year of its release.

Nedelheimers

As a presenter at the 1982 Tony Award show, Elizabeth Taylor greatly amused the audience with her apparently involuntary fracturing of the names she read aloud. One of them was theater owner James Nederlander, whose name somehow became "Nedelheimer." Nederlander himself thought it was so funny he changed the name of his restaurant in the Manhattan theater district to "Nedelheimers."

Paul Neshamkin

Paul Neshamkin was the tutor hired by Elizabeth Taylor in the mid-1960s for her four children. Between the demands of her career and those of husband Richard Burton, the household was continually on the move, and Taylor became aware that the children's education was suffering. Liza had not started to read even though she was seven; and Maria, who had frequently been hospitalized for surgery to correct her crippled hip, still spoke nothing but German. It was Neshamkin's responsibility to see that the children caught up with the classroom knowledge they needed.

Never Poor

Mike Todd, who had been through several fortunes by the time he married Elizabeth Taylor, and spent another one buying her presents, liked to joke that he had often been broke, but never poor.

New Back Problems

According to the statements Elizabeth Taylor made at a press conference in the spring of 1989, the back pain she suffered the previous year, so intense that it drove her back to dependency on prescription drugs, was caused by a compression of the first lumbar vertebra. The actress has suffered from a bad back for years; though she underwent a spinal fusion in 1956, she continues to experience pain and weakness in her back. At this stage doctors can only try to alleviate the symptoms as they arise, and medication for pain is one of their chief weapons. In the course of treatment for the drug dependency caused by the medication, Taylor's intake of pain pills had to be greatly reduced, with the result, she said, that "I'm still in a lot of pain, but I'm coping with it. I'm learning to live with the pain. It hasn't been easy, but I'm okay."

Paul Newman

Paul Newman costarred with Elizabeth Taylor in the 1958 film version of *Cat on a Hot Tin Roof*, in which she gave an unforgettable performance as Maggie the Cat opposite Newman as her husband Brick. Newman, himself a box-office idol of long standing, was born in Cleveland in 1925, did his undergraduate work at Ohio's Kenyon College and then studied drama at Yale. At the time he costarred with Taylor, he was best known for his Broadway work, including the lead in Tennessee Williams's play, *Sweet Bird of Youth*. His only previous screen appearance had been in *Somebody Up There Likes Me*, in which he played the leading role of boxer Rocky Graziano.

Newman was direct in his praise of Taylor as an actress. Admitting that he had not expected much of her, he says he was bowled over by her ability to respond intuitively to the camera. Her low-key approach to rehearsal had caused him concern that she might not be able to reach the emotional pitch needed for their big scenes—but when the cameras started rolling, Taylor rose magnificently to the demands of the role.

Nibbles and Me

In 1945, Elizabeth Taylor published her first book, a slight volume about the adventures of her pet chipmunk entitled *Nibbles and Me*. The book was hokey, but the pet was genuine, a pert little creature that Taylor had trained to live on a long string leash and sleep at the foot of her bed. The girl had frequently been photographed with Nibbles, so interest was high when it was announced that her book about the chipmunk would be published.

The publisher of *Nibbles and Me* was Duell, Sloan and Pearce, to whom the young star of *National Velvet* wrote an ingenuous letter headed "Dear Mr. Editor." The slim volume, priced at one dollar and illustrated with pictures drawn by Taylor, supposedly originated as an essay written for her teacher at the MGM school, Miss Birdine Anderson. It tells of the love between Elizabeth and Nibbles, and the fun they shared. The book has a rather sad ending, since Nibbles goes the way of all chipmunks, but the author is philosophically brave. After suffering a broken heart, she walks and talks with "Mummie" and finally concludes, "And then I knew just as I knew before that in reality there is no death. I know that he would always live in my heart— and that another one would come to me . . . not to take his place but to bring the same sense of love to me and he did—and I knew him immediately and I named him Nibbles. Not Nibbles the second but just Nibbles—my favorite chipmunk."

Night Watch

Night Watch was a 1973 movie starring Elizabeth Taylor and Laurence Harvey. The two had wanted to work together again ever since their success in *Butterfield 8*, and they were well aware that Harvey's battle with cancer might make this the last film he ever appeared in. (It was; he died before the picture was released.) So they both agreed to do *Night Watch* for no money up front, just a percentage of the hoped-for profits, simply because it was the opportunity they had been looking for.

The movie was based on a play by Lucille Fletcher, one of the gritty psychological thrillers in which she specialized. Taylor played a woman who says she sees a murder in a neighboring house, then finds that both her husband (Laurence Harvey) and her best friend (Billie Whitelaw) think she has imagined it. That apparently leads her to wonder about the death of her first husband, and whether or not she is coming unhinged. To underscore the unexpected nature of the plot twists, the ads for the movie announced that no patrons would be seated during the last twenty minutes of the movie. It ends with Taylor revealing that her seeming confusion was all an act to lure her husband and his mistress, her best friend, into revealing their treachery. Then she gleefully knifes them both.

The review in *The New York Times* was quite complimentary. "Elizabeth Taylor, and about time, has got herself a good picture," it began, going on to say that Taylor "churns up a fine, understandable lather of nerves." But most other critics were negative, castigating the script, the direction, and the lack of "nuance" in Taylor's performance in the difficult double-edged role of the wife. The movie sank out of sight quickly, and there were no profits with which to pay the stars.

Louis Nizer

In the 1960s, Louis Nizer was one of the top lawyers in the country. At the height of the Taylor–Burton romance, he flew to Rome to consult with Elizabeth on the subject of divorce. Interestingly, he also met with Eddie Fisher. It was Nizer who released the terse announcement of the couple's impending divorce.

"No More Marriages"

Elizabeth Taylor and Richard Burton were married while he was appearing on stage in Toronto in the leading role in *Hamlet*. At the first performance after the wedding, Burton came out as usual to take his curtain calls. After several bows, he stepped forward and spoke to the audience. "I would just like to quote from the play," he told them. "Act 3, Scene 1: 'We will have no more marriages.'"

No Relation to Robert Taylor

Elizabeth Taylor made two movies with actor Robert Taylor: *Conspirator*, in which she played his wife; and *Ivanhoe*, in which she played a woman who loved him. Fans repeatedly wondered whether the two Taylors were related. The answer is no. Elizabeth is a true Taylor, using the name she was born with. Robert Taylor was renamed in Hollywood, abandoning forever his original identity: Spangler Arlington Brugh.

Not-So-Lucky Liz

In late 1956, after Mike Todd and Elizabeth Taylor had announced their engagement, he leased a Lockheed Lodestar and named it *The Lucky Liz*. He let Elizabeth redecorate the interior, at a reported cost of $100,000. Todd was traveling on *The Lucky Liz* on the night of March 22, 1958, when the plane crashed, killing all aboard.

Taylor and Mike Todd, Jr. later filed a lawsuit against the company from which Todd had leased the plane, claiming the firm's negligence had caused the accident. They eventually settled for $40,000, which was held in trust for Todd and Taylor's daughter Liza.

Dr. Max Nussbaum

Dr. Max Nussbaum, of the Temple Israel in Hollywood, was the rabbi who supervised Elizabeth Taylor's study of Judaism and then presided over the ceremony that converted her to that faith, in the spring of 1959. He also conducted her wedding to Eddie Fisher.

-O-

O Fie

O Fie was a Pekinese that was for many years part of the Taylor–Burton household.

"Ocean"

During the filming of *Cleopatra*, as Richard Burton and Elizabeth Taylor fell in real-life love, he began to call her by a private nickname, "Ocean."

An Odd Triangle

At the height of the scandal over the romance of Elizabeth Taylor and Richard Burton on the set of *Cleopatra*, a rumor surfaced that their involvement was just a cover for Taylor's affair with the director of the film, Joe Mankiewicz. According to a story told by Burton's biographer, Hollis Alpert, Burton responded with a joke: The next day on the set, he went up to the director and said, "Mr. Mankiewicz, do I have to sleep with her again tonight?" Mankiewicz, who found the whole thing funny, told his press agent to put out a release contradicting the rumor. The real truth, the agent should say, was that the Taylor–Burton romance was a cover for the hot affair going on between Mankiewicz and Burton!

Old Bond Street

Elizabeth Taylor's parents, Francis and Sara Taylor, moved to London in the 1930s because Francis was sent there to open an art gallery for his uncle, Howard Young. The gallery was located on posh Old Bond Street, at Number 30. It was upstairs, in a quiet suite of rooms, discreetly paneled and conservatively furnished.

On the Rocks

During the Burton years, Elizabeth Taylor's habitual drink was Jack Daniels on the rocks. She usually told the bartender to make it a double. After divorcing Burton, she switched to a new favorite: Stolichnaya vodka on the rocks.

The Only Game in Town

In 1970, Elizabeth Taylor costarred with hot male sex symbol Warren Beatty in *The Only Game in Town*. Actually, Beatty was second choice; the part had originally been intended for Frank Sinatra, but after production was delayed by a Taylor illness, Sinatra dropped out of the project and Beatty was signed instead.

The plot hinges on a romance between a none-too-successful Las Vegas chorine and a piano player who seems intent on gambling away every last dime. The dancer (Taylor) is involved in an affair with a married man, but slowly she finds herself succumbing to the breezy charm of the piano player (Beatty). In the end, these two bruised people conclude that togetherness is the only game in town. The movie was better than its reception, which was lukewarm at best; it lost more than $8 million. Taylor's box-office draw had been tarnished by a string of pretentious failures, and director George Stevens had bombed badly with his previous film, *The Greatest Story Ever Told*. So audiences for the most part ignored the movie.

In fact, *The Only Game in Town* was a charming film, with Taylor and Beatty at their best in this blend of comedy and romance. It was based on a play by Frank Gilroy (who also wrote the screenplay), and kept the small cast and limited sets of the stage version. Reviews of the performance by the two stars were good. *Variety* called it one of Taylor's best characterizations, and *Cue* said she was "colorfully convincing." Several reviewers, among them Pauline Kael, also noted that Taylor was looking better than ever—even though they all agreed that it was hard to believe her as a working woman living in a tacky little apartment. Kael added, "Miss Taylor has a sweetness and, despite her rather shapeless look, a touching quality of fragility (like some of the women stars of an earlier era, as she gets older she begins to have a defenseless air about her) but the plot makes her ridiculous."

Only the Men She's Been Married To

At the time of Elizabeth Taylor's highly publicized romance with Richard Burton, many aspersions were cast on her moral character. She commented sorrowfully, "The irony is that the morality I learned at home required marriage . . . so I got married all those times and now I'm accused of being a scarlet woman. I've only slept with the men I've been married to. How many women can make that claim?"

Oscar Presenter in 1949

The first time Elizabeth Taylor was asked to present an Oscar was at the 1949 Academy Awards show. The beautiful seventeen-year-old came on stage to the strains of "Did You Ever See A Dream Walking?" and handed out the Oscar for Best Costume Design. Unfortunately, this was before the ceremonies were televised, so our only souvenir of the occasion is a photo of Elizabeth, gowned in what looks like a prom dress, sitting with her escort Glenn Davis, both of them looking bored to tears.

Oscar Presenter in 1970

Elizabeth Taylor fans treasure their memories of the 1970 Academy Awards ceremonies, broadcast on television, at which she was one of the presenters. The star had rarely looked better. Trim and tanned, she was dressed in an organdy Edith Head creation in a divine shade of pale blue, her hair piled atop her head. Around her neck she wore her latest acquisition, the fabulous Cartier diamond, hanging from a diamond necklace that was a major piece in its own right. Taylor was radiant, despite her deep disappointment that husband Richard Burton was once again a losing nominee (for *Anne of the Thousand Days*) in the Best Actor category.

Hilda Jenkins Owen

Hilda Jenkins was a sister of Richard Burton. She married a local boy, carpenter Dai Owen, and settled down in Pontrhydfen, Wales, where Richard had grown up. He and his wife, Elizabeth Taylor, made periodic visits to Hilda, who cooked them many of Richard's favorite dishes and spoke to her brother in his native Welsh. According to Hilda,

Elizabeth always enjoyed these visits. The star often sent her old clothes to her sister-in-law, although they hardly seemed appropriate for life in a small Welsh village. But Taylor and Burton invited Hilda and her husband to visit them regularly in London, to attend some movie premier or other glamorous event, so perhaps the clothes came in useful on those occasions.

Oxford University

In the 1940s, young Richard Burton was in a training program in the Royal Air Force. One phase of the training was a six-month course at Exeter College, Oxford University. Burton loved Oxford so much that thereafter he liked to give the impression he had been a regular student there.

During the years that Elizabeth Taylor was married to Richard Burton, she shared in his attachment to Oxford. The Burtons together bought a building to serve as a rehearsal hall for the Oxford University Dramatic Society, and they both appeared in the OUDS production of *Doctor Faustus* that Burton later turned into a film. They also contributed the money necessary to save *Isis*, the Oxford magazine.

-P-

Pacific Palisades

When Elizabeth Taylor and Nicky Hilton returned from their honeymoon, they settled down in a rented house in Pacific Palisades. It was furnished, right down to the sheets and towels, by items from the warehouse of the Hilton Hotels. When they separated, it all went back to the company.

Pal

In *Lassie Come Home*, Elizabeth Taylor costarred with Lassie—except that the feminine role of Lassie was actually played by Pal, a male collie. Although Pal lived to be nineteen, he retired when he was five, and the role of Lassie was taken over by his son. All the screen and TV Lassies were related, and all were owned and trained by Rudd Weatherwax, who was always mentioned in the title credits.

Pamela Brown

Pamela Brown was the name of the cat Elizabeth Taylor had during her marriage to Richard Burton. The name came from the actress who costarred with Burton on Broadway in *The Lady's Not for Burning*.

Louella Parsons

Louella Parsons was one of Hollywood's leading gossip columnists, nationally syndicated in the Hearst newspapers, when she first met young Elizabeth Taylor, a child actor at MGM. Elizabeth's mother had arranged the meeting, saying that her daughter was anxious to meet Jimmie, Louella's cocker spaniel. For years thereafter Louella Parsons—like all other Hollywood columnists—wrote frequently about the life and loves of Elizabeth Taylor. She was a guest at Taylor's first wedding, to Nicky Hilton, and publicly exclaimed "I told you so!" when the marriage ended in divorce. Parsons, who liked to call herself "Love's Undertaker," also chided Liz for her choice of aging Michael Wilding as Husband Number Two, and was outraged when Taylor "stole" Eddie from Debbie for Wedding Number Four. Later, she was the first to publish reports of the attraction between Taylor and her *Cleopatra* costar on location in Rome in 1960.

Louella Parsons, born in 1893, also wrote and published two volumes of memoirs. An outspoken admirer of Mussolini before World War II, she often used derogatory racial epithets in her stories. Hollywood insiders told stories of her frequent malapropisms—for example, she spoke of a dying star falling into a "comma"—that had to be edited out of her columns. Parsons entered a nursing home in 1965 and died in 1972, at the age of 79.

Although Elizabeth Taylor had earlier courted Parsons's good opinion, she denounced the gossip columnist after her death in 1972. "She was dumpy, dowdy and dedicated to nastiness. Forget anybody that stood in her way. And her voice . . . so irritating. You just wanted to smack her." Ironically, in 1988, Taylor played the role of Louella Parsons in a made-for-TV movie called *Malice in Wonderland*.

Partial Hysterectomy

In 1968, Elizabeth Taylor underwent a partial hysterectomy in a London hospital.

Pasadena

When the Taylor family first moved to Los Angeles on the eve of World War II, they lived in a modest house in Pasadena, east of Los Angeles. In those days, Pasadena was still largely agricultural, and Sara Taylor's parents had moved there from Kansas to settle on a chicken ranch. Later the Taylors moved to Pacific Palisades, and finally to a house in Beverly Hills bought with Elizabeth's movie earnings.

Passion

In 1988, Elizabeth Taylor introduced her fragrance, Elizabeth Taylor's Passion. Created for her by Parfums International, Passion comes in a violet bottle reminiscent of the color of the star's eyes and contains rich floral notes mixed with sensual undertones. Passion is priced at $165 an ounce for the perfume and $25 an ounce for the eau de toilette. Taylor receives a fixed percentage of every bottle sold as part of her licensing agreement with the company that makes it, and in turn, she gives a part of her earnings to the AIDS Foundation.

The print ads for Passion include a close-up portrait by Norman Parkinson of Taylor at her most glamorous, dripping with diamonds from Harry Winston. Later ads for the Passion line of scented bath products feature a photo of the star in a pool tinted purple by a sunset, wearing nothing but a fortune in emerald jewelry from Harry Winston and accompanied only by a pensive leopard in the background; the picture echoes the famed shot of Taylor in a pool and emeralds used by Helmut Newton for the cover of his published collection of celebrity photos. The television commercials featured closeups of Taylor reciting lines from Shakespeare, interspersed with her own comments that relate to the fragrance.

In 1989, Taylor introduced her line of men's fragrance products, called Passion for Men. At a press conference in Paris to promote the new line, she said, "Passion is just the way I like my men to smell." She added that her message to men was, "Just be passionate about the whole thing."

Unfortunately, the promotion of all Passion products hit a snag shortly after their introduction, when it was discovered that Annick Goutal, a French perfumer, was already marketing a scent with the same name. Taylor's company sued to obtain freedom to use the name, and Goutal countersued to prevent Taylor's product from being sold. In a peculiar compromise, Federal District Judge Robert W. Sweet ruled that Taylor's Passion could not be sold in fifty-five retail outlets that would carry Goutal's perfume of the same name. The Taylor Passion continues to sell briskly in more than 1,200 stores.

William Pawley, Jr.

Bill Pawley was Elizabeth Taylor's first official fiance, when she was just seventeen. William Pawley, Jr. was the son of a former U.S. ambassador to Brazil and Peru, and himself a prosperous businessman, vice-president of a family-owned Florida bus line. His eligibility was emphasized by the fact that he had been one of the founders of the exclusive Miami Bachelors Club. Elizabeth met the twenty-eight-year-old

Pawley through her great-uncle, Howard Young, at a birthday party Young threw for her at his winter home on Star Island, near Miami. Pawley arrived for their first date in his own boat, and soon romance blossomed under the Florida sun, at the Pawleys' family home on Sunset Island.

In the spring of 1949, Elizabeth broke off her relationship with Glenn Davis, the former football hero, when he returned from Korea. Shortly thereafter, she accepted a three-and-a-half–carat diamond engagement ring from Pawley. When she showed it to reporters, she told them that Bill called it "a nice piece of ice." However, the love between this pair was not strong enough to surmount the obstacles facing them—primarily the fact that Bill wanted her to move to Florida and be Mrs. Pawley, while she was still reveling in the glamour and fame of being movie star Elizabeth Taylor. When she insisted on accepting the part of Angela Vickers in *A Place in the Sun*, instead of retiring from her career as they had previously agreed she would, Bill Pawley told first Elizabeth and then the press that the engagement was off.

According to Kitty Kelley, Bill Pawley made a flying visit to California to accost Elizabeth on the day of her wedding to Nicky Hilton in May 1950. Pawley, who became a leader of the Moral Rearmament movement, did not fall off the Eligible Bachelor list until his 1974 marriage.

Peanuts

Elizabeth Taylor is a longtime fan of the *Peanuts* comic strip, and it's always the first thing she reads in the morning paper.

People Covers

In 1989, *People* celebrated its fifteenth anniversary and paused to reflect on a few notable statistics. Among them was the fact that the person who had appeared most frequently on the cover of the magazine was Elizabeth Taylor, with eleven covers to her credit.

The Peregrina Pearl

In January, 1969, (the same year he bought the Cartier diamond) Richard Burton bought Elizabeth Taylor the famous Peregrina Pearl when it was auctioned at the Parke-Bernet Gallery in New York. He paid $37,000 for the gem, which was said to have been discovered by Spanish explorer Balboa. It was originally part of the Spanish crown jewels, then King Philip gave it as a wedding present to his bride, Queen Mary Tudor of England. Most recently, it had belonged to the English Duchess of Abercorn, a lady-in-waiting to Queen Elizabeth II. Appropriately for such a well-traveled gem, its name means "The Wanderer." The historic pearl was nearly destroyed by one of Elizabeth's dogs; the Pekinese was found glumly chewing on the necklace just in time to save it. Taylor usually wears it as a pendant, on a diamond necklace that was also a gift from Burton.

Perfect Thirty-Sevens

Elizabeth Taylor turned from a girl into a woman very quickly, and entirely in the public eye. In an era that focused on bust measurements as a symbol of womanly attraction, she was proud to say she had "perfect thirty-sevens." Those perfect thirty-sevens remain one of her most striking attributes, as recent photos of Taylor in décolleté dresses attest.

Pills Prescribed in 1988

In the spring of 1989, certain of Elizabeth Taylor's doctors came under investigation for allegedly prescribing excessive quantities of potentially dangerous drugs for her (and other patients as well). According to news stories in print at the time, the star had received prescriptions for more than 10,000 pills in the first ten months of 1988. She was taking dozens of pills daily, some of them in amounts considered by physicians to be life-threatening. Taylor subsequently entered Hazelden Clinic in Minnesota to recover from her prescription-induced addictions. She expressed indignation about the huge doses of medication she had been prescribed, and a willingness to cooperate with police investigations of her doctors' activities.

The Pink Diamond

Shortly after Elizabeth Taylor married Richard Burton for the second time, he gave her a rare pink diamond. The twenty-five–carat stone cost more than $1 million. Taylor immediately announced that she planned to sell the diamond to build a hospital in Botswana as a permanent tribute to their renewed love. Nothing ever came of the hospital, and within months, when Taylor and Burton separated again, the diamond became the subject of bitter argument over its ownership.

A Pisces

Elizabeth Taylor, born on February 27, is a Pisces, the zodiac sign that astrologers claim is destined to experience both Heaven and Hell on earth. A Pisces is an "old soul," pained by sadness and ugliness in human existence and desirous of escaping it—sometimes through meditation or artistic creation, sometimes through drugs and alcohol. Born with an instinctive awareness of life's troubles, the Pisces views other people's failings with sympathy and compassion. Taylor's friend Montgomery Clift, a knowledgeable follower of astrology, once characterized Elizabeth as "a real Pisces—dreamy, sentimental, all female."

According to astrologer Linda Goodman, in her book *Love Signs*, "To Pisces, love is unselfish submission of the ego to the desires of the one needed to become Whole." She explains, "The Fish gains more pleasure from giving than from receiving, more happiness in serving than in being served. Yet enigmatic Neptune [Pisces's ruling planet] tests the Pisces soul with the lure of multiple sexual and romantic experience—floating from one affair to another."

Perhaps one reason that Elizabeth Taylor has not always been lucky in love is her Piscean nature. Her beauty, her femininity, and her fragility attract men who desire to protect and serve her, yet she is happiest when she can be the one who gives and serves—as was frequently the case in her relationship with Richard Burton. Moreover, her old soul's sympathy for human failing makes her a magnet for weak men, yet she needs another strong person, like Mike Todd, if she is to be able to submit her own ego and become whole through her union with another. Thus, for example, Elizabeth Taylor could marry Eddie Fisher because she thought he needed her, only to grow unhappy because he lacked the strength she needed in a true partner.

A Place in the Sun

In 1951, MGM released the powerful melodrama, *A Place in the Sun*, starring Montgomery Clift, Elizabeth Taylor, and Shelley Winters. The movie was based on the highly regarded novel by Theodore Dreiser, *An American Tragedy*, and told the story of an ambitious young man (Montgomery Clift) who sees a world of wealth and power opening before him and falls in love with that world's embodiment, the rich and beautiful Angela Vickers (Elizabeth Taylor). All that stands in his way is the girlfriend who works in a factory (Shelley Winters). Pregnant by him, she nags him to make an honest woman of her. With murder on his mind, he takes the factory worker out in a boat, causes it to capsize, and then swims for shore, leaving her to her fate. Later, he faces charges of murder brought by a relentless district attorney (Raymond Burr) and must answer to his own sense of guilt as well.

Elizabeth Taylor actually filmed *A Place in the Sun* before *Father's Little Dividend*, but MGM released the comedy first, to capitalize on the popularity of *Father of the Bride*. Much of the movie was shot on location at Lake Tahoe and at Cascade Lake, Nevada; the actual filming ran for more than four months. It was so cold on location that the crew had to hose off patches of snow before the stars could film scenes wearing bathing suits and summer clothes.

Although the director who initiated the screen version of Dreiser's novel, George Stevens, had originally hoped to get Grace Kelly for the role, he later said he considered Taylor the ideal Angela Vickers. "The part calls for not so much a real girl as the girl on the candy box cover, the beautiful girl in the yellow Cadillac convertible that every American boy sometime or other thinks he can marry." Stevens thought that the greatness of Dreiser's story lay in the fact that it was a morality play that meant different things to different people. "The thing that interested me most about *Place*," he later confided, "was the relationship of opposing images: Shelley Winters busting at the seams like sloppy melted ice cream as against Elizabeth Taylor in a white gown with blue ribbons floating down from the sky."

Critics, who had previously commended Elizabeth Taylor's talent for light comedy, had to expand their definition of her abilities in light of her strong performance as Angela Vickers. A character determined to have her own way, and win the man she is attracted to, she is nevertheless an appealing and even somewhat innocent young woman. Taylor succeeds in portraying the naivete of a sheltered daughter of the rich, suggesting a dreamy and romantic outlook that exists independently of her spoiled selfishness. Taylor has always said that on the set of *A Place in the Sun* was the first time she had ever seriously tried to be an actress. Her real mentor, she explained, was Montgomery Clift, a former Broadway actor who had already received great acclaim for his screen performances. "I watched Monty," she commented. "I watched how much time he spent on concentration—which has since become the key to my kind of acting, if you can call it acting." Elizabeth was also helped by veteran director Stevens, who had a reputation for his ability to make his women stars look good on the screen. Although he sometimes lost his patience with Taylor's effort to extend her acting abilities—he once told her coldly to remember they were not making *Lassie Comes Home to a Place in the Sun*—Stevens was for the most part supportive and encouraging, and the results show he did coax out of her one of her very best performances.

The critic of *The New York Times* called Elizabeth Taylor's performance in *A Place in the Sun* "the top effort of her career." He added, "It is a shaded, tender performance and one in which her passionate and genuine romance avoids the pathos common to young love as it sometimes comes to the screen." *Variety* said Taylor's "histrionics are of a quality so far beyond anything she has done previously that Stevens' skilled hands on the reins must be credited with a minor miracle." *Time* said, "Actress Taylor plays with a tenderness and intensity that may surprise even her warmest fans." *Boxoffice* announced that she deserved an Academy Award, but apparently the majority of their professional colleagues did not agree. Although Montgomery Clift, Shelley Winters, George Stevens, and the film itself were all nominated for Oscars, Taylor's name was not on the list of nominees. Stevens won Best Director, Michael Wilson and Harry Brown won the award for their screenplay, and cinematographer William C. Mellor, costume designer Edith Head, and score composer Franz Waxman also took home the coveted gold statuettes. The fact that Elizabeth Taylor held her own in a movie of this quality helped boost her reputation as a serious actress, eventually leading to the dramatic roles of the later 1950s that would put her own name on the list of Oscar nominees.

Planned Hostage Exchange

Elizabeth Taylor, often the subject of Arab terrorist threats because of her support for the state of Israel, once learned that she was the target of a plot to kidnap her as a hostage. The terrorist group's intention was to exchange Taylor for captive Arab skyjacker Leila Khaled. Taylor minimized the dangers in her public statements, but she remained under constant guard by Scotland Yard for weeks, until it was judged that the threat had subsided.

Playboy Pictures

In 1962, while Elizabeth Taylor was in Rome filming *Cleopatra*, she agreed to appear in a scene in which she was massaged in the nude by her handmaidens. Other than her then husband, Eddie Fisher, and the necessary cast and crew, the only person allowed on the closed set was Taylor's good friend, Roddy McDowall, who had a supporting role in the movie. Taylor agreed to let McDowall photograph her nude and in a transparent gown. With her consent, the photos were published in the January 1963 issue of *Playboy*.

Pneumonia Threatens to Take Liz's Life

In the winter of 1961, Elizabeth Taylor contracted a near-fatal case of pneumonia. She was in London at the time, with husband Eddie Fisher and her four children, shooting scenes in an English studio for the MGM film *Cleopatra*. She had invited her parents to join them, for a gala family celebration on February 27, the date of her own birthday as well as that of her son, Christopher Wilding. Elizabeth had been through a number of illnesses early in the winter, including a long cold, an abscessed tooth, and the Asian flu. Shortly before the birthday party, in her suite at the Dorchester Hotel, she turned blue and started gasping for breath. Then she lapsed into unconsciousness.

Taylor was rushed to the hospital (a journey recorded by press photographers), where doctors estimated she was only minutes away from death. They performed an emergency tracheotomy, which gave her some relief in her tortured breathing, but her condition continued to deteriorate. The diagnosis was acute staphylococcus pneumonia, and Taylor was not responding to the antibiotics she was being given. She was fed intravenously and given blood transfusions to combat an underlying anemia, but doctors despaired of saving her.

Elizabeth was near death when Sara Taylor came to her hospital room and began reading her daughter the writings of Mary Baker Eddy, the founder of Christian Science. At the same time, Elizabeth was given a new experimental antibiotic, which Eddie Fisher had located in America and arranged to have flown over. After several days on the brink, Elizabeth finally rallied and eventually began to recover. She later recalled, "Four times after the initial time, I stopped breathing. When I came to that last time, it was like being given sight, hearing, touch, sense of color. Like I was, I don't know, twenty-nine years old but had just come out of my own womb. I knew that I wanted more in my life than what I had."

Elizabeth's Taylor's mother always credited Christian Science practice with saving Elizabeth's life, whereas Elizabeth at the time said it the devotion of her husband that pulled her through. Fisher modestly credited her recovery to the imported antibiotic. Probably the lions' share of the credit is due to Elizabeth herself and her strong will to fight.

During the crisis, the entire world had waited anxiously for bulletins from the London Clinic, where Elizabeth Taylor was hospitalized, and a huge volume of mail poured in to wish the stricken actress well.

Poetry Reading

In the summer of 1964, Elizabeth Taylor collaborated with Richard Burton in a poetry reading in New York. The event was a benefit to raise money for the drama school run by Burton's mentor, Philip Burton, and tickets were $100 each. It took a great deal of courage for Elizabeth to face a live audience composed primarily of celebrities connected to the world of New York theater—as she put it, "I knew that 85 percent of them had come there and spent a great deal of money to see me fall flat on my face"—and to put herself in a position where she would be compared to one of the acknowledged masters of a difficult art. Richard was so concerned about his wife's performance that he wouldn't even attend the same rehearsals.

Taylor, looking gorgeous in a one-shoulder taffeta gown, stumbled at first, but gained confidence as she went on. Among her selections were "The Ruin'd Maid" by Thomas Hardy and "Three Bushes" by William Butler Yeats. Midway through the evening, British actress and wit Bea Lillie cracked, "If she doesn't get worse soon, they'll all be leaving." At the end of the evening, even Elizabeth Taylor's severest critics had to admit that she had acquitted herself admirably.

Poker Alice

In 1987, Elizabeth Taylor starred in a made-for-TV movie with friend George Hamilton, called *Poker Alice*. In this lighthearted Western, she played a religious woman, a highborn Bostonian, who accidentally manages to win a brothel in a game of five-card stud. Later she falls in love with a bounty hunter, played by Tom Skerritt. Her snappy dialogue included such lines as, "Poker isn't work for me. When I sit in on a poker game, I don't cast shadows. I'm too good to cheat." An easily forgotten production, *Poker Alice* garnered respectable ratings and mediocre reviews. *The New York Times* assessment? "A bland romp."

"Pooters"

John Warner had many nicknames for his wife Elizabeth Taylor: among them was "'Pooters."

"Portrait of a Man"

One of the best-known paintings in Elizabeth Taylor's art collection is "Portrait of a Man" by Dutch master Franz Hals. According to a story related by Taylor biographer Brenda Maddox, Francis Taylor found the painting in a London junk shop and bought it for £100. Taylor inherited the picture on her father's death.

Jane Powell

Jane Powell was one of the bright young stars at MGM when Elizabeth Taylor was under contract to the studio. Powell, born Suzanne Burce in 1929, began her career on radio as a child, and started acting in movies when she was fifteen. Powell was best known for her soprano voice and her petite blonde good looks.

Elizabeth Taylor and Jane Powell costarred in *A Date with Judy*, a 1948 MGM vehicle for the studio's young musical talent. The two girls became friendly enough to act as bridesmaids in one another's weddings. Powell's career peaked in 1954, when she had the lead role in *Seven Brides for Seven Brothers*, and by the end of the fifties, she retired for a time. She reappeared in the mid-1970s, doing regional theater and revivals of Broadway musicals.

Premiere of Doctor Faustus

The New York premiere of *Doctor Faustus* in 1967 was a gala event. Elizabeth Taylor, wearing a caftan and an impressive array of jewelry, attended with husband Richard Burton and special guests Senator Robert F. Kennedy and his wife Ethel.

President Harry S. Truman

In 1946, child star Elizabeth Taylor was invited to the White House to meet President Harry S. Truman and to participate in a radio broadcast with Mrs. Truman to launch the March of Dimes campaign. Later, thirteen-year-old Elizabeth confided that she thought the President looked like MGM studio head Louis B. Mayer!

The Prince of Wales Feathers

In 1987, after the death of the Duchess of Windsor, her jewels were auctioned by Sotheby's in what was called "the sale of the century." The jewels, which were appraised at $3 million, brought ten times that figure at the sale. One of the most desirable items was a yellow gold pin set with diamonds in the shape of the three feathers that are the insignia of the Prince of Wales, the title held by the duke for many years before he ascended to the throne in 1936 and took the title of King Edward VIII. That pin was purchased by Elizabeth Taylor, who later explained that she wanted it as a memento of the friendship she and Richard Burton had with the Windsors. Perhaps it was also a way to remember Welsh-born Burton; for him, the insignia always had a special meaning.

Taylor's winning bid for the piece was $623,327, phoned in from the pool of her California home. The price was approximately ten times the intrinsic value of the stones themselves, but of course the intangible value of the duchess's jewelry, the closest thing to crown jewels that will ever come on the market, is immense. After her purchase, Liz remarked ruefully, "I feel so guilty, it seems so indulgent. I've never spent that much on myself before." Rumor has it that the rival bidder who finally dropped out was none other than Diana, the Princess of Wales!

Since her purchase, Elizabeth Taylor has frequently been photographed wearing the pin. It adorns her right shoulder in some of her television commercials for her fragrance, Passion.

Princess Elizabeth of Yugoslavia

Princess Elizabeth of Yugoslavia is actually of English descent, a second cousin to Prince Charles, the heir to the throne of Great Britain. At the time she met Richard Burton in the fall of 1974, she had been married and divorced twice—once to the American Howard Oxenberg, with whom she had two children, one of whom (Catherine) would grow up to be an actress; and once to the British banker Neil Balfour. Burton, who had just been divorced from Elizabeth Taylor for the first time, pursued the princess so skillfully that they became engaged within three weeks. Taylor offered the couple distant congratulations. Princess Elizabeth broke the engagement four months later after learning of her intended's on-location fling with a *Playboy* cover girl, Jeanne Bell. Burton's continued drinking also influenced her decision. "I didn't realize," she said later, "that it takes more than a woman to make a man sober."

In an interesting sidelight, it appears that Princess Elizabeth and Elizabeth Taylor were friends when they were children. The princess's father, Prince Paul of Yugoslavia, had been an Oxford roommate of Victor Cazalet, the friend of Francis and Sara Taylor who introduced them and their children into English society. So the two little girls were childhood playmates, and they stayed in touch until the princess's involvement with Richard Burton put an end to their acquaintance.

Princess Grace Suite

During the New York run of *Hamlet*, which opened in the spring of 1964, just after the marriage of Elizabeth Taylor and Richard Burton, the couple lived in the Princess Grace Suite of the Regency Hotel. The eight-room suite was decorated with eighteenth-century French furniture and cool pastel colors.

Private Lives

Late in 1982, Elizabeth Taylor and Richard Burton announced they were planning to work together on the stage, costarring in a theatrical production of *Private Lives*. The play was written by Noel Coward, who they said once told them they reminded him of the leading characters, Amanda and Elyot, a couple who discover they can't live together and can't live apart. Coward, who had worked with Taylor and Burton in the screen disaster *Boom!*, especially admired Taylor as an actress, calling her "a million percent professional."

Coward's play tells the story of a divorced couple who both remarry. Their honeymoons coincidentally take place in the same hotel, and they end up meeting and falling in love again. The supporting cast of *Private Lives* included Kathryn Walker, John Cullum, and Helena Carroll. Milton Katselas directed (although he was fired just before the play opened); Elizabeth Taylor and Zev Bufman produced. Costumes were designed by Tony- and Oscar-winner Theoni V. Aldredge.

Taylor subsequently confided that she thought both she and Burton had made a terrible mistake in appearing in *Private Lives*. They were not comfortable in their roles, they were not comfortable in a comedy, and most of all, seven years after their divorce, they were not comfortable with each other. Moreover, Burton was in poor health at the time; he died only months after the show closed in late 1983.

Reviews were savage. When the play opened on the road, in Boston, a local critic said, "Elizabeth Taylor was perfectly terrible—a caricature of a Coward heroine, inside a caricature of an actress, inside a caricature of Taylor." When the play moved to Broadway, claws were equally sharp. Frank Rich in *The New York Times* said the stars looked "whipped and depressed" as they went through the motions of appearing on the stage. "Miss Taylor lists about, her hands fluttering idly, like a windup doll in need of a new mainspring." John Simon said snidely that Taylor was such a bad actress it was obvious that her entire film career "is clearly attributable to her former face, her former directors, and the cutting room." Clive Barnes, calling the pace of the play "funereally lugubrious," complained that Taylor had the energy for the part but lacked the stage technique, while Burton had the techinique but lacked the energy. *Time*'s review, titled "King Midas Calls the Tune," said, "Liz and Dick are almost as inept at playing themselves as they are at re-creating Coward's characters." The reviewer concluded that Taylor had created her character as a blend of Mata Hari and Lady Macbeth.

The play left Broadway for a national tour, which was canceled midway through. Taylor almost immediately entered the Betty Ford Center for treatment of drug dependency, which had made her miss a number of performances. Burton, visibly frail on the stage, died in less than a year.

Purchase, New York

When Elizabeth Taylor was Mrs. Eddie Fisher, the singer bought a home for them in Purchase, New York. The white brick house had thirteen rooms and stood on five acres of land that included tennis courts and a swimming pool.

-Q-

QE3

In the 1980s, the media often called Elizabeth Taylor "QE3," a not very complimentary allusion to her bulk.

Quarantine

In 1968, when Elizabeth Taylor and Richard Burton returned for a stay in London, her dogs were not allowed to enter the country because of the British policy of quarantining animals for six weeks. So that she would not be parted from her pets, Taylor chartered a yacht and moored it on the River Thames as a floating kennel for the six-week quarantine. Burton told reporters it cost them $21,600 to house the dogs. It was a gesture that reaped considerable negative publicity.

-R-

Raintree County

Raintree County was the second of the movies in which Elizabeth Taylor costarred with Montgomery Clift. As in their first collaboration, *A Place in the Sun*, Taylor played a young woman whose beauty and charm lures Clift away from the path of duty. A Southern belle visiting friends in Indiana, she has an affair with a schoolteacher (Clift) and manipulates him into abandoning his childhood sweetheart (Eva Marie Saint) and marrying her. Then he discovers, rather like Mr. Rochester in *Jane Eyre*, that his new bride has inherited her family's tendency toward madness. During the Civil War, he fights for the Union and she goes back home to the South and disappears. Dutifully, he searches for her, finds her in a mental institution, and takes her home again. The story ends—not a moment too soon!—with the wife's accidental drowning during a fit of lunacy, which frees the hero to return to Eva Marie Saint. Clift privately called the plot a "soap opera with elephantiasis."

Raintree County was based on a similarly lengthy novel that was a best-seller in 1947. MGM acquired the rights as soon as it was published, paying author Ross Lockridge, Jr., like his hero an Indiana schoolteacher, the unheard-of sum of $150,000. Shortly thereafter, Lockridge, unable to cope with such sudden and gargantuan success, killed himself. MGM put the project on a back burner until 1956. Then they asked Millard Kaufman to write a screenplay and assigned Edward Dmytryk to direct. *Raintree County* was the most expensive film MGM had yet made, with 119 speaking parts and a budget of more than $5 million. The studio had hoped for another *Gone with the Wind*. After all, *Raintree County* too was a romantic movie with Civil War battles, location footage of old Natchez plantations, and all the trappings of the Old South. It had Elizabeth Taylor at her most beautiful, paired with Montgomery Clift, the only male costar whose looks could rival hers. Alas, midway through the production, that ceased to be the case. Driving home from a dinner party at the home of Taylor and her second husband, Michael Wilding, Montgomery Clift crashed his car and badly injured his head. He underwent weeks of treatment, including plastic surgery, but his face was never fully repaired.

Work on the movie was suspended for awhile, and then MGM decided simply to shoot the remainder of Clift's scenes, using long shots wherever possible, and hope that audiences wouldn't notice the difference in the star's looks. Of course they did. There was a difference in his acting too, in part due to the heavy doses of painkillers he had to take to keep going, and perhaps also to his own reaction to his ruined beauty. MGM exec Dore Schary has recalled, "About half of *Raintree* was shot when the accident occurred. Yes, Monty was in terrible shape, yes, he'd lost his looks and was going to have to adjust to a new face. Yes, we considered replacing him." Schary added, "After conferring with Elizabeth and with Monty's doctors as well as with Monty himself, we all decided it would kill him to take him off the picture. Elizabeth was afraid he might kill himself if he wasn't allowed to go back to work."

Was the whole effort worth it? Most critics agreed that the movie was too long, the plot too diffuse, and the characterization too shallow. Box-office receipts were disappointing, too. But critics generally praised Taylor's characterization of the "vain posey shallow young thing whose only asset is her beauty" (Bosley Crowther in *The New York Times*). Peter Baker called Taylor's performance outstanding, adding that she revealed "depths of feeling and intelligence such as we have never seen from her before." *The New York Herald Tribune* called her the best of the actors.

The movie had one exciting result for Elizabeth Taylor—she was nominated for an Academy Award. She was happy to be recognized by her peers in the movie industry as a genuine actress rather than only a star. And in fact, her performance was a high-voltage portrayal of a woman who remains fascinating and attractive even though she is a total lunatic. While Clift, playing the sensitive hero, broods and Eva Marie Saint simpers, Taylor holds the screen with her dark passions.

Elizabeth Taylor watched the Oscar ceremonies on TV the night after husband Mike Todd's funeral in 1958, only to learn she had lost to Joanne Woodward's tour de force in *The Three Faces of Eve*. It was a difficult loss for Taylor, although she handled it bravely, and sent Woodward a spray of white orchids with a card signed by "Elizabeth Taylor Todd, and Mike too."

The "Real" Fathers of Elizabeth Taylor

Elizabeth Taylor once said candidly that her real fathers were Benny Thau, the MGM executive who managed her career, and Jules Goldstone, her agent during the MGM years.

Reconciliation with Burton

Elizabeth Taylor and Richard Burton were first divorced in June 1974. She then lived openly with Henry Wynberg; Burton, briefly engaged to Princess Elizabeth of Yugoslavia, shared his rented villa with a former *Playboy* model, Jeanne Bell. As 1975 wore on, Burton and Taylor spent more and more time talking on the telephone. In August, when she returned from Russia, where she had been filming *The Blue Bird*, they met in Switzerland, ostensibly to discuss business. The next day, they announced their reconciliation and immediately began to live together again. Less than two months later, they remarried. The London *Times* rejoiced, "We happily join the millions of staunch Taylor–Burton subjects to wish the couple god-speed, for they have the marvelous ability to make a make-believe world even more unbelievable but oh so delicious. Long may they be able to cast their wonderful spell."

Within months, the Burtons had separated again, this time for good.

Reconciliation Gift

Elizabeth Taylor and Richard Burton separated in the summer of 1973 and reconciled briefly in time for Christmas. Richard's gift to his wife to mark the event was a thirty-eight–carat colored diamond, a rich cognac brown similar in hue to her favorite Jack Daniels.

Reflections in a Golden Eye

Elizabeth Taylor starred in the 1967 screen adaptation of Carson McCuller's novel, *Reflections in a Golden Eye*. Much of Taylor's original interest in the project was due to the fact that she felt it would be an ideal vehicle for her ailing friend, Montgomery Clift. Not only did she fight to have him cast in the part of her husband, she even volunteered to put up her million-dollar salary in lieu of insurance, which the producers were unable to get with Clift in the production. Sadly, Clift died only weeks before production was scheduled to begin.

The sorrowful Taylor, locked into a lucrative contract that forced her to continue, helped director John Huston and producer Ray Stark look for a replacement. They found that most Hollywood stars (Richard Burton included) were reluctant to take on the role of the repressed homosexual Major, lest it damage their careers. It was Marlon Brando who finally dared to take that risk. The strong supporting cast included Brian Keith and Julie Harris.

Reflections in a Golden Eye should get an "A" for effort, but unfortunately, the final product was not as great as the sum of the individual talents behind it. The quirkiness of the characters evoked no emotional response from the audience, and reviewers were nearly unanimous in their agreement that the movie was a failure. (So were audiences, who stayed away from the box office.) Taylor's performance was commended by some reviewers. Judith Crist called her "very good as the trollopy young woman" and Pauline Kael called her "charming as a silly sensual Southern lady." Others were more critical. *Variety* complained that Taylor's dialect obscured some vital plot points. Arthur Knight, writing in *Saturday Review*, said, "Her virulent scenes in *Virginia Woolf* revealed her full capabilities; but when she shrieks 'You son of a bitch!' at Brando in this one, she might still be playing *National Velvet*." A balanced view came from Bosley Crowther in *The New York Times*. "Elizabeth Taylor is erratic, showing genuine arrogance and cruelty in some scenes, but too often letting her bitchy housewife be merely postured and shrill." On the whole, a perfectly respectable performance notwithstanding, *Reflections in a Golden Eye* further damaged Elizabeth Taylor's bankability.

Renouncing Her American Citizenship

Although Elizabeth Taylor was born in London, she was an American citizen. But in the 1960s, when she was married to Richard Burton, she decided to renounce her citizenship and become British. "It's not that I love America less," she said, "but I love my husband more." Aware of the negative publicity that her action would garner, she managed to keep it quiet for several years. Later, the IRS alleged that the real reason she had renounced her citizenship was to avoid U.S. taxes—and filed suit to get some of those taxes back.

In 1977, after Taylor married John Warner, she applied for naturalization papers and once again became an American citizen.

Replacing the Elephant Tusk

When Elizabeth Taylor married Richard Burton for the second time, in 1975, the ceremony took place in Botswana and the couple exchanged rings made of native ivory. Several days later, when the Burtons returned to London, Richard replaced the simple ring with one set with seventy-two diamonds.

Return Engagement

In 1978, Elizabeth Taylor starred in a TV movie first presented on NBC, called *Return Engagement*. She played the role of a professor of ancient history who is concealing the fact that she used to be a famous musical star. One of her students, a role played by Joseph Bottoms, learns of her secret and persuades her to appear in a college variety show; he, of course, ends up acting as her dancing partner. The ensuing dance number is more than a little embarrassing. Rex Reed claimed it looked "like a mating dance between Jughead and Kate Smith." The tentative affair never gets off the ground, but both professor and student are left with warm memories. The movie was written by James Prideaux and directed by Joe Hardy.

In an interview at the time the movie was first aired, Bottoms revealed that he was cast in the movie because Taylor had seen him in the part of a resistance fighter in *Holocaust* and asked for him as her leading man. "She's kind and generous," he commented. "Some people in this business in her position wouldn't give you the time of day. She always has time for people."

Once again, reviewers seemed to be under the impression they were assigned to comment on Elizabeth Taylor's looks rather than her performance. After they got past that issue, they generally commended Taylor's interpretation of the role. John J. O'Connor in *The New York Times* called her "marvelously appealing", adding, "There is an admirable element of sassy determination, of what used to be called gumption, in her performance." Bernie Harrison commented that "Taylor is still one of our very best actresses." Rex Reed, complaining about the script, added, "No matter how inane the material becomes, she rises above it, and in the process manages miraculously to make it work."

Anne Revere

Anne Revere played Elizabeth Taylor's mother in *National Velvet*, a role for which she won an Oscar as Best Supporting Actress. Later, she played Montgomery Clift's mother in *A Place in the Sun*, in which Clift commits a murder out of love for Elizabeth Taylor. Revere, who also won an Oscar for portraying Jennifer Jones's mother in *The Song of Bernadette*, maintained that the character of the mother in *National Velvet* was seriously lacking in dimension. "Such a mother never existed," she pronounced. But *Time* called her performance "perhaps the best mother ever seen in a moving picture." Revere's promising career ended in 1951, when she was a victim of the Hollywood blacklist during the McCarthy era.

Revisiting MGM

In a 1977 interview, Elizabeth Taylor talked about her feelings when she passed the old MGM lot. "When I have time to stop I say hello to the cops on the gate at MGM. Some of the same ones are still on the gate as when I worked there. But it's very depressing, the concrete streets at the studio with the weeds busting through. When I was a child, it was like fairyland. You'd walk into the commissary and there'd be 2,000 people, Roman senators and Indians, and I would drop my knife and fork and just weep."

Debbie Reynolds

Movie star Debbie Reynolds was born Mary Frances Reynolds on April 1, 1932, in El Paso, Texas. Her family moved to California when she was eight. She won the Miss Burbank contest in 1948 and was offered a movie contract with Warner Brothers, where her first film was *The Daughter of Rosie O'Grady*. Two years later, Reynolds moved to MGM, at that time famed for its production of musicals. Her big break came at seventeen, when she was cast as the ingenue in *Singin' in the Rain*. She acknowledges the role star Gene Kelly played in her success in that movie. "He had to work so hard with me. I was talented but so young and still so untrained . . . Gene was hard on me. He had to be. He was a huge star and he had to be tough making a picture that he had 'created.' I give him all the credit for *Singin' in the Rain* and for helping me learn the best way I possibly could."

After a long engagement, she married singer Eddie Fisher on September 18, 1955. The wedding took place at Grossinger's resort in the Catskills, where Fisher's own career in show business had begun, and the bride wore the wedding dress Helen Rose had designed for her when she appeared opposite Frank Sinatra in *The Tender Trap*. She later said of Fisher, "He had a sweetness, a boyishness. Why else did all those women go for him?" The couple had two children: Carrie Francis in 1956 and Todd Emmanuel in 1958. The

Fishers, nicknamed "America's Sweethearts," made one movie together, *Bundle of Joy*, which bombed at the box office. Eddie and Debbie were divorced in 1959, after Eddie humiliated Debbie publicly in his pursuit of his new love and next wife, Elizabeth Taylor.

In 1960, Debbie married California businessman Harry Karl, owner of a chain of shoe stores. "I wasn't looking for grand passion," she subsequently explained. "I was looking for someone who would love and take care of Carrie and Todd. I also wanted someone who would look at me with adoration and think I was the greatest thing since 7-Up." In the 1970s, Debbie discovered that Harry was a compulsive gambler and a bad businessman. Before the marriage ended, her own earnings had gone to cover his debts, in the millions of dollars. In 1984, Reynolds married her third husband, Virginia real estate developer Richard Hamlett.

Among the best-known movies of Debbie Reynolds's career were *Three Little Words*, *The Affairs of Dobie Gillis*, *The Tender Trap*, *Tammy and the Bachelor*, *The Gazebo*, and *The Second Time Around*. She continues to appear in regional theater as well as on television. In 1989, she toured with a company of *The Unsinkable Molly Brown*, a role she played in the movie twenty-five years earlier (for which she won an Oscar nomination). Her daughter Carrie is a successful actress and author; her son Todd is a movie sound engineer.

Rhapsody

In the five-year period between *A Place in the Sun* (1951) and *Giant* (1956), Elizabeth Taylor, then one of MGM's brightest stars, inexplicably appeared in a long string of undistinguished movies. One of them was *Rhapsody*. In this 1954 vehicle, she played a rich young woman (surprise!) torn between her love for a pianist (John Ericson) and her obsession with a darkly handsome violinist (Vittorio Gassman)—both of whom turn away from her because of her overtly manipulative behavior. In the end, she marries the pianist, nearly destroys him, and then nobly devotes herself to rehabilitating him and his career.

As critics rightly noted, most of the plot was merely an opportunity to give Elizabeth Taylor a new outfit (designed by Helen Rose) or a change of mood. Bosley Crowther of *The New York Times* apparently thought that was enough. "Miss Taylor never looked lovelier than she does in this high-minded film," he raved. "Her wind-blown black hair frames her features like an ebony aureole, and her large eyes and red lips glisten warmly in the closeups on the softly lighted screen. Any gent who would go for music with this radiant—and rich—Miss Taylor at hand is not a red-blooded American. Or else he's soft in the head." Otis L. Guernsey, Jr. saw the same phenomenon but drew a different conclusion. "Music goes into one of Elizabeth Taylor's shell-pink ears and out the other in *Rhapsody* . . . The point of the story is to show off Miss Taylor wearing attractive gowns, sobbing in loneliness, or radiant at a concert. It is a ravishing show of feminine charm, in vivid color, but director Charles Vidor has evoked hardly a single honest gesture or expression . . . Even her evident and genuine beauty seems at times to be a fake."

The Richard Burton Cocktail

One joke about Richard Burton's legendary drinking during the years he was married to Elizabeth Taylor was the recipe for the "Richard Burton cocktail." It began "Take twenty-two tequilas . . ."

Joan Rivers

In the late 1970s, Joan Rivers made a virtual career out of her Elizabeth Taylor fat jokes. For example, she claimed that Elizabeth wanted to go to McDonald's but got stuck in a golden arch. Some years later, after Taylor was once again svelte, she and Rivers met at a Hollywood party. According to Taylor's account, Rivers told her how wonderful she looked and then asked Taylor to think about why Rivers had told so many jokes about the star's weight. Taylor's response indicated that she found it hard to believe that Rivers's only motive was helping Taylor see that she ought to lose weight.

Riviera Country Club

Before production began on *National Velvet*, Elizabeth Taylor took lessons every day at the Riviera Country Club to prepare her to ride in the steeplechase scenes. She loved horses, and had been riding since she had her first pony at the age of three. But the jumps required a technical expertise she needed to learn. Her teacher was an Australian named Snowy Baker, and Taylor was a diligent student. In fact, she practiced so often that the studio, fearing an accident, finally grounded her until shooting began.

The Roles That Got Away

Like most actresses, Elizabeth Taylor hasn't always gotten the roles she wanted to play. Among those she lost were: Maria in *The Barefoot Contessa*, which went to Ava Gardner; Lillian Roth in *I'll Cry Tomorrow*, a role that went to Susan Hayward—and won her an Oscar; the princess that made Audrey Hepburn a star in *Roman Holiday*, and won her an Oscar, too; Elizabeth I in *Young Bess*, which went to Jean Simmons, on the grounds that Taylor's voice was too shrill and accent too American; and Dulcinea in the film version of *Don Quixote* that Mike Todd planned to make.

Room Service

It was reported in a New York newspaper that when Elizabeth Taylor stays at her favorite hotel in the city, the Plaza Athenee, she regularly runs up room service bills of $2,500. That led to a funny article by Roy Blount, Jr., who was commissioned by *Traveler* magazine to find out what $2,500 worth of room service at the Plaza Athénée would buy. Blount and his lady friend entertained friends for cocktails and dinner, without stinting on champagne or caviar; ate shrimp and langoustines; called up the manicurist; and tipped lavishly. Their total room service bill for one day: a paltry $1,497.18. As the writer concluded, "I don't know how Taylor does it."

Mickey Rooney

One of Elizabeth Taylor's most memorable costars was Mickey Rooney, who played the part of the jockey Mi Taylor in *National Velvet* in 1944. At that time, child star Rooney was already Number one at the box office. He had twice been nominated for an Oscar, for his performances in *Babes in Arms* and *The Human Comedy*. He had also been given a special Oscar in 1939 for "his significant contribution in bringing to the screen the spirit and personification of youth," as well as a second special Oscar in 1942 for the wholesome Andy Hardy series.

Born in a theatrical boarding house in 1920, to parents who worked together as a vaudeville team, Rooney was signed in 1935 to an MGM contract by David O. Selznick, and for the next ten years, his career was watched over carefully by studio head Louis B. Mayer. The box-office appeal of the youngster with the red hair and the cocky grin was immense. He regularly stole scenes from such distinguished costars as Spencer Tracy and Judy Garland.

National Velvet was one of the most successful films of Rooney's career. After it was completed, he enlisted in the army to serve his country in World War II. When he returned two years later, his career had passed its zenith. But Rooney has remained a durable Hollywood figure. He starred on stage in *Sugar Babies* with Ann Miller, and has played leading roles in several TV movies. His presence has been a highlight of several recent tributes to Taylor's movie career.

Roscoe Award

In 1950, after the release of *Conspirator*, in which Elizabeth Taylor played the wife of a Communist traitor, the Harvard *Lampoon* gave her its Roscoe Award, "for so gallantly persisting in her career despite the total inability to act."

Helen Rose

Designer Helen Rose created some of Elizabeth Taylor's most memorable gowns. MGM assigned her to design the star's clothes in *Father of the Bride*, including the beautiful wedding dress Taylor wore in the climactic scene. It was such a success that MGM commissioned Rose to design the dress for the star's real-life wedding to Nicky Hilton. Later, she also designed the dress Grace Kelly wore for her marriage to Prince Rainier of Monaco.

Helen Rose dressed Taylor in several subsequent movies, including *Father's Little Dividend*, *The Last Time I Saw Paris*, and *Cat on a Hot Tin Roof*. She also designed two more bridal outfits for Taylor: the suit she wore to marry Michael Wilding and the chiffon dress in which she was married to Mike Todd. Rose became a part of the star's inner circle, even accompanying her on the nightmare trip to Chicago to bury Mike Todd. In 1966, Helen Rose introduced her own line of retail clothes. The author of a book of memoirs, *Just Make Them Beautiful* (her instructions from boss Louis B. Mayer at MGM), she died in 1985.

Rosemond

Elizabeth Taylor's middle name is Rosemond. She was given the name in tribute to her paternal grandmother, by all accounts another beauty in the family, whose maiden name was Elizabeth Rosemond.

Royal Command Performance

In 1967, *The Taming of the Shrew*, starring Elizabeth Taylor and Richard Burton, was selected for a Royal Command Performance at London's Odeon Theater. The Burtons were formally presented to the royal family, and then the movie royalty adjourned to an all-night party in their suite at the Dorchester Hotel. About 150 members of Burton's family from Wales had been invited to attend the bash.

Peggy Rutledge

Peggy Rutledge was for many years Elizabeth Taylor's private secretary and confidante. Rutledge, who had once worked for Bob Hope's wife, Dolores, was recommended by Taylor's agent, Jules Goldstone. Early in 1951, Peggy became both secretary and roommate after Taylor's separation from Nicky Hilton. Rutledge first located the apartment into which the two women moved and then took on a variety of duties that ranged from cleaning up the kitchen after Taylor's occasional experiments as a cook to trying to clean up the star's language (at the request of MGM).

Peggy Rutledge stayed with Taylor throughout the Wilding years, but when Mike Todd entered Elizabeth Taylor's life, Rutledge was no longer needed.

-S-

Salems

Elizabeth Taylor smokes Salem cigarettes. Wherever she goes, a fresh pack is always out on the table, with several cigarettes pushed up already, in case she decides she wants to smoke. She says smoking is the one vice she has never been able to give up.

Sally in Her Alley

Sally in Her Alley was a film that MGM planned to make in 1946, costarring the fourteen-year-old Elizabeth Taylor. Both Taylor and her mother thought that Elizabeth was wrong for the part, which required singing and dancing skills the girl did not possess. Together, they went to see studio exec Louis B. Mayer to tell him Elizabeth was miscast, and suggest that she be reassigned to another picture—or at least given some coaching for the song and dance demands. Mayer was insulted by their temerity and behaved with typical arrogance. The meeting ended with Mayer screaming at Sara Taylor, and Elizabeth running out of his office.

After all that drama, the movie was never made.

Chen Sam

Chen Sam is Elizabeth Taylor's publicist. She met Taylor in 1975, when Richard Burton came down with malaria while in South Africa making a movie and Taylor hired Sam, a pharmacist, to be flown into the bush to look after him. After several years on Taylor's payroll, Chen Sam opened her own public relations agency. She was hired by John Warner to help with his 1978 campaign, and thus traveled with Taylor throughout the state of Virginia. Elizabeth Taylor claims that the campaign trail, which caused her to gain weight, affected Chen Sam the same way. The publicist regained her own trim figure by following Taylor's diet. Taylor remains her most valued client.

The Sandpiper

In 1965, Elizabeth Taylor worked again with director Vincente Minnelli, who was responsible for *Father of the Bride* and *Father's Little Dividend*. The movie was *The Sandpiper*, and Taylor's costar was Richard Burton. Although the world-famous lovers were by this time married, the movie's plot alluded to the moral controversy surrounding their adulterous romance. It told the story of a not-too-successful artist living in a beachfront house and her affair with an impeccably upright man who is not only married (to Eva Marie Saint) but also the headmaster of a school for boys and, to top it all off, an Episcopalian minister. By the end of the movie, he has given up career, marriage, *and* affair to try to find himself. Apparently audiences found it easy to identify the actions of Burton's character with the events of his real life. There was an outcry about the immorality of the script, and the voyeuristic experience of seeing the movie—all of which helped make it a success at the box office. Burton always maintained the only reason he and Taylor appeared in the movie was their desire for the large salaries they were paid.

In fact, *The Sandpiper* made money for all concerned,

because it had good box office. Reviews of the movie were mixed, in part because many critics seemed to believe they were reviewing the lives of the stars rather than the film itself. Pauline Kael acknowledged, "Listening to lines like, 'I never knew what love was before,' and 'I've lost all my sense of sin,' it was impossible to separate this unconvincing performance from what we know about the performers." She added, "The whole absurd enterprise up there on the screen seemed to be a vast double-entendre." Judith Crist sniped, "Miss Taylor and Mr. Burton were paid $1,750,000 for performing in *The Sandpiper*. If I were you, I wouldn't settle for less for watching them." And John Simon, known for his cruel comments about actors' physical presences, said, "It is possible to get one's kicks merely out of watching Miss Taylor, who has grown so ample that it has become necessary to dress her almost exclusively in a variety of ambulatory tents." One person who was outspoken in his praise of Taylor's acting was Vincente Minnelli. He commented publicly on how much she had grown professionally in the fifteen years since he had worked with her before, saying, "Her talent as an actress has developed almost beyond belief."

Gaston Sanz

In the 1960s, Gaston Sanz was the chauffeur for the Burton household, driving Richard and Elizabeth back and forth to the studio every day (his salary usually being written into Taylor's contract for each film). Sanz traveled everywhere with the Burton family, and served as a kind of household organizer in each new place they went to make their movies. Gaston, also a judo expert, was nicknamed "Five-by-five" in reference to his chunky build.

The Sapphire Brooch

One of the gems in Elizabeth Taylor's jewel box is a forty-carat rich blue sapphire, set as a pin. It was a 1969 gift from Richard Burton, who purchased it from the London firm, Collingwood Jewelers, for $65,000. According to unconfirmed rumors, the pin once belonged to a member of Britain's royal family.

Satchmo

Satchmo was a black toy French poodle belonging to Elizabeth Taylor in the 1960s, named in tribute to the great jazz artist, Louis Armstrong.

Scent of Mystery

As a favor to Mike Todd, Jr., the son of her late husband, Elizabeth Taylor made a brief cameo appearance in a movie he produced in 1960, called *Scent of Mystery*. The name was intended to promote the unusual fact that the movie was made in Smell-O-Vision, with various aromas—coffee, cigarette smoke, shoe polish, and so on—sprayed into the air in the theater at appropriate moments. The plot hinges on the search for a missing heiress. She turns up at the end of the movie, played by Elizabeth Taylor. It was intended as a surprise for the audience, so she received no billing and no advance publicity, and the stills from the movie show only her back, never her face. Critics rightly concentrated on the novelty of Smell-O-Vision rather than the quality of the movie, as apparently there was little more than the smell of the picture to attract audiences.

The Schoolhouse on the Lot

As a child star at MGM, Elizabeth Taylor attended the red brick schoolhouse (once a bungalow belonging to producer Irving Thalberg) run by the studio on their 167-acre Hollywood lot. The incongruities of the situation were striking. Taylor remembers, "On the set, the teacher would take me by the ear and lead me into the schoolhouse. I would be infuriated; I was sixteen and they weren't taking me seriously. Then after about fifteen minutes I'd leave class to play a passionate love scene as Robert Taylor's wife."

Lizzie Schwartzkopf

One of Mike Todd's favorite pet names for Elizabeth Taylor was "Lizzie Schwartzkopf." It means "Blackhead" in German.

A Scoop for Louella Parsons

Louella Parsons was the Hollywood gossip columnist who first broke the story of the romance between Elizabeth Taylor and her *Cleopatra* costar Richard Burton. "It's true," she trumpeted, "Elizabeth Taylor has fallen madly in love with Richard Burton. It's the end of the road for Liz and Eddie Fisher. They will part as soon as a property settlement can be worked out." All principals initially denied the story, but it was only a matter of time until the truth of Parsons's scoop was apparent.

The Screen Persona

Foster Hirsch, in his book on the films of Elizabeth Taylor (one in the series *The Pictorial Treasury of Film Stars*, published by Galahad Books) reflected on the nature of Elizabeth Taylor's screen persona. "What *is* it about the screen persona of Elizabeth Taylor that gives her so much trouble keeping a man?" he asks. "Is she too pushy? Too idle? Too dumb? Too demanding? At one time or another, her characters are guilty of all these charges, but there's something else—some deep-rooted metaphysical lack, perhaps—that dooms her to unfulfillment." Hirsch goes on, "Like many legendary actresses, Taylor has her secrets. *She* may know who she is, but she isn't about to tell all to us. The Taylor women, then, are always somewhat remote. That is their allure, but it is also their downfall. Men lose interest."

Secret Ceremony

In 1968, Elizabeth Taylor starred in a movie directed by Joseph Losey called *Secret Ceremony*. Taylor played a woman worn out by life on the streets who has come to view the male sex as her enemy—or as she summed up the role earthily, "I play a dikey prostitute in this one." A deranged young woman (Mia Farrow) believes she recognizes the streetwalker as her mother, and insists on bringing her back to the decaying grandeur of her London townhouse. The two women are locked in a *folie à deux*, from which burly Robert Mitchum attempts to rescue Mia Farrow, but the subtext of the movie is the difficulty of separating fantasy from reality. Intended as an "artistic statement," the film lost most of its audience early in the picture. Taylor and her costars all came in for heavy criticism, and that aimed at Taylor was particularly unkind. Rex Reed, for example, said, "The disintegration of Elizabeth Taylor has been a very sad thing to stand by helplessly and watch . . . She has become a hideous parody of herself—a fat, sloppy, yelling, screeching banshee." Penelope Mortimer said, "In spite of her skill, I have an irresistible compulsion to think of her as the Queen Mother playing charades. Whatever the part, she is often and inescapably Elizabeth Taylor." Roger Greenspun commented that her misreading of every line approached the sublime. This movie was the final blow to Taylor's reputation as a box-office draw, and thereafter she was virtually unbankable.

Separation from Richard Burton

In the summer of 1973, the problems in Elizabeth Taylor's marriage to Richard Burton had progressed to the point that she decided they should separate for a time. After a failed attempt to patch things up in a borrowed house on Long Island, Taylor returned to New York City and issued the following statement:

> I am convinced it would be a good and constructive idea if Richard and I are separated for awhile. Maybe we have loved each other too much—I never believed such a thing was possible. But we have been in each other's pockets constantly, never being apart but for matters of life and death, and I believe it has caused a temporary breakdown of communication. I believe with all my heart that the separation will ultimately bring us back to where we should be—and that's together. I think in a few day's time I shall return to California, because my mother is there, and I have old and true friends there too . . . Wish us well during this difficult time. Pray for us.

The announcement was issued on July 4. Less than a month later, Elizabeth flew to join Richard at the Italian villa belonging to Sophia Loren and her husband Carlo Ponti. The reconciliation lasted only days.

"Sex Is Absolutely Gorgeous"

The mature Elizabeth Taylor has been outspoken about her enjoyment of sex. In one interview she said, "I think sex is absolutely gorgeous. I don't make any bones about sex being wonderful. Anyone who says that it isn't is either mentally sick or afraid he or she can't measure up."

Silly Sketch with Bob Hope

In 1982, Elizabeth Taylor agreed to appear in one of Bob Hope's TV specials. She took part in a silly hospital sketch that starred Hope, actor Tony Geary of *General Hospital* (with whom Taylor was rumored to be romantically involved), and her ex-husband, Richard Burton.

Silver Bear Award

In 1972, Elizabeth Taylor won the Silver Bear, the German equivalent of the Oscar awarded at the Berlin Film Festival, for her performance in *Hammersmith Is Out*.

The Slob Club

As a teenager, Elizabeth Taylor was isolated by the glamour of her image, and had virtually no genuine social life, let alone any real dates. She and her friend Betty Sullivan (daughter of Ed, then a syndicated columnist) formed a club they called the SLOB club: Single Lonely Obliging Babes.

"Sonny Boy"

One of Elizabeth Taylor's names for her boyish husband Eddie Fisher was "Sonny Boy." It was actually his childhood nickname.

Sara Southern

Sara Southern was the stage name used by Elizabeth Taylor's mother during her own acting career. In the early 1920s, she was part of a repertory company established in Los Angeles by character actor Edward Everett Horton; later she appeared on stage in New York and London. Her reviews were excellent and she had a following of fans. One of her greatest successes was in a play called *The Fool*, about a faith healer who cures a young crippled girl, the role Sara always played.

When Sara married Francis Taylor, she left the stage. One British critic wrote of that decision, "Marriage has robbed the theatre of the beauty, grace and ability of Sara Southern."

Southern Accent

Elizabeth Taylor has long been commended for the authenticity of her southern accent, and the woman who taught her that accent was Marguerite Littman. A native of New Orleans, she was a friend of Tennessee Williams, and as a favor to him, she undertook to tutor Barbara Bel Geddes for her role as Maggie in the original Broadway version of *Cat on a Hot Tin Roof*. Her fame as an accent coach spread, and she was hired to help Elizabeth Taylor prepare for *Raintree County*. Her hints for sounding southern include, "Make the *e* sound like *i*. Hit the verb, slur the pronouns, drop the *g*s in the *ing*s, and come down on the first part of a word hard. Chair is CHAY-uh—and take a long time to add the end syllable. Drag out and dramatize the adjectives." Taylor told Littman that the southern accent "took like a vaccination."

The Spa at Palm-Aire

In the summer of 1979, Elizabeth Taylor checked in for a three-week stay at The Spa in Palm-Aire, near Pompano Beach, Florida. She had gained weight steadily since her 1976 marriage to John Warner, a circumstance that had diminished her self-image and made her the butt of innumerable unkind jokes. Although her stay was cut a few days short by the death of second husband Michael Wilding, whose funeral in England she decided to attend, Taylor succeeded in losing twenty pounds and looked wonderful by the time she left.

Unfortunately, her return to her old life in Washington soon caused her to regain much of the weight she lost. It was not until she returned to work, playing Regina in *The Little Foxes* on the stage, that she got her weight under control.

Spinal Fusion

On December 8, 1956, Elizabeth Taylor underwent a spinal fusion. The surgery, which took four hours, was performed by an orthopedic specialist at the Harkness Pavilion in New York City. Three crushed spinal discs were removed, and bone from her hip and pelvis used to create a fused column to support the area. Taylor had suffered from back problems since she was a teenager; according to one account, the pain started after she fell so often learning to ride a horse for *National Velvet*. A later injury on the set of *The Last Time I Saw Paris* made matters worse, and then she fell down the gangplank of a yacht (belonging to English media magnate Lord Beaverbrook) while out with her fiancé, Mike Todd.

Todd was at Taylor's side during her recovery, speeding the process with specially catered food and Old Masters to hang on the wall of her hospital room. When Elizabeth was well enough to leave, they flew to Mexico, where she was quickly divorced from Michael Wilding. Within days, she married Todd—but she was still so weak she had to be carried down the aisle.

John Springer

During the time Elizabeth Taylor was married to Richard Burton, both had the same publicist, a young man named John Springer, who had previously represented Montgomery Clift. One of Springer's most taxing assignments was handling the publicity of the Taylor–Burton wedding in Montreal in early 1964—and then breaking the news to Sybil Burton in New York. Springer continued to work for Richard Burton until his marriage to Suzy Hunt. Springer has said of his famous employer, "It's hard to become Elizabeth's friend, but once you are, Elizabeth never forgets you."

St. Elizabeth

St. Elizabeth is the patron saint of queens.

The Start of All the Health Problems

Elizabeth Taylor began to have health problems while only in her teens. On the MGM lot, after her success in *National Velvet*, she complained of various ailments such as a cough, a bloodshot eye, an irritation of the skin. Each of these problems was treated with the utmost seriousness: Doctors were called in to examine the young star, and studio execs wrote anxious memos debating whether she should continue working or go home for a rest.

Writer Kitty Kelley has noted that Taylor's first period of illnesses coincided with the time her parents separated, in late 1946, when the teenager was emotionally upset and needed attention. Looking at her lifelong pattern of illnesses, it is easy enough to interpret them as a sustained call for attention and help—help in bearing the burden of being Elizabeth Taylor.

Statue at Madame Tussaud's

Madame Tussaud's in London is the best-known exhibition of wax figures in the world. Established in the early 1800s, it now attracts more than two million visitors a year. There is a section of the museum devoted to film stars, and in 1967, a statue of Elizabeth Taylor was added to the collection. The hardest part, the museum said, was getting the color of the eyes to match the fabled violet Taylor orbs.

Status Symbols on the Set of Virginia Woolf

According to Kitty Kelley's biography of Elizabeth Taylor, the pecking order of the stars of *Who's Afraid of Virginia Woolf?* was made symbolically evident. Warner Brothers gave Elizabeth Taylor the best dressing room, and stocked it with $800 worth of fine champagne. Her husband Richard Burton had the next-best dressing room, with a bottle of aged Scotch. Costars George Segal and Sandy Dennis could count themselves lucky to find a $2.95 bottle of German white wine in their small dressing rooms.

Dennis Stein

Dennis Stein is a bicoastal businessman with whom Elizabeth Taylor had a brief romance after they were set up on a blind date. In December 1984, Elizabeth accepted a twenty-carat engagement ring from Dennis, a friend of Frank Sinatra, and toasted the event with a glass of iced tea. Stein, a former garment salesman, was a partner in the revitalized Astoria Studios and was also involved in a subsidiary of Technicolor, owned by financier Ron Perelman. Two months afterward, the engagement was over. Taylor later told a reporter, "Let's just say I almost made a mistake—but I didn't."

George Stevens

George Stevens was the director who evoked several of the best screen performances of Elizabeth Taylor's career. Born in 1904 in Oakland, California, Stevens made his stage debut at the age of five, performing in his actor father's company. As a cameraman at Hal Roach's studio, he worked on many of the *Laurel and Hardy* shorts. His first big directorial success was *Alice Adams*, starring Katharine Hepburn in the title role, followed by the Astaire-Rogers hit, *Swing Time*. Stevens won his first Oscar in 1951 for *A Place in the Sun*, which also garnered excellent reviews for female lead Elizabeth Taylor. His second Oscar also came from a movie starring Taylor, *Giant* (1956). Many thought he should also have won for his direction of *Shane* in 1953. The last movie Stevens ever directed was the Elizabeth Taylor–Warren Beatty vehicle, *The Only Game in Town*. Stevens died in 1975.

Stevens was initially criticized for casting Elizabeth Taylor in *A Place in the Sun*. She was only seventeen, and she had yet to prove herself as a serious actress in adult roles. He later explained, "Liz was a teenager, but she had all the emotional capabilities. She had the intelligence, sharp as a tack. She was seventeen and she had been an actress all her life. So there was no problem there. The only thing was to prod her a bit into realizing her dramatic potential." He did this by bullying Taylor—as he was to do again when he directed her in *Giant*. The actress was angry at the time, but she didn't hold a grudge and even asked for him as a director again in the future. She knew he could draw out her best as an actress.

Dean Stockwell

Dean Stockwell was a child actor under contract to MGM at the same time young Elizabeth Taylor was there, and the two became friends. Born in California in 1936, Dean made his stage debut when he was seven, with his brother Guy, two years younger. In 1945, a year after Taylor's success in *National Velvet*, it was Dean's turn in the limelight, winning praise for his performance in *Anchors Aweigh*, a Gene Kelly vehicle. As an adult, he continued to act, but found few movie roles; his career shifted to acting in television dramas. He was formerly married to actress Millie Perkins.

Streaked at the 1974 Award Ceremonies

In 1974, Elizabeth Taylor was one of the presenters at the annual Academy Awards ceremonies. Just before she walked on stage to deliver the Oscar for the Best Picture, a streaker raced across the stage. The ever-suave David Niven thanked the streaker for sharing his "shortcomings" with the TV audience and then calmly introduced Taylor.

Stripper Scandal

To film the movie *Giant*, Elizabeth Taylor went to the little town of Marfa, Texas, for location shooting. While she was away from husband Michael Wilding and their two sons, a story appeared in a tabloid that Wilding and a friend had hired two strippers to perform their act one evening beside the pool at the Wildings' house. The appearance of the story was a blow to Taylor and to her image of herself as a happily married woman. Whether or not there was any truth to the story, a point that is not clear, it was a humiliation to Taylor.

Suddenly Last Summer

As an actress, Elizabeth Taylor seemed to have a particular affinity for the heroines of Tennessee Williams. Perhaps the most dramatic Williams role she played was Catherine in *Suddenly Last Summer*, a 1959 movie produced by Horizon and distributed by Columbia Pictures. Taylor, still under contract to MGM, was lent out by that studio for the fee of $500,000. That was the highest sum ever paid for the services of an actress, but most of the money went to MGM, which in turn paid Taylor only her regular salary of $5,000 a week. She started work on the movie while she was still on her honeymoon with fourth husband Eddie Fisher.

Catherine is an attractive young woman accused of madness by her aunt, Violet Venables (Katharine Hepburn). For much of the movie, Venables tries to persuade a doctor, played by Montgomery Clift, to agree to have the young woman lobotomized. But the audience quickly senses that Catherine is perfectly sane, even though she cannot yet face her memories of the horror of her cousin Sebastian's death. Eventually, Catherine comes to grips with the past and recalls how Sebastian was the victim of a cannibalistic attack by the Arab boys who were the target of his amorous attentions. At the end, we see that it is Sebastian's mother, Mrs. Venables, whose sanity has been shattered.

Suddenly Last Summer had an atmosphere of mystery and danger, wonderful dialogue, and great performances from Taylor and Hepburn. Montgomery Clift was a brooding presence, but reports from the set that he was shockingly ill and often unable to remember his lines seem substantiated by his unfocused performance. Rumor had it that the director, Joseph L. Mankiewicz, treated Clift badly, and that costars Taylor and Hepburn resented the torture the director inflicted on someone so obviously helpless. Whatever the stresses and strains during the filming, the finished product remains a classic. Taylor received her third Oscar nomination for her role as Catharine, and Hepburn was also nominated. They both lost to Simone Signoret for her work in *Room at the Top*.

Although reviewers were obviously uncomfortable with some of the subject matter—madness, homosexuality, and cannibalism didn't fit the wholesome world view that characterized the 1950s—they agreed that Taylor proved her merit as an actress. As the reviewer of *The New York Herald Tribune* said, "If there were ever any doubts about the ability of Miss Taylor to express complex and devious emotions, to deliver a flexible and deep performance, this film ought to remove them." Arthur Knight said, "Elizabeth Taylor, as the beleaguered heroine of a New Orleans nightmare, works with an intensity beyond belief; hers is unquestionably one of the finest performances of this or any year." The *Los Angeles Examiner* said, "Elizabeth Taylor plays with a beauty and passion which make her the commanding young actress of the screen." Taylor was also called "most effective," "rightly roiled," and "courageously whole hearted."

Summit Drive

When Elizabeth Taylor became pregnant with her second child, she and husband Michael Wilding realized they had outgrown their first home. They sold it and bought a second, located on Summit Drive in Beverly Hills just down the road from David O. Selznick. It was an eight-room house with a swimming pool, priced at $150,000. Designed by architect George MacLean (who later claimed he'd had Taylor in mind when he was creating it) and built of beige stone, adobe, and glass, the house featured a huge fireplace, interior fieldstone walls, and an indoor garden. There was also a view of the distant Pacific. Like many of Taylor's houses, it was filled with dogs that were given the run of the house and allowed to sit—or relieve themselves—anywhere they chose.

Sweet Bird of Youth

In the fall of 1989, Elizabeth Taylor starred in a TV movie version of *Sweet Bird of Youth*, broadcast on NBC-TV. She played the part of the aging movie legend, Princess Alexandra Del Lago, a character whose life in some ways parallels her own. The author of the play on which the movie was based, Tennessee Williams, once told Taylor she ought to play the part, as did the actress who pioneered the role on stage and in film, Geraldine Page. Producer Linda Yellin mused, "With Elizabeth Taylor in the part, the piece keeps moving from fiction to reality. The Princess has a line, 'By the time I was thirty-one, I was a living legend.' The line has a special resonance when a real legend plays a legend.

This is a play about the difficulty of aging, of moving beyond youth, and it adds layers to have Elizabeth Taylor, who is dealing with those very same issues."

The film's director, Nicolas Roeg, whose previous credits include *The Man Who Fell to Earth* and *Don't Look Now*, called Taylor the archetype of a Tennessee Williams' heroine. "I can't think of any other star of her stature. Such astounding beauty and talent—you don't often find that in one person." Taylor herself commented that the role "came at exactly the right time in my life. Finally I'm the right age [fifty-seven] and it was really nice because the producers didn't want me to lose weight."

Taylor's costars included Mark Harmon as the gigolo, Chance Wayne, with whom Alexandra becomes involved (this was the role played by Paul Newman in the 1962 feature film version); Cheryl Paris as Chance's former girlfriend; Rip Torn (husband of the late Geraldine Page) as the girlfriend's father, who engineers a brutal revenge for her unwanted pregnancy; and Valerie Perrine as his own girlfriend. Elizabeth Taylor's son Michael Wilding had a small role as a Hollywood producer. The screenplay was written by Gavin Lambert. Taylor's wardrobe, consisting largely of delectably lacy negligees, was designed by Nolan Miller.

The movie was shot on location in Los Angeles, using a Catholic school that was converted to resemble the Royal Palms Hotel, a lush Florida resort in which much of the action is set. The year is supposed to be 1959, and one journalist invited to visit the set noticed that it had been decorated with old magazines, including an issue of *Life* with Debbie Reynolds on the cover, published at the height of the scandal over Liz and Eddie. Taylor also noticed the magazine and commented, "God, 1959. I remember it well."

Reviewers seemed to have a hard time separating the actress from the character she played, and spent most of their space musing about the similarities—when they weren't speculating about how much weight she might have gained recently. John Leonard, writing in *New York*, outlined the problem: "It's difficult, of course, to look at Elizabeth Taylor in anything and not see Taylor, even when she's supposed to be someone else. She's a palimpsest of all the

revisions we've made of our fantasies about her over the decades. We're watching *National Velvet, Ivanhoe,* and *Cleopatra*; Eddie Fisher, Richard Burton and Malcolm Forbes." Leonard concludes that the real problem is that *Sweet Bird of Youth* is not a good play, an opinion other reviewers also voiced.

Those who were able to review Taylor's performance rather than her personality were mostly laudatory. "She knows just how far toward parody to take Alexandra," said Hal Rubenstein, "and dangles her over the cliff of caricature, bringing her back just in time to knock you flat. And she's damn funny, a game comedienne."

Sybil Sticks with Richard

Sybil Burton was very reluctant to divorce her husband Richard Burton, even though he was openly living with Elizabeth Taylor by early 1963. She told the press, "I would never allow the father of my children to become the fifth husband of Elizabeth Taylor. I'm going to have him bound hand and foot . . . I'm not going to cut the leash, and when I get him back, I'll be two million dollars richer." In the end, though, Sybil capitulated and gave Richard the divorce he sought, in early 1964.

"Sybil's Folly"

In 1966, Richard Burton bought a home for Elizabeth Taylor in England. (Since he was officially a resident of Switzerland, for tax purposes, the house could not be his.) He purchased it with the money he saved in alimony after ex-wife Sybil married rock star Jordan Christopher in 1965, and therefore he nicknamed it "Sybil's Folly."

-T-

Tallulah Did It First

Tallulah Bankhead was a legendary actress, best known for her deep raspy voice and her exaggerated mannerisms, who originated both of the roles Elizabeth Taylor played on the stage. Tallulah was the first Regina in *The Little Foxes*, and the first Amanda in *Private Lives*, so Taylor's performances were inevitably compared with Bankhead's. The fact that Tallulah was already a legend made her tough competition for Taylor. Tallulah also originated the leading role in Tennessee Williams's play, *The Milk Train Doesn't Stop Here Anymore*, which was turned into Taylor's screen vehicle, *Boom!*

Tallulah Bankhead was born in Alabama in 1903, and made her New York stage debut when she was still in her teens. Stardom quickly followed, and she became the toast of both London and New York. Many imitated her unmistakable voice, as well as her theatrical gestures and her uninhibited behavior in private life, but there was only one "Tallu." One of the most famous photographs of the actress shows her sitting on a piano while President Harry Truman played. Of her handful of movies, only *Lifeboat* (1944) is still likely to be seen on TV or in revival theaters. The actress died in 1968.

The Taming of the Shrew

In 1967, Elizabeth Taylor and Richard Burton starred in a film version of Shakespeare's *The Taming of the Shrew*. The director was Italian operatic director Franco Zeffirelli, and the coproducers were Taylor and Burton. Burton explained why the couple had taken on the responsibility: "Whilst Elizabeth and I both wanted to do this film, no outside producer, for Shakespeare, would put up the kind of money we can demand." That amount was rumored to be $3 million per film; by forming their own production company, the stars were able to pay themselves their usual salary, eventually recouped from the film's profits.

Burton had long wanted to turn Shakespeare's comedy into a movie, even going so far to announce in the late 1950s that he would star in a screen version of *The Shrew* with Marilyn Monroe as his Kate. There was a certain amount of derision when it was announced that he would do the film with Elizabeth Taylor, whose name was not usually associated with Shakespeare. As it turned out, *The Taming of the Shrew* was a delight for Elizabeth Taylor fans. Once again, she played a shrew, but in contrast to her previous film, *Who's Afraid of Virginia Woolf?*, she was a sexy shrew, an attractive shrew, a shrew well worth the effort of taming. Taylor gave an interview during the movie's production that illuminated her concept of the character: "She's the eternal female. She wants to acquiesce but she doesn't know how. She adores Petruchio but you know she's never going to be tamed." It's easy to see how strongly the actress identified with the role.

Burton couldn't resist making a few cracks about his wife's work in *The Taming of the Shrew*. "She shows definite Shakespearean feeling," he pontificated, "the only difficulties being some of the bard's words that are alien to her. For instance, 'how durst thou' is not common talk in California." Although Taylor *was* obviously a bit uneasy with the Shakespearean dialogue, she nevertheless threw herself into the part, and made her Kate a memorable character despite some weakness in scenes with long speeches. She also looked so lovely every minute she was on camera that it scarcely mattered what she said.

Most reviewers praised Taylor fairly. "She's a buxom delight when tamed," was *Variety*'s conclusion. *Time* punned, "In one of her better performances, Taylor makes Kate seem the ideal bawd of Avon—a creature of beauty with a voice shrieking howls and imprecations." Critic Hollis Alpert said, "The challenge to Taylor must have been a big one. She had to contend with her husband at his absolute best in a role for which he is extremely well suited. Well, not only has she managed it, she has come through the ordeal with honor. She has held nothing back in attacking the role with blazing fury."

The Taming of the Shrew remains a popular film on television and in revival houses, and many Liz fans think it's one of her very best vehicles.

Francis Taylor

Francis Taylor was Elizabeth Taylor's father. Born in 1900 in Arkansas City, Kansas, he was the son of a prosperous merchant who moved west from Indiana in 1890 and made a place for himself in his new community, joining the Presbyterian Church and the Masonic Lodge. Francis grew up in a substantial brick house, considered one of the nicest in town. He left Arkansas City (without graduating from high school) to go to St. Louis and work for his aunt's husband, Howard Young, who owned a thriving art gallery there. Later Young went to New York to compete in the art market there, and Francis Taylor went with him. Francis was an extremely handsome young man, with a striking profile, prematurely gray hair, and bright blue eyes framed by thick dark lashes.

In New York he met by chance, and quickly married, fellow Arkansas City native Sara Warmbrodt, in 1926, when she was thirty and he was twenty-six. Soon after their marriage, Francis's wealthy uncle sent the attractive young couple to Europe. Taylor's mission was to buy Old Masters paintings from impoverished European families, to be sold in New York to wealthy Americans. After a period of travel, during which they lived in luxury hotels, Francis and

Sara settled down in Hampstead Heath, in north London, where their first child, Howard Taylor, was born in 1930. On the instructions of his uncle, Francis opened a gallery on Old Bond Street and concentrated on the English market. Two years later, the couple's daughter Elizabeth was born, on February 27, 1932. Taylor sent his family back to the United States on the eve of World War II, and joined them in Los Angeles after settling his affairs in London. He opened his own gallery in the old Chateau Elysee, where he specialized in the work of the English portraitist Augustus John. He later moved to premises in the basement of the prestigious Beverly Hills Hotel.

In November 1946, Francis Taylor and his son Howard went to live in Wisconsin with his uncle. It was an unofficial separation from his wife, who had been having a rather public affair with Michael Curtiz, the director of *Life with Father*, in which Elizabeth Taylor played the female ingenue. Sara and Francis were reconciled two years later. Francis closed his gallery, which had become more of a hobby than a business, and retired in 1956. He died in 1968.

Howard Taylor

Howard Taylor is Elizabeth Taylor's brother. Born in 1930, the little boy with the blond curls and angelic expression was considered to be an even more attractive child than his beautiful younger sister. Their mother Sara tried to push Howard toward a career in the movies, but he was so opposed to the idea that on the day he was to have a screen test, he shaved his head bald. He did agree to play a walk-on part in Elizabeth's childhood hit, *National Velvet*, but otherwise shunned the glamorous world of Hollywood. Still Howard remained close to his sister, attending her wedding to Mike Todd in Acapulco with his wife Mara, and hurrying to her side when Todd was killed less than two years later. Howard Taylor became a professor of oceanography at the University of Hawaii, and Elizabeth sent her sons to his island home for long visits. Howard paid her a visit in Sardinia when she was there in 1968 filming *Boom!* and agreed once again to play a walk-on part. He remains close to his famous sibling.

Sara Warmbrodt Taylor

Sara Warmbrodt was born in Arkansas City, Kansas, in 1896. Her father, of German immigrant background, worked in a laundry as an engineer; her mother gave music lessons to supplement the family income. Sara left her hometown at the earliest possible opportunity, not even waiting to graduate from high school, to pursue a career on the stage. Her first stop was Georgia Brown's dramatic school in Kansas City. Then, using the name Sara Southern, she made it into stock companies as a supporting player, and worked her way up to genuine successes in starring roles in New York and London. She gave up her career in 1926 when she married Francis Taylor. The couple traveled extensively in Europe on business for several years, then settled down in London, where their son Howard was born in 1930 and their daughter Elizabeth in 1932.

In 1939, the Taylors returned to the United States to escape the approaching European war. They moved to Los Angeles, where Francis opened an art gallery and Sara was able to visit her parents, who had moved away from Kansas and purchased a chicken ranch in nearby Pasadena. Sara Taylor became a stereotypical "stage mother" when her daughter entered films. She accompanied the girl on the set and acted as Elizabeth's own personal director. The studio appointed her Elizabeth's official chaperone, and she was paid 10 percent of her daughters's salary even after Elizabeth was married to Michael Wilding and had become a mother herself. Elizabeth once told an interviewer, "Perhaps for a few years [my parents] loved me too much. I was too much a part of their lives. They had no lives of their own, especially my mother."

On the set with Elizabeth during the filming of *Life with Father*, Sara met and fell in love with her daughter's director, dashing Hungarian Michael Curtiz. The romance ended when the picture was finished, but it caused problems in the Taylor marriage, which led to a separation in late 1946—a break that lasted two years, until Sara fell ill and asked Francis to hurry to her bedside. The reconciliation was announced the next day by gossip columnist Hedda Hopper.

Sara Taylor was her daughter's closest adviser for many years, but their relationship was damaged at the time that Elizabeth divorced Nicky Hilton, against her mother's wishes. The star's subsequent romance with director Stanley Donen widened the breach between disapproving mother and her daughter, and even though Sara continued to collect part of Elizabeth's salary as her companion and chaperone, she had to give up her duties and stay in touch with her daughter through intermediaries. A number of years passed before the two women were once again in direct communication. Sara was not invited to her daughter's wedding to Michael Wilding. The rift was repaired by the time Taylor married Mike Todd, but of course by then the relationship had changed. Elizabeth never again deferred to her mother's guidance.

After the death of Francis Taylor in 1968, Sara moved to Palm Desert. She has continued to see her famous daughter regularly.

The Taylor Connection in Films

Elizabeth Taylor has costarred in seven films with other performers also named Taylor: Robert Taylor in *Conspirator* and *Ivanhoe*; Don Taylor in *Father of the Bride* and *Father's Little Dividend*; Rod Taylor in *Giant*, *Raintree County*, and *The VIPs*. The cast of *Cat on a Hot Tin Roof* included an actor named Vaughn Taylor. In two of her films, Elizabeth's brother Howard Taylor had a small part: *National Velvet* and *Boom!*

Telegraphic Exchange with Frank Sinatra

In 1961, the whole world watched as Elizabeth Taylor, stricken with pneumonia, fought for her life in the London Clinic. Messages of support and encouragement poured into the star's hospital room, one of them a telegram from Frank Sinatra. It was terse: "WIN," Frank told her.

When Taylor had recovered enough to look at some of her mail, she spotted the telegram from the famous singer and promptly sent him a one-word message in return: "DID."

The Telephone Call from Debbie

In Debbie Reynolds's autobiography, *Debbie: My Life*, the star revealed how she finally confirmed the truth of the rumors about her husband Eddie Fisher's involvement with family friend Elizabeth Taylor. In the fall of 1958, less than six months after Mike Todd's death, Eddie was in New York, singing at a hotel, and Debbie was in Hollywood with the children. Elizabeth Taylor was also in New York, staying at the Plaza Hotel. Debbie tried to call Eddie late at night at his New York apartment, and got no answer. Her next move was to dial the Plaza Hotel and ask to be connected to Elizabeth Taylor's suite. When she identified herself as Debbie Reynolds, the switchboard told her there was no answer.

Debbie wrote that she just *knew* Eddie and Elizabeth were there, but that Eddie had warned the switchboard not to put her calls through. So she waited ten minutes and called again. This time she pretended to be Dean Martin's secretary calling for Eddie in Elizabeth's suite. In seconds, Eddie picked up the phone.

"Well hiya, Dean, whatcha doin' callin' me at this time of the night?" he said sleepily, according to Debbie.

"It's not Dean, Eddie, it's Debbie."

"Oh . . ." Then, says Reynolds, her husband started to yell at her for daring to call him at Elizabeth's hotel. He tried to pretend he had just dropped by, but Debbie refused to be fooled. Finally, he admitted that he loved Taylor and said he would fly back to California to talk to Debbie face to face about ending their marriage.

Terrorist Threat

In late 1972, Elizabeth Taylor was filming the TV movie, *Divorce: His/Divorce: Hers*" in Munich, Germany. The summer Olympics had been held in Munich only weeks earlier, with the horror of the massacre of Israeli athletes in the Olympic Village. Three of the Arab terrorists were in a German jail awaiting trial, and there was a fear that other terrorists might try to kidnap a hostage to exchange for them. Elizabeth Taylor seemed a likely candidate—world famous, she was also a highly publicized convert to Judaism and supporter of the state of Israel. Thus she was put under armed guard while she worked in Munich, which she accepted with becoming nonchalance. Her husband, Richard Burton, was more forthright about his feelings. "I'd kill anyone who tried to hurt her," he said fiercely. No one did.

Testifying in Congress

In 1987, Elizabeth Taylor appeared before a House subcommittee to testify about the importance AIDS education for the American public. Representative Ron Wyden had asked for the star's help when Congress stalled a bill intended to provide money for mailing an AIDS education booklet to millions of American homes. Taylor shared her personal views on the subject with the committee members: "I'm a single woman, and I think before embarking on a new relationship, I would have the AIDS test myself. I would ask my partner to have the AIDS test before embarking on an intimate relationship."

"That Face"

During Elizabeth Taylor's marriage to Eddie Fisher, she often sat at a table near the stage for the singer's live performances at night clubs in Las Vegas and New York. In tribute to his beautiful wife, Eddie would sing, directly to her, the tender song, "That Face." Audiences flocked to the clubs for that glimpse of an intimate moment between the most famous lovers of the fifties.

Benjamin Thau

Benjamin "Benny" Thau was the MGM executive who supervised Elizabeth Taylor's career and maintained a long and friendly relationship with the star.

Thierry

Thierry is the makeup artist assigned to prepare Elizabeth Taylor for the cameras for the demanding close-up portraits used in the promotion of Passion perfume. Although Taylor is skilled at applying her own makeup, and often does so for public appearances, this time she relied on a pro—and the results were startlingly youthful and glamourous.

Thirtieth Birthday Party

Elizabeth Taylor turned thirty while she was in Rome making the movie *Cleopatra*. Although she had already become involved with Richard Burton, her husband Eddie Fisher threw a party in honor of the occasion, just as if their marriage were unthreatened. The party was held in a Roman nightclub called the Hostaria del' Orso. Guests included Taylor's friend and fellow cast member Roddy McDowall, director Joe Mankiewicz, and Hume Cronyn and Cesare Danova, also in the *Cleopatra* cast. Fisher gave her an expensive diamond ring as a birthday present. Within a month, the Fishers were permanently separated.

There's One Born Every Minute

Elizabeth Taylor's first screen appearance was in a minor—*very* minor—comedy made by Universal Pictures in 1942. Aimed at the juvenile market, it was called *There's One Born Every Minute*. (It was originally titled *Man Or Mouse*.) Taylor costarred with Carl "Alfalfa" Switzer, one of the original cast members of *Our Gang*, as two of the children of Lemuel P. Twine, owner of the Twine Tasty Pudding Company and also candidate for mayor. As the title of the picture and the name of its leading character (played by Hugh Herbert) suggest, the movie was steeped in the ethos of W.C. Fields; and both Taylor and Switzer played the kind of bratty and horrible children typically encountered in Fields's vehicles.

The adult Elizabeth Taylor characterized her role in *There's One Born Every Minute* as "a beastly child who slung rubber bands at ladies' and gentlemen's bottoms." She and Alfalfa also sang an undistinguished duet. The movie was so lightly regarded by one and all that it was never reviewed, not even in the trade publications, so all we know about the contemporary opinion of young Miss Taylor's screen debut comes from the Universal press release that called her their "nine-year-old singer and dancer." This was to be the only movie Elizabeth Taylor made while under contract to Universal. The studio allowed her option to lapse after *There's One Born Every Minute* was released. Coincidence?

The $30 Million Marriage

Some years after Richard Burton's final estrangement from Elizabeth Taylor, he commented that their ten years together had cost him $30 million. Burton biographer Melvyn Bragg suggests that the actor may have underestimated the cost.

From another point of view, it might be considered only fair that Burton spent so much of his income on Elizabeth Taylor, since the reason he was able to earn such large sums was due in large part to the publicity surrounding their romance.

Marshall Thompson

Marshall Thompson was one of the young actors on the lot at MGM with Elizabeth Taylor in the 1940s. Although he was seven years older than Elizabeth, he was her first "official" date (arranged by the studio), escorting her to the premier of MGM's *The Yearling*. According to legend, Thompson was also the young man who gave Elizabeth Taylor her first *off*-the-screen kiss. Supposedly, they went on a real date, from which Taylor came home and told her mother rapturously, "He kissed me! He really kissed me!" But that was the limit of their romance. Some years later, Marshall's wife Barbara was one of Taylor's bridesmaids in her wedding to Nicky Hilton.

Thompson, born in Illinois in 1925, began his movie career playing naive juveniles in such films as *Gallant Bess* and *The Romance of Rosy Ridge*. Later, he became identified with action films such as *To Hell and Back*. A starring role in *Clarence the Cross-Eyed Lion* led to being cast as a regular on the *Daktari* television series.

Liz Thorburn

Elizabeth Taylor's home in Los Angeles is run by Liz Thorburn. Miss Thorburn formerly worked for Princess Margaret at Kensington Palace and likes to joke, "I've gone from a princess to a queen." One of Thorburn's responsibilities is to plan appetizing low-calorie meals for Taylor. Many of her recipes were included in Taylor's diet book, *Elizabeth Takes Off*.

Tipps

One of Elizabeth Taylor's happiest memories of her youthful career as an actress came from the days when she was preparing for her role in *National Velvet*. Every morning she got up early to take her riding lessons and practice for the difficult steeplechase scenes, which she loved. Afterward, her mother took her to a nearby restaurant called Tipps, where she always ordered the farm breakfast: two fried eggs, hamburger patties, hash-brown potatoes, and a stack of silver-dollar pancakes.

Elizabeth "Liza" Frances Todd

Liza Todd is the daughter of Elizabeth Taylor and her third husband, Mike Todd. Liza was born prematurely by Caesarean section in a Connecticut hospital on August 6, 1957, weighing barely five pounds, and she spent her first few weeks of life in an incubator. Her proud father told reporters that "the baby is so beautiful she makes her mother look like Frankenstein." After the death of Mike Todd, Liza was briefly adopted by her mother's next husband, Eddie Fisher, who later filed papers to ask for partial custody as part of his divorce settlement with Elizabeth Taylor; he subsequently dropped his request. Liza studied art at London's Middlesex Polytechnic School, and is today a sculptress, married to painter Hap Tivey, with whom she has one child, a son named Quinn. They live near Rhinebeck, up the Hudson River from New York City.

Mike Todd

Mike Todd was Elizabeth Taylor's third husband. He was born Avrom Hirsch Goldenbogen, the son of a Hasidic rabbi, on June 22, 1907. He grew up in Minneapolis, where he worked as a shoeshine boy and a carnival pitchman before the family moved to Chicago when he was a teenager. Too impatient to graduate from high school, he changed his name to Mike Todd and then went on to produce strip shows, burlesques, and finally legitimate musicals. His early theatrical successes included *Star and Garter*, *Something for the Boys*, and *The Hot Mikado*, an adaptation of the Gilbert & Sullivan operetta starring black tap dancer Bill "Bojangles" Robinson. Todd explained his formula as "dames and comedy." "I believe in giving the customers a meat and potatoes show. High dames and low comedy. That's my message."

In 1945 Mike Todd entered the movie business and in 1951 he formed Thomas-Todd Productions with veteran newscaster Lowell Thomas. Todd was one of the original partners in the wide-screen process Cinerama, but he sold out and formed his own company with rival wide-screen process, Todd-AO. His most successful productions were *Oklahoma!* in 1955 and *Around the World in 80 Days* in 1956.

Elizabeth Taylor had met Mike Todd at several Hollywood parties, and even spent a weekend on his yacht with a large group of guests that included her husband but didn't know him well, until the news media announced her separation from Michael Wilding in the summer of 1956. Todd immediately called and said he had to see her. On the day of the meeting, he took her to a private office at MGM, where he sat her down and, according to Elizabeth, "started in on a spiel that lasted about a half an hour without a stop, saying that he loved me and that there was no question about it, we're going to be married." Her reaction? "I thought, 'Oh, well, he's stark raving mad. Jeez, I've got to get away from this man.'" But Todd continued to pursue Taylor, calling her long-distance every night she was away on location, and finally, when she had a break in her shooting schedule, he sent his plane to pick her up and take her away for a week's vacation. At the end of that time, they were engaged. Mike gave Elizabeth a twenty-five–carat diamond to celebrate the fact.

Elizabeth Taylor and Mike Todd were married February 2, 1957, in Acapulco. Taylor was Todd's third wife. His first, Bertha Freshman, had married him when he was seventeen and she was sixteen; the mother of his son, Michael Todd, Jr., Bertha died inexplicably during minor surgery. His second wife, with whom he was already involved before his first wife died, was actress Joan Blondell; they divorced after two years of marriage at a time when he was forced to declare bankruptcy. (Blondell's assets went down the drain along with his.) At the time he met Taylor, Todd was engaged to actress Evelyn Keyes.

Mike and Elizabeth's daughter Elizabeth "Liza" Frances was born on August 6 in the year of their marriage. The marriage itself lasted just 413 days. On March 22, 1958, Todd boarded his private plane, *The Lucky Liz*, to fly to New York where he was being given an award as Showman of the Year. The plane crashed en route, killing Todd and three other people.

"Todd Almighty"

Elizabeth Taylor's third husband, Mike Todd, was affectionately called "Todd Almighty" by his Hollywood associates.

Mike Todd's Engagement Ring

On October 17, 1956, Elizabeth Taylor and Mike Todd announced their engagement. She joyously displayed her ring to reporters: a 29.7-carat diamond for which her fiancé had paid $92,000. He had already given her a $30,000 pearl ring as a mark of his affection, and he was to give her many more gems, including an elaborate diamond tiara, during their all-too-brief marriage. Elizabeth told reporters after Todd's death, "I think he liked to see me in pretty jewelry."

Mike Todd's Wedding Present

When Elizabeth Taylor married Mike Todd in 1957, he gave her a present to mark the occasion. It was a diamond bracelet worth about $80,000.

Mike Todd, Jr.

Mike Todd, Elizabeth Taylor's third husband, had a son from his first marriage, called Mike Todd, Jr., who was three years older than Taylor. He and his stepmother became great friends, and he was her chief comforter after Todd was killed in a plane crash. But Mike Jr. had a home and family in Chicago and eventually returned to them. Elizabeth Taylor, still in need of someone to talk to about her terrible loss, turned to her husband's good friend, Eddie Fisher.

Mike Jr. took over the reins of his father's business, and in 1960 he produced a movie called *Scent of Mystery* in the new process he called Smell-O-Vision. The theaters that showed the film were equipped with spray nozzles that released various aromas, such as peppermint and new leather, into the air at appropriate moments in the film. As a favor, Elizabeth Taylor appeared in a cameo role at the end of the movie, although even that surprise failed to attract many viewers to the box office. Smell-O-Vision proved to be an idea whose time had not yet come.

Mike Jr.'s wife Sara, born in 1931, died in 1972 at the early age of forty-one, and it was Taylor's turn to comfort her stepson. He continues to make his home in Chicago.

Too Much Hair

Elizabeth Taylor's mother says that when the star was born, she was covered with dark hair—all over her body, even her ears. "She was the funniest-looking baby I have ever seen," reminisced Sara Taylor, but according to some family insiders, Sara was not laughing but crying over her hirsute baby girl. It was Elizabeth's brother Howard who was considered the beautiful child in the family during their early childhood. It was not until Elizabeth was four or five years old that her beauty began to attract as much favorable comment as her brother's.

Torch Song

Torch Song was a 1953 MGM movie that costarred Michael Wilding, then married to Elizabeth Taylor, and Joan Crawford. Crawford, returning to MGM after a decade-long absence, was extremely sensitive about whether she would still be treated as a great star. One day, Elizabeth Taylor visited her husband on the set and failed to say hello to Joan. That made Joan so angry she tried to have Taylor barred from future visits. Crawford was unsuccessful.

Trashing the Plaza Hotel

In 1951, after her divorce from Nicky Hilton, Elizabeth Taylor made a visit to New York, checking into a luxurious suite at the famed Plaza Hotel. Apparently there was some misunderstanding about the bill, and the incensed Taylor decided to move immediately to the St. Regis. According to a story told by Kitty Kelley, she and friends Montgomery Clift and Roddy McDowall first packed her bags and then trashed the Plaza suite, ripping down the curtains and unscrewing the bathroom fixtures.

Trouble with the IRS

Elizabeth Taylor, then married to Richard Burton, became a British citizen in the 1960s. She said the reasons were personal, involving her marriage to Richard Burton and their need to be near his home in England (although Burton had already became a legal resident of Switzerland in a move he frankly admitted was meant to dodge British income taxes). In the early 1970s, the IRS said the reason she had claimed foreign citizenship was to evade U.S. taxes, and asked for $350,000 in back taxes. A settlement was eventually reached.

Tubal Ligation

At the time Elizabeth Taylor entered the hospital for the premature birth of her third child, daughter Liza Todd, she was having a difficult labor. Her two previous children, the sons of Michael Wilding, had been delivered by Caesarean section, and it was decided to repeat the procedure for this delivery. Doctors worried about Taylor's health, especially in view of the fact that she had undergone complicated spinal fusion surgery less than a year before. They recommended to her husband, Mike Todd, that she should not have any more children, and he reluctantly gave them permission to perform a tubal ligation after delivery. Taylor later said that waking up to learn she could no longer have children was the worst shock of her life.

"Tubby"

Richard Burton liked to play down the role Elizabeth Taylor's great beauty had in their passionate relationship. As if to prove it, he often called her "Tubby."

Pat Tunder

Pat Tunder was a chorus girl at the New York nightclub, the Copacabana, with whom Richard Burton was reportedly involved during the Broadway run of *Camelot*. Early in 1962, when Burton's affair with Elizabeth Taylor was hanging in the balance, Richard and Pat turned up on the set of *Cleopatra*, after a Paris weekend. Elizabeth coldly informed Richard that the presence of an outsider on the set was annoying; Burton reportedly responded by warning her not to get his Welsh temper up. But within a few days, Richard and Elizabeth had made up, and Pat Tunder left Rome— and Burton's life.

The Twisted Ring

The plane crash that killed Mike Todd was so violent that few objects survived. One that did was the wedding ring Elizabeth Taylor had placed on his finger the day they were married—but the heat of the fire after the crash had melted and twisted the ring. It was later given to his widow, and Elizabeth Taylor wore the ring on her hand every day for years, many of them during the period she was married to Todd's good friend, Eddie Fisher. She finally stopped wearing the ring regularly after she married Richard Burton, but photographs reveal that she continues to don it occasionally.

-U-

Under Milk Wood

Under Milk Wood was a noble attempt to create a film version of the radio play written in 1945 by Welsh poet Dylan Thomas. He had originally written it to be performed by himself and Richard Burton, and after his death, writer/director Andrew Sinclair decided to try to bring it to the screen. Richard Burton quickly agreed to appear in the movie, taking a low salary to hold the costs down but asking instead for a percent of the gross. Friend and fellow actor Peter O'Toole, who had once appeared in the radio version, also signed on.

Elizabeth Taylor agreed to do a cameo as Rosie Probert, a lady of easy virtue. She was familiar with the radio version, which was also available on record; in fact, according to one report, she claimed that every time she listened to her husband's rich voice declaiming the poetic phrases of Dylan Thomas, she experienced an orgasm.

Under Milk Wood was filmed in a little over a month, in the summer of 1971; it was not released in the United States until 1973. The general consensus by critics was that the movie was not as artistically successful as the radio play, but that it was worth seeing nevertheless. Audiences apparently did not agree, for it never did well at the box office. The reviews of Taylor's performance were for the most part negative. *Saturday Review*'s critic said, "With her heavy blue eye makeup, modish hair-do and tentlike gown, Mrs. Burton looks as though she belongs in the audience at the Academy Awards, rather than in a grave in Llareggub." Judith Crist's view was a bit more balanced: "The only outsider seems to be Miss Taylor, all movie star with the blue eye shadow and surplus hair—but in the arms of the young Captain Cat, and perhaps in his dreams, she becomes possible."

Universal Pictures

Elizabeth Taylor's first screen test was at Universal Pictures, in early 1942, when she was ten years old. At that time, child stars were big business in Hollywood, and Universal hoped the beautiful child might be another Deanna Durbin or Judy Garland. They gave her a contract and cast her in *There's One Born Every Minute*, opposite Carl Switzer, who played Alfalfa in *Our Gang*. Apparently the studio was discouraged by that movie's lack of success, for they allowed Elizabeth's option to lapse. One reason for the decision was given by the studio's casting director, who said, "Her eyes are too old; she doesn't have the face of a kid." The following year, Taylor was signed by MGM.

Unnecessary Appendectomy

Late in 1957, Elizabeth Taylor decided to have her appendix removed. She had suffered abdominal pains a few weeks earlier while in Hong Kong with husband Mike Todd, and she insisted on having the surgery when they returned to Hollywood. It was performed at the Cedars of Lebanon, and Todd stayed in the room next to hers for the full week she was in the hospital. Years later, Taylor confessed that she knew she didn't really need the appendectomy, but it was the only way she could think of to spend time alone with her workaholic husband.

Victory at Entebbe

Elizabeth Taylor made a brief appearance in the 1976 TV movie, *Victory at Entebbe*. It was based on the real-life drama played out the year before at the Entebbe airport, when terrorists took a planeload of travelers hostage and the Israelis eventually rescued most of them. Taylor and Kirk Douglas played the cameo roles of the Jewish parents of a teenaged hostage (Linda Blair).

Raymond Vignale

Raymond Vignale was a Frenchman who came to work for Elizabeth Taylor and Richard Burton as a temporary secretary in the 1960s. He ended up staying with Taylor for ten years. "Monsieur Raymond" was never a favorite with Richard Burton.

Villa at Celigny

During the years that Richard Burton was married to Elizabeth Taylor, they spent many happy days at her home in Gstaad, Switzerland. Burton also owned a home in Switzerland, at Celigny, near Geneva, which he had bought in the mid-1950s. It was about seventy miles from Taylor's house, and that proximity had been convenient in the days before they were married, when they wanted to give the appearance of leading separate lives. After their divorce, Burton continued to reside in the villa on the edge of town, and in accordance with the instructions in his will, he was buried in the churchyard in Celigny. His widow, Sally Burton, still owns the villa.

Villa Papa

The Villa Papa was the pink marble mansion Elizabeth Taylor and Eddie Fisher rented in Rome when she went to Italy to film *Cleopatra*. Located on the famed Appian Way, it had fourteen rooms, a swimming pool and a tennis court, and a huge staff, including one woman who did nothing but ironing. The villa was tucked away amid acres of pines, although they proved to be no barrier to the eager paparazzi. Elizabeth and Eddie entertained in the Villa Papa frequently—and Richard and Sybil Burton were regulars on the guest list.

Violet Eyes

Of all Elizabeth Taylor's attributes, perhaps the most famous is her "violet eyes." Of course, her eyes are not *really* violet, but they are an unusual shade of blue that photographs with a slight violet tinge.

The V.I.P.s

The V.I.P.s was the first of the movie vehicles designed specifically to capitalize on the fame of Elizabeth Taylor and Richard Burton as the world's best-known lovers. Burton had already been signed by MGM for his role, and Taylor, who had followed her lover back to London after the filming of *Cleopatra* was finished, suggested she would like to play the part of his wife in order to be near him. By that time, Burton was openly living with Taylor in a London hotel, while still going back home to his wife and children on a regular basis.

Audiences were riveted by the parallels between life and art as they watched the character played by Taylor plan to leave her husband to go away with the man she has fallen in love with, (Louis Jourdan). Ultimately she decides to stay and try to make the marriage work. The glossy script, by Terence Rattigan, was convoluted and full of improbable coincidences made acceptable by his wit and professionalism.

The best part of the movie is the large supporting cast, including everyone from Michael Hordern to Maggie Smith. Margaret Rutherford won an Oscar for Best Supporting Actress for her role as an eccentric English aristocrat. Reviewers were negative about both Burton and Taylor in *The V.I.P.s*, but it was a success at the box office—perhaps because of the continuing publicity focused on the costars' romance.

The Vulgarity of Her Jewels

Someone repeated to Elizabeth Taylor an oft-voiced criticism of her vulgarity in wearing such large diamonds all the time. She replied simply, "Would you have me any other way?" She also liked to point out that the perception of vulgarity was all relative. For example, Princess Margaret once teasingly told Taylor the Krupp diamond was the most vulgar thing she had ever seen. Taylor responded by asking the princess if she'd like to try on the ring. As Princess Margaret moved her hand back and forth to catch the reflection of light in the perfect thirty-three–carat stone, Taylor said wryly, "It's not so vulgar now, is it?"

-W-

War of the Posters

When Elizabeth Taylor and Richard Burton were filming *The Taming of the Shrew* in 1966, they teased each other by printing a series of fake publicity posters to hang in their shared dressing room. First, Elizabeth tacked up an announcement:

>Now on location in Rome
>ELIZABETH TAYLOR
>in
>THE TAMING OF THE SHREW
>and introducing
>Richard Burton

Burton countered with a creation of his own:

>RICHARD BURTON
>in
>THE TAMING OF THE SHREW
>Directed by Richard Burton
>Produced by Richard Burton
>Scripted by Richard Burton
>Edited by Richard Burton
>Cinematography by Richard Burton
>A RICHARD BURTON FILM

Elizabeth had the last word:

> ELIZABETH TAYLOR
> Academy Award Winning Actress
> and Shakespearean Coach
> To
> RICHARD BURTON
> IN
> THE TAMING OF THE SHREW

Warhol Diaries

After the death of pop artist Andy Warhol, it was learned that he had for more than a decade dictated diary entries about the rich and famous people he met. An avid celebrity collector, he loved gossip—and recorded it for posterity. An excerpt of the diaries was published in mid-1989, and it was inevitable that one of the subjects of his interest was Elizabeth Taylor. He reported meeting the star at a party held in her honor at New York's Studio 54, and wrote, "Liz looked like a—bellybutton. Like a fat little Kewpie doll." Later that same year, he added that he had learned that her husband, Senator John Warner, was no longer having sex with her.

Senator John William Warner

John William Warner, the United States senator who was the sixth husband of Elizabeth Taylor, was born in Washington in 1927. His father was a noted obstetrician, his uncle the dean of St. Albans Episcopal Church. Warner attended St. Albans School but eventually dropped out and graduated from public high school. He later put that down to youthful rebelliousness. He enrolled in the Navy at seventeen, in 1944, and spent two years as a cook. He attended

Washington and Lee University on the G.I. Bill, studying engineering and receiving a B.S. in 1949. Warner then went to the University of Virginia to study law, interrupting his studies to enlist in the Marines and serve in Korea during the "conflict." He rose to the rank of captain before returning to Virginia to finish the work needed for his law degree.

Upon graduation, Warner served as a clerk for a federal judge, then worked for the U.S. attorney's office. In 1968, after eight years of private practice, Warner was appointed Under Secretary of the Navy by the Nixon administration, and served as secretary of the navy from 1972 to 1974. That year, he was appointed head of the American Revolution Bicentennial Commission. Warner was elected to the Senate in 1978, where he still serves.

John Warner has two daughters and a son from his first marriage in 1968, to heiress Catherine Mellon; they divorced in 1973. He met Elizabeth Taylor in Washington in the summer of 1976. On the surface they seemed ill suited: he was Republican and Episcopalian, she Jewish and Democratic. But Warner, who had previously dated Barbara Walters (who called him "a genuinely nice man, devoted to his children") had the kind of strength Taylor admired. They were married on December 4, 1976, and for a wedding present, the bride gave the groom two cows and a bull. Warner was promptly dropped from the pages of *The Social Register*. Elizabeth was by her husband's side during his campaign for the Senate in 1978.

Taylor has said that she truly loved the first few years of life on the Virginia farm. "It's just the kind of life I always wanted to lead. It reminds me of Kent, where I grew up in England. It's the same kind of country, with rolling hills, and even the trees are the same." The trouble in their marriage seems to have begun after Warner was elected senator. In her book *Elizabeth Takes Off*, Taylor wrote that thereafter she felt she'd become redundant. "Like so many Washington wives and so many other women at different times in their lives, I had nothing to do. The image the public had of me, and my own self-image, was shot." The Warners separated in late 1981 and were officially divorced on November 5, 1982. According to an announcement made at the time, "No cash or property exchanged hands."

Watching Cleopatra

Elizabeth Taylor has said that she realized *Cleopatra* was the low point of her career even before the shooting was finished, and she intended never to see the movie at all. Then, she explained, the British government trapped her by asking her to host members of the Bolshoi Ballet at a special screening of *Cleopatra* in London shortly after the movie's release. Taylor's recollection: "Afterwards, I raced back to the Dorchester Hotel and just made it into the downstairs lavatory and I vomited."

Wedding Number One

Elizabeth Taylor's first wedding, to Nicky Hilton, took place at 5 PM on May 6, 1950, at the Church of the Good Shepherd on Santa Monica Boulevard in Beverly Hills. More than 3,000 fans lined the sidewalk to catch a glimpse of the bride, radiant in a $3,500 white satin gown with a plunging neckline inadequately camouflaged by white chiffon, a gift from MGM and created for her by costume designer Helen Rose. The wedding dress required twenty-five yards of satin, with a fifteen-yard satin chiffon train. The silk illusion net veil was attached to a Juliet cap of seed pearls. Helen Rose also created the yellow organdy dresses worn by the bridesmaids and the bronze chiffon gown for the mother of the bride.

The bride was given away by her father, Francis Taylor, and attended by maid of honor Anne Westmore, as well as by six bridesmaids: Jane Powell, Nicky's sister Marilyn, Elizabeth's brother's fiancée Mara Reagan, her movie stand-in Marjorie Dillon, Ed Sullivan's daughter Betty, and Marshall Thompson's wife Barbara. The bride carried a huge bouquet of white orchids, wore a blue garter, and tucked her mother's lace handkerchief in her sleeve. The Roman Catholic ceremony, conducted by Monsignor Patrick J. Cancannon, omitted the traditional nuptial mass, because Elizabeth had not been baptized in her husband's faith. The altar was banked with yellow and white spring flowers.

One of those attending the wedding was Spencer Tracy, who had recently given Taylor away on screen in *Father of the Bride*. He commented, "I've been to many weddings, but this was the flossiest. Elizabeth and young Hilton made a charming couple—he's handsome and she was even lovelier than in our movie. Elizabeth had a cold and slight fever and had to wipe her brow occasionally, but then everyone was using a handkerchief. Ginger Rogers, Greer Garson—even I had to reach for mine. When it was all over, I heard a studio publicist say, 'I wish I'd had the hankie concession, that wedding was the tearjerker of all time.'"

The reception for 600 guests was held at the Bel Air Country Club (and paid for by MGM). The new Mr. and Mrs. Conrad Nicholson Hilton cut a five-tiered wedding cake with a silver knife adorned with ribbons and flowers. Then Elizabeth changed into her going-away dress, a sleek blue gabardine number designed by Edith Head, covered by a matching mink stole. The newlyweds spent a quiet week in Carmel, California, and then flew to New York to embark on the *Queen Mary*. The honeymoon itinerary included Paris, London, Rome, and the Riviera.

Wedding Number Two

On February 21, 1952, Elizabeth Taylor married her second husband, English actor Michael Wilding. The wedding was a civil ceremony conducted by J.D. Halliday, the registrar at Caxton Hall, in London's Westminster district. The bride wore a dove-gray suit designed by MGM's Helen Rose (who had also designed Taylor's wedding dress when she married Nicky Hilton). It had a tiny waist and a wide skirt; the collar and cuffs were white organdy. A demure pearl necklace and a fetching little cap embroidered with pearls and flowers completed the ensemble, and the bride carried a small bouquet of lilies of the valley. One unkind reporter said, "The bride wore a dove gray suit and the bridegroom wore an air of surprise."

Elizabeth Taylor's only attendant for the ten-minute ceremony was Anna Neagle, the fifty-ish actress with whom Wilding was professionally linked. No members of the Taylor family were present, although both of Wilding's parents attended. The bride arrived for the ceremony alone, in a Rolls-Royce, as befitted a Hollywood star, and was greeted by a throng of several thousand fans standing outside the red-brick public building. As the newlyweds emerged, the fans surged around them, ripping Taylor's hat off her head. The bride was heard to whisper to her new husband, "Hold me tighter."

The reception was held at Claridge's, one of London's poshest hotels, where the bride told a reporter, "I'm glad to be British again." Champagne flowed, and the newlyweds received congratulations from a small list of guests. Afterward, they spent the night at the Berkeley Hotel in London, ordering a supper of pea soup, bacon and eggs, and champagne. The next day they left for a ten-day honeymoon in the French Alps. While there, they celebrated the bride's twentieth birthday with a candle on a cup of creme caramel. Wilding joyously sang ten choruses of "Happy Birthday" to his bride.

Wedding Number Three

On February 2, 1957, Elizabeth Taylor married husband number three, Mike Todd. The wedding took place in Acapulco, a few days after Taylor had obtained a fast divorce in Mexico City. The ceremony was held at an oceanside villa belonging to Fernando Hernandez. The bride wore a chiffon dress in a lavender-blue color that matched her eyes, and she carried white orchids. (Like the dresses she had worn for her two previous weddings, the gown was designed by MGM's Helen Rose.) Her only attendant was matron of honor Debbie Reynolds. Debbie's husband Eddie Fisher was one of two best men for the groom, the other being the Mexican comedian Cantinflas, star of Todd's movie, *Around the World in 80 Days*. Taylor, who had undergone a spinal fusion operation just two months earlier, was carried down the aisle by Todd and Cantinflas, to protect her healing back. The civil ceremony was performed by Acapulco's mayor.

At the reception, guests drank twenty-five cases of champagne and ate spicy Mexican food. The bride displayed her gift from the groom, an $80,000 diamond bracelet, and then fireworks, with the couple's intertwined initials, lit up the night sky. Eddie Fisher sang the "The Mexican Wedding Song." Among those present were Taylor's parents, her brother Howard and his wife Mara, and Mike Todd, Jr. and his wife Sara.

Wedding Number Four

Elizabeth Taylor was married to fourth husband Eddie Fisher in the Temple Beth Shalom in Las Vegas on May 12, 1959, in a Jewish ceremony. It was conducted by Rabbi Max Nussbaum, who had earlier supervised Taylor's conversion to Judaism. The bride was given away by her father, and chose as her only attendant her sister-in-law Mara Taylor. Mike Todd, Jr. served as Eddie Fisher's best man. In front of seventeen guests, Eddie and Elizabeth stood under the traditional flower-bedecked canopy, or chuppah, to exchange their vows. The bride wore a moss-green chiffon dress, designed by Jean Louis, with a high neck, long sleeves, and its own hood as the required head-covering. She carried a bouquet of yellow and green orchids. Outside, angry ex-fans picketed the Temple, outraged at Liz for home-wrecking Debbie's happy marriage and at Eddie for letting it happen.

After the ceremony, the couple flew first to Los Angeles, then to New York. After a night at the Waldorf-Astoria Hotel, they boarded a plane for Spain, where they embarked on the yacht *Olnico*, borrowed from producer Sam Spiegel, for a peaceful Mediterranean cruise.

Wedding Number Five

Elizabeth Taylor married Richard Burton in a small ceremony on March 15, 1964. The couple left Toronto, where they were staying while Burton appeared on stage as Hamlet, and chartered a plane to Montreal, in the province of Quebec, where all marriages were deemed religious matters and required no civil license (and therefore no chance for the press to learn their plans and descend on the event). The wedding took place in their suite at the Ritz-Carlton Hotel, and was conducted by a Unitarian clergyman, Reverend Leonard Mason. The bride wore a chiffon dress in bright yellow, designed by Irene Sharaff, who had created her costumes for *Cleopatra*; the groom had a matching daffodil boutonniere. Taylor's hair was pulled back in a braid and intertwined with Roman hyacinths. Her jewelry consisted entirely of gifts from the groom: an emerald pin worth $150,000 he had given her on the set of *Cleopatra*, an emerald and diamond necklace that had been a birthday present, and a matching pair of emerald and diamond earrings that were his wedding present. The bride had no attendants; the best man was Bob Wilson, the groom's valet. Guests included the bride's parents and the groom's agent, Hugh French. After the ceremony, a small reception was held in the hotel suite.

Wedding Number Six

Elizabeth Taylor and Richard Burton remarried on October 10, 1975, in a ceremony that took place on a river bank outside Kasane, Botswana (near Johannesburg, where they had gone with Peter Lawford and Ringo Starr to attend a celebrity tennis tournament). The site was close to famed Victoria Falls, in the Chobe National Park, a game preserve. As the bride had explained to the groom, they would take their vows "in the bush, amongst our kind." The bride wore a flowing chiffon dress given to her by her late brother-in-law Ivor Jenkins, green trimmed with beads and guinea-fowl feathers. In her hair were leaves and more beads. The groom wore white pants and red silk turtleneck jersey. The couple exchanged rings made of ivory from a native elephant and then toasted the event with champagne.

Actually, that was the second ceremony of the day. The couple had been officially married that morning in a brief civil ceremony in the office of the District Commissioner, Ambrose Masalila. At the time, the groom told the press, "There is no meaning to my life if she is not standing beside me. She is my sunrise and my sunset." Later, he confessed that he was drunk at the time and that the wedding was "like a huge dream. I remember thinking: What am I doing here? Odd place to be married, in the bush, by an African gentleman. It was very curious. An extraordinary adventure, doomed from the start."

Wedding Number Seven

Elizabeth Taylor was married to John Warner on the grounds of his Virginia estate, Atoka Farm, on December 4, 1976. The ceremony was conducted by Episcopalian clergyman Reverend Neale Morgan, who described the whole event as a very simple one: "No music, nothing but the lowing of the beasts." The bride wore a lavender cashmere dress with a matching coat trimmed in silver fox. Gray suede boots and a lavender turban completed the ensemble.

Wedding Number Eight

July 27, 1991, Elizabeth Taylor announced plans to marry Larry Fortensky on October 5 at Michael Jackson's Santa Ynez Valley estate. "Larry and I finally decided we wanted to spend the rest of our lives together . . . I always said I would get married one more time and with God's blessings, this is it, forever." The bride's outfit? By Valentino. The groom's? Versace. Giving the bride away? Michael Jackson.

The Welsh Hour

By all accounts, Richard Burton was a moody man, often given to bouts of melancholy that he tried to drown in drink. Elizabeth Taylor called these dark passages "the Welsh hour" and did her best to remain at her husband's side and offer him comfort while the gloom was upon him.

Westport Estate

After Mike Todd married Elizabeth Taylor, he leased an estate in Westport, Connecticut, in case they wanted to spend time in New York. The twenty-acre property had tennis courts and a swimming pool. Their daughter Liza was born in a nearby hospital.

What Elizabeth Taylor Finds Sexy in a Man

Elizabeth Taylor revealed in one interview what she found sexy in a man: "It has to do with warmth, a personal givingness, not self-awareness . . . It's what he says and thinks."

When Richard Burton First Saw Elizabeth Taylor

Although Richard Burton and Elizabeth Taylor first actually met on the set of *Cleopatra*, he later revealed that he remembered seeing her years earlier. It was at a party at the home of Stewart Granger and Jean Simmons, sometime in 1952, after Elizabeth had divorced Nicky Hilton and before she had fallen in love with Michael Wilding. Burton recalled being so bowled over by her beauty that he became self-consciously aware of his own physical shortcomings, and tried to cover up his pockmarked face with his hand. Then he heard her talk, in the salty language she had already learned to employ, and was shocked. He left the party with a generally unfavorable opinion of his wife-to-be.

Where Will Elizabeth Taylor Find Her Final Rest?

When Elizabeth Taylor falls in love, she plans to be with her man forever. And she really means *forever*; for her, commitment extends to death—and beyond. When she loves a man well enough to link her life with his, she also wants to lie beside him for her final rest. Over the years, she has made various arrangements for her burial. At one time, she told friends she wanted to be buried next to Mike Todd, in the cemetery near Chicago where he lies near his parents. During her marriage to John Warner, she announced they had already picked out suitable burial spots on Atoka Farm, his Virginia estate.

It was when she was married to Richard Burton that she gave most thought to her final resting place. She and Burton bought adjacent plots in the small cemetery in his hometown, Pontryhydfen, Wales, and told the world they would be side by side throughout eternity. But of course by the time Richard Burton died, he and Taylor had been estranged for nearly a decade. He was buried in the Swiss cemetery near his home at Celigny, a decision based in large part on the fact that returning his body to Wales would open up the possibility of having to pay British taxes on his estate. Apparently his last wife, Sally Hay Burton, was concerned enough about Taylor's intentions (after the divorce from John Warner) to announce her own plans to be laid to rest beside Richard. Sally designed a memorial for his grave that included a double stone. "That's my plot," she told reporters pointedly. "I'll be buried beside him." Taylor, who has continued to send roses to her former husband's grave, has remained silent about her current plans for eternity.

The White Cliffs of Dover

The White Cliffs of Dover was a 1944 movie from MGM made for the purpose of paying homage to the brave spirit of our British allies as they continued to bear the brunt of World War II. In the tradition of the studio's previous wartime success, *Mrs. Miniver*, it told the story of a family's sacrifice for country. Irene Dunne played a young American woman who falls in love with and marries titled Sir John Ashwood (Alan Marshal). He is killed serving his country in World War I, leaving her to raise their young son. When the boy grows to manhood, he too serves his country; a soldier in World War II, he is wounded and subsequently dies. The movie ends with a speech from his mother that emphasizes her belief that the deaths of the two men she loved the most were not in vain.

Elizabeth Taylor was cast in another English role: young Betsy, the sweet country neighbor who becomes a friend and playmate of the heroine's son, played by Roddy McDowall. In scenes of lyrical beauty set in a flowering meadow and on the shore of a rustic pond, the two children share a case of puppy love that presages a later adult romance (at which time the characters are played by June Lockhart and Peter Lawford). Taylor's scenes illustrate MGM art director Cedric Gibbons at his best, creating a romantic vision of playmates in an idyll of childhood.

Unfortunately, those who edit old movies to fit the television format often deem those childhood scenes expendable, and it is very difficult to find a print of *The White Cliffs of Dover* that includes Elizabeth Taylor. Nor are there reviews that mention her performance. Most reviewers, caught up in wartime sentiment, praised the film excessively.

"Who the Hell Cares about Eddie Fisher?"

At the time of Elizabeth Taylor's involvement with Eddie Fisher, she and his wife Debbie Reynolds stopped speaking to one another, even though they had been close friends during Taylor's marriage to Mike Todd. Debbie had been Elizabeth's matron of honor at her wedding to Mike, and had been one of the first to comfort Elizabeth after Mike's death. The two women remained estranged for some years, thanks to the bitterness of the Reynolds–Fisher breakup. But then Elizabeth fell in love with Richard Burton, and herself went through a hostile divorce with Fisher. Meanwhile, Debbie had remarried and found her own (fleeting) happiness with Harry Karl.

In 1963, the two women discovered they were fellow passengers on the *Queen Elizabeth*, traveling to Europe, and somehow it seemed it was time to bury the hatchet. The two couples agreed to have dinner together, and after a few moments of nervousness, both women giggled and felt at ease. According to Debbie, her husband Harry poured everyone a glass of Dom Perignon champagne. "Elizabeth held up her glass and said, 'Just look how you lucked out and how I lucked out. Who the hell cares about Eddie Fisher!'"

Who's Afraid of Virginia Woolf?

Elizabeth Taylor won her second Oscar for the role of Martha, the impossibly difficult wife in *Who's Afraid of Virginia Woolf?* The movie was closely based on the succesful Edward Albee play, which had on Broadway starred Uta Hagen as Martha and Arthur Hill as her husband George. Many of Hollywood's best dramatic actresses, including Bette Davis (playwright Albee's first choice, with James

Mason as her costar) wanted to play Martha on the screen, and when it was announced that Taylor had won the role, there was a general expectation that her portrayal of the savagely bitchy wife would make Martha too sweet, too "Hollywood." Many insiders speculated that the movie would be a box-office failure and a financial loss as well, especially in view of the fact that half of its total cost of $5 million had to be paid in salary to Burton and Taylor. Elizabeth Taylor couldn't possibly be wroth that amount of money in a black-and-white film where she was forty pounds overweight, wearing a gray-streaked wig, and dressed in frumpy clothes. Could she?

Taylor proved her detractors wrong. Under the direction of Mike Nichols, in his first movie assignment, she turned in a stellar performance. She was ably supported by Richard Burton in the role of her husband (Jack Lemmon, the producer's first choice, had turned the part down), and George Segal and Sandy Dennis as the couple's friends. By all accounts, the period of filming was a tense one. Taylor knew she was taking a big risk in tackling the part of Martha; Burton was anxious about what the role of henpecked husband would do to his image; Mike Nichols was worried about the technical aspects of directing his first film; producer Ernest Lehman feared that the salaries of the two stars might be more than a black-and-white movie about a depressing couple could recoup. Trying to relieve some of the tension on the first day of filming, Lehman sent Taylor two dozen white roses, and then enigmatically sent director Nichols a whip. Later, both Burton and Taylor confessed that they were taking their characters home at the end of the day, to the detriment of their personal lives. After working in the Hollywood studio for weeks, the cast and crew traveled to Smith College in Massachusetts to finish shooting.

All four leads in the movie were nominated for Academy Awards. Taylor won Best Actress, and Dennis won Best Supporting Actress. The movie also won three other Oscars for cinematography, costumes, and set decoration. Neither Segal nor Burton won in their categories. In addition to her Oscar, Taylor also received in recognition of her fine performance the New York Critics Circle prize, the National Board of Review award, the British Film Critics

Award, the Silver Mask of Italy as best actress in a foreign film, and the Foreign Press Association Award.

Critical comment reinforced Taylor's triumph. "Easily the finest performance of her career," said William Weaver; Stanley Kaufman opined that "she does the best work of her career, sustained and urgent." *Variety* commented that she "earned every penny of her reported million plus. Her characterization is at once sensual, spiteful, cynical, pitiable, loathsome, lustful and tender." *Time*, calling her "loud, sexy and vulgar," agreed that she achieved "moments of astonishing tenderness."

Who's Afraid of Virgina Woolf? helped restore some of the professional credibility Elizabeth Taylor lost through *Cleopatra*, and it also gave a new direction to her roles in the future. She was to play many a shrew in forthcoming movies.

Why She Married Nicky Hilton

Years after the fact, Elizabeth Taylor explained why she married Nicky Hilton when she was just eighteen. She said she felt trapped in her life of a young Hollywood star and concluded, "I only had two ways of running away from everything: Go to college or get married. I got married at barely eighteen. I really *did* think that being married would be like living in a little white cottage with a picket fence and roses."

The Wife of Bath

Critic Stanley Elkin mused on the power of Elizabeth Taylor's stardom in a 1964 article for *Esquire* and concluded that her movie persona was that of the Wife of Bath, Chaucer's earthy and wholly feminine heroine in *The Canterbury Tales*. Elkin says, "In each important role since puberty . . . she has been either wife or mistress, a woman as involved in the giving of love as the Magi in the giving of gifts. Beautiful as she is, she has been not the pursued as much as the pursuer." According to Elkin, "woman" is Elizabeth Taylor's metaphor.

Interestingly, critic Pauline Kael made much the same comparison. She once called Taylor "Beverley Hills Chaucerian" adding, "and that's as high and low as you can get."

Aileen Getty Wilding

Aileen Getty married Christopher Wilding and thus became Elizabeth Taylor's daughter-in-law. Aileen is the daughter of John Paul Getty, Jr., and the granddaughter of the oil man who founded one of America's largest fortunes. Aileen, born in 1959, lived through the childhood ordeal of seeing her brother, John Paul Getty III, kidnapped in a highly publicized case in which the kidnappers sent the family one of the boy's ears to motivate them to pay the ransom quickly. Aileen and Christopher were the parents of two sons, Caleb, born in 1984, and Andrew, born in 1985. When the couple separated two years after Andrew's birth, temporary custody of the children was awarded to their father. During divorce proceedings, rumors began to surface that Aileen was addicted to cocaine, that she had engaged in sexual orgies, and that she had had a bisexual lover who died of AIDS. In an official statement that had obviously been carefully worded, Elizabeth Taylor said of her soon-to-be ex–daughter-in-law, "I am deeply distressed over the public reports regarding Aileen Getty's health. The pending divorce between my son Christopher and Aileen does not change my feeling for Aileen. My love, concern, and support for her well-being continues."

Christopher Wilding

Christopher Edward Wilding is the second son of Elizabeth Taylor and her second husband, British actor Michael Wilding. He was born, by Caesarean section, in England on February 27, 1955, coincidentally his mother's twenty-third birthday, and weighed just five pounds twelve ounces. After private tutoring in his childhood, he attended boarding school in England and then took his undergraduate degree at the University of Hawaii. He worked for a time as a still photographer. He married the former Aileen Getty, of the wealthy oil dynasty, and the couple had two sons: Caleb, born in 1984 and Andrew, born in 1985. The couple separated in 1987, with custody of the children going to their father. Christopher currently works as a film editor in Hollywood.

Laele Wilding

Laele Wilding, born in 1971, was Elizabeth's first grandchild, daughter of her son Michael Wilding and his then-wife Beth. Beth says that Elizabeth was an indulgent grandma—as she has continued to be with all five of her grandchildren.

Michael Wilding

The recently divorced Elizabeth Taylor met British actor Michael Wilding when she was in England in 1951 for the location shooting of *Ivanhoe*. Although she returned to Hollywood within a few months, she did not get over her attraction to the suave Englishman, nineteen years her senior. "I wanted the calm and quiet and security of friendship," she later explained. From his point of view, he said, "I thought I'd guide this trembling little creature along life's stony path."

It took the determined Taylor months to induce Wilding, long separated from his first wife but only recently divorced, to marry her. One reason for his hesitation was that he was involved with Marlene Dietrich and didn't want to give her up. Another was that he was reluctant to break his ties to England, where he was well known as an actor and could count on earning a good living. Taylor solved the second problem by getting MGM to offer him a contract to work in Hollywood. It appears that Marlene solved the first problem by making it clear that she had no intention of ever divorcing her husband and marrying again.

Early in 1952, Elizabeth Taylor boarded a plane for London, making the public announcement, "I am going to Michael. I adore him. We'll be married at the end of the week." This was news to Wilding, who had not yet proposed to her, and he was further startled when she bought an expensive sapphire and diamond engagement ring and announced it was a gift from him. Taylor was a beautiful woman, and a star of the first magnitude; Wilding was flattered and intrigued. So he soon acquiesced to her plans, and they were married on February 21, 1952, in London's Caxton Hall.

The couple settled down in Hollywood, where Elizabeth was a big star and her new husband was virtually unknown. At first, they were very happy. Elizabeth later recalled, "Even though there was a large difference in age, we were so much alike in so many ways. We both loved animals and nature. We both were babes in the woods where economics were concerned. We worried constantly about money and had to borrow from the studio." In a very short time, the marriage was in trouble. Wilding explained to a journalist, "The happiest years of my marriage were when Liz was so dependent on me. Now I follow her around and I hate it." He later commented that he thought their divorce was inevitable. He concluded sadly, "It's the tyrants who seem to make a success of marriage." Liz admitted after the divorce, "I'm afraid in those last few years I gave him rather a rough time. Sort of henpecked him and probably wasn't mature enough for him."

The marriage produced two sons: Michael Howard, born January 6, 1953; and Christopher Edward, born on February 27 (his mother's birthday), 1955. By Christopher's first birthday, the relationship between his parents had completely deteriorated. On July 19, 1956, MGM made public an anouncement by the Wildings that they had separated. "Much thought has been given to the step we are taking . . . We are in complete accord in making this amicable decision." Soon thereafter, Taylor became engaged to Mike Todd. When she and Mike discovered she was pregnant, he insisted on a speedy Mexican divorce rather than waiting the year it would take for a California decree. Always a gentleman, Wilding agreed to a divorce in Mexico City on January 30, 1957, and then Elizabeth Taylor and Mike Todd were married in Acapulco a few days later. Wilding helped with the arrangements but returned to California before the ceremony. He and Taylor remained good friends for the rest of his life.

Michael Charles Gauntlet Wilding was born in the little town of Westcliff-on-Sea in England's Essex county on July 23, 1912, the son of an army officer and an actress. He could trace his family back to the Archbishop of Canterbury and even to that ancestor of many royals, John of Gaunt. Educated in private schools and holding a degree from Christ Church College at Oxford, he was a portrait painter before he became an actor, and he happily returned to painting at the end of his life. His first success was in the 1946 English film, *Piccadilly Incident*, costarring Anna Neagle. Thereafter he was professionally linked with Neagle and her actor/manager husband, Herbert Wilcox.

Wilding married four times. His first wife was actress Kay Young, whom he married in 1937 and divorced in 1952 (having been separated since 1945). Elizabeth Taylor was his second wife. At the time that Taylor married Eddie Fisher, Wilding took a third wife, society beauty Susan Nell. In 1962, that marriage too ended in divorce. His fourth wife was British actress Margaret Leighton, whom Wilding married in 1964, after a much-publicized friendship with Faye Dunaway. They were still married at the time of Leighton's death in 1976. Despite his many marriages and affairs, there were persistent rumors in Hollywood about Wilding's homosexuality. When gossip columnist Hedda Hopper published one of these stories, Wilding sued for libel and won $100,000.

After his divorce from Elizabeth Taylor, Michael Wilding continued to appear on the stage, in movies, and on TV, and he also acted as a theatrical agent; one of his first clients was Richard Burton. Although his reviews were always favorable, Michael Wilding will probably be best remembered as a husband rather than an actor. After several years of frail health, Wilding died following a fall in his London home in July 1979. Taylor, along with their two sons, attended his funeral in Chichester, England. She also sent a large floral tribute with a card that read, "Dearest Michael, God bless you. I love you, Elizabeth."

Michael Howard Wilding, Jr.

Michael Howard Wilding Junior is the eldest child of Elizabeth Taylor, from her marriage to British actor Michael Wilding. Michael Jr. was born by Caesarean section on January 6, 1953, a year after the couple were wed. The proud mother adored her beautiful baby boy, who weighed seven pounds, five ounces at birth, and later told the press, "I was absolutely idiotic with pride. You would have thought I was the only woman who had ever conceived and carried a child."

As a teenager in the late 1960s, Michael went through a rebellious phase, and after he was asked to leave his English boarding school, he was sent to Hawaii to live with Elizabeth's brother Howard and his wife. There Michael met Beth Clutter, a keypunch operator, whom he married in 1970, when he was seventeen and she was nineteen. Taylor and husband Richard Burton attended the wedding at Caxton Hall in London (where Taylor had married Michael's father in 1952) at which the groom wore a burgundy velvet caftan and Taylor a white dress that eclipsed the bride's. Afterward, the Burtons held a champagne reception for the newlyweds at London's Dorchester Hotel, their own favorite place to check in. Hoping that marriage would settle Michael down, his mother gave him a $75,000 house in London, as well as a Jaguar in which to get around the city.

Elizabeth was thrilled when Beth in 1971 gave birth to a baby girl named Laele, Taylor's first grandchild. Shortly thereafter, Michael rejected his mother's values, left the London house, and took his family to live in western Wales, where he started a commune and renounced his American citizenship. The marriage floundered, and Beth returned to her native Portland, Oregon, with the baby. Michael then lived with a common-law wife, Johanna Lykke-Dahn (called Jo) with whom he had a second daughter, named Naomi. For a time, Michael was part of a rock group called Solar Ben. Despite the clash over Michael's new values, Taylor visited her son at the commune. Michael's present wife is Brooke Palance, daughter of actor Jack Palance. She is herself an actress and a producer.

Michael, of course, has been familiar with movie sets since he was a baby. He worked briefly as a photographer's assistant on *X Y & Zee*, in which his mother starred, and eventually found his way to an interest in acting after leaving the commune. He got a role on a daytime soap, performed in an off-Broadway production, and played the part of a Hollywood producer in his mother's TV movie, *Sweet Bird of Youth*. In the fall of 1989, Michael Wilding joined the cast of TV's long-running prime-time soap, *Dallas*, in the role of Alex Barton. Barton, an Englishman who owned a Dallas art gallery, took a particular interest in the artistic career of J.R. Ewing's wife Callie, until J.R. forced him to leave Dallas forever.

Brook Williams

Brook Williams, the son of actor Emlyn Williams, was a close friend and employee of Richard Burton for many years. Brook was himself an actor, and very knowledgeable about movies. He headed Richard's production company, he acted as his confidant, he organized his household. His last duty was giving the eulogy at Richard's funeral.

Emlyn Williams

Emlyn Williams, born in 1905, was a Welsh actor who also established a reputation as a playwright and stage director. His best known work as a writer is *The Corn Is Green*, made into a movie in 1945 starring Elizabeth Taylor's good friend, Roddy McDowall. Williams appeared as an actor in *Ivanhoe*, in which Taylor had a lead role. But the chief connection between Taylor and Williams came through Richard Burton.

In 1943, Emlyn Williams was casting his play, *The Druid's Rest*, and chose young Richard Burton for one of the roles. (Burton was understudied by Stanley Baker, later to become a well-known actor himself.) Burton and Williams remained good friends for years, and Emlyn's son Brook worked for Burton for many years as his production manager and general aide. There was a period of coolness between Emlyn Williams and Richard Burton at the time Burton married Elizabeth Taylor. Williams unkindly called her a third-rate chorus girl. But Taylor went to great lengths to charm her husband's old friend, and when Williams got to know Taylor personally, he became one of her staunch supporters. He also became a fan of her screen performances, saying, "I have always thought her fame obscured her talent, which is very great."

Tennessee Williams

Throughout her adult career, Elizabeth Taylor has been closely linked professionally to famed playwright Tennessee Williams. One director called her "the quintessential Tennessee Williams heroine." Taylor starred in three of Williams's works when they were translated to the big screen: *Cat on a Hot Tin Roof*; *Suddenly Last Summer*; and *The Milk Train Doesn't Stop Here Anymore* (retitled *Boom!*). She also starred in the 1989 TV movie version of *Sweet Bird of Youth*.

Although Williams himself had some reservations about her portrayal of his heroines, he responded warmly to Taylor as a person. They first met after she had finished *Cat on a Hot Tin Roof*, and she recalls that they hit it off immediately. "We both had odd senses of humor," she explained.

Thomas Lanier Williams was born in Mississippi in 1911. He was the one to change his name to Tennessee, in a reference to his family's place of origin. His first play to appear on Broadway was *The Glass Menagerie*, in 1945. It received great critical acclaim and won the New York Drama Critics Award as best play of the season. Williams then warned his audience, "In this play, I have said all the nice things I have to say about people. The future things will be harsher." Indeed, his subsequent works scandalized many with their thinly veiled references to homosexuality and moral depravity. Perhaps the best known of his works is *A Streetcar Named Desire*; others include *The Rose Tattoo* and *Orpheus Descending*, with a central character reportedly based on Elvis Presley. Williams was a winner of the Pulitzer Prize for drama.

Williams once told reporters that he thought Taylor was totally miscast as the heroine in peril in the screen version of *Suddenly Last Summer*. Taylor played the part of a young woman who was used by her homosexual cousin as bait to attract men into his orbit, a ploy that ends in disaster on a beach on Morocco, where a horde of Arab urchins attacks, kills, and cannibalizes the cousin. Williams remarked, "I think it stretches credulity to believe that such a hip doll as our Liz wouldn't know she was being used for something evil. I think Liz would have dragged Sebastian home by his ears and so saved them both from considerable embarrassment."

Tennessee Williams and Maggie the Cat

In 1958, when the movie was released, Tennessee Williams told reporters he thought Elizabeth Taylor was the best of all the actors in the film of *Cat on a Hot Tin Roof*, and in 1965 he said in an interview that he thought Elizabeth Taylor had been "brilliantly cast" as Maggie. Eight years later, he reversed his decision: "Elizabeth Taylor was never my idea of Maggie the Cat."

Wilshire Boulevard

After Elizabeth Taylor's separation from Nicky Hilton, she decided not to return to live in her parents' home. She had learned to value her independence, and she resented her mother's pressuring her to reconcile with Nicky, and later to stop seeing her new beau, director Stanley Donen. So the divorcee rented a five-room apartment on Hollywood's Wilshire Boulevard, and moved in with her secretary, Peggy Rutledge. It was a modestly comfortable place, with interesting neighbors; newlyweds Janet Leigh and Tony Curtis had an apartment downstairs. Taylor remained there until her marriage to Michael Wilding.

Bob Wilson

Bob Wilson was Richard Burton's valet and stage dresser during the 1960s. He served as Burton's best man in his 1964 wedding to Elizabeth Taylor. When his wife Sally became ill while the Wilsons were traveling with the Burtons, Elizabeth Taylor arranged for her to be flown back to New York, entered in Columbia Presbyterian Hospital, and treated by the best physicians—all at the star's expense. Wilson left Richard Burton after his marriage to Suzy Hunt.

Winning the Second Oscar

Elizabeth Taylor won her second Oscar for *Who's Afraid of Virginia Woolf?*, released in 1966. When the award ceremonies were held in the spring of 1967, Taylor agreed to attend. She had already received several other critical awards for her performance as the virago Martha, and hoped she would carry off her second Oscar. But husband Richard Burton, who was a nominee in the Best Actor category for his role in the same movie, was still on the Riviera, working on *The Comedians*, and it would be difficult for him to get away. Moreover, he felt he was not likely to be a winner of the Academy Award, since most of the other critical awards of the year had been won by his competitor, Paul Scofield, for his fine performance in *A Man for All Seasons*. In the end, Taylor decided not to go without her husband. So she learned of her win over the phone. Her award was accepted by Anne Bancroft.

Winning her second Oscar put Elizabeth Taylor in a small group of two-time winners. At the time they were: Luise Rainer, Olivia De Havilland, Vivien Leigh, and Ingrid Bergman. Later, Katharine Hepburn managed to exceed them all with a total of three Oscars for Best Actress.

Winter Kills

In 1979, Elizabeth Taylor made a cameo appearance in the movie *Winter Kills*. Based on a novel by Richard Condon, best known for his *Manchurian Candidate*, the move tells the story of the attempts by the half-brother of an assassinated president to track down the conspirators responsible for the murder. Taylor was on screen so briefly that she was unbilled, playing a Washington hostess who helped the late president in his pursuit of nubile young women. Vincent Canby called the movie "a funny, paranoid fable," and other critics also praised the film. It was not a success at the box office, however, and it did nothing to restore Taylor's bankability.

Women Elizabeth Taylor Admires

In a 1973 interview, journalist Liz Smith asked Elizabeth Taylor to name the women she most admired. They were: Ethel Kennedy, Katharine Hepburn, and Golda Meir.

Henry Wynberg

Henry Wynberg was a used-car dealer with whom Elizabeth Taylor was involved in the mid-1970s. Wynberg, born in Holland and five years younger than Taylor, was introduced to her in 1972 through Peter Lawford. Divorced from actress Carroll Russell since 1967 and the father of one son, he had a roster of previous lady friends that included Tina Turner and Dewi Sukarno. As Taylor's marriage to Burton deteriorated, Wynberg made it clear he was ready to step into her life. Her affair with him in 1973, while still married to Burton but living apart from him, was public knowledge. Elizabeth and Henry cruised the Mediterranean on the *Kalizma* and were entertained by Princess Grace when they stopped at Monaco. After she divorced Burton in 1974, Taylor and Wynberg lived together in a rented house in Beverly Hills. The romance ended when Taylor remarried Burton, but Henry remained on friendly terms with her, and offered her emotional support as the second Burton marriage fell apart.

Unsurprisingly, Richard Burton was always a critic of Wynberg. When friends told Burton that Wynberg was rumored to be a man of unusual sexual endowment, Burton made a naughty crack: "I'm sure that like the used cars he sells, it will fall off at just the psychological moment."

A public postscript to the relationship came in late 1989, when Henry Wynberg sued Elizabeth Taylor and Cheseborough–Pond, makers of her fragrance, Passion, for $2.4 million. Wynberg claimed that in 1975, he and Taylor signed a contract that gave him the exclusive right to license her name for a perfume and related products.

Her response was a disdainful "Don't even ask me to talk about it," as she devoted herself to "Passion"—ately promoting her name brand. In three years, as of early 1991, it became one of America's ten top fragrances.

In early December, 1990, Wynberg suddenly, inexplicably dropped the suit just as it was about to go to trial. With full media in attendance, Liz announced that she was vindicated and that she did not make any kind of a financial settlement. This "no settlement" settlement was greeted with disbelief, especially in the fragrance industry. Wynberg and his lawyers had spent three years in various facets of litigation, motions and legal procedures at an estimated cost of at least six figures.

Quipped John G. Ledes, publisher and editor of the prestige trade magazine, *Cosmetic World*, "Is the world now to believe that Henry Wynberg, better known as 'the beau between the Burtons' and his lawyers, who had won every legal round until this point, rolled over and cried 'forgive us our legal trespasses' and took not a dime?"

X Y and Zee

X Y and Zee was a 1972 movie starring Elizabeth Taylor. Made in Britain, where it was titled *Zee & Co*, it was based on an original screenplay written by novelist Edna O'Brien. The story revolves around the crisis in a marriage when the husband (Michael Caine) becomes involved with another woman (Susannah York) and contemplates leaving his wife, played by Elizabeth Taylor. O'Brien's screenplay is tough, funny, salty to the point of occasionally being lewd. Its flavor is conveyed by the opening lines of the novelization published in 1971: "She sang while she played, Zee did. Always—'My love is a red red prick.'"

Directed by Brian Hutton, the movie was a modern take on the classic triangle plot. It did have a surprise ending, in which the wife seduces the mistress, and, the movie implies, thereby wins her husband back. Dressed in early-seventies "trendy" clothes, Taylor looked as beautiful as ever—although there were reports she had asked for a body double in the movies's one seminude scene.

Veteran critic Pauline Kael considered this role to be one of Elizabeth Taylor's best performances. She observed, "At the beginning of *X Y and Zee*, Elizabeth Taylor, peering out of blue lamé eyeshadow like a raccoon, seemed ridiculous and—well, monstrous. But as the picture went on, I found myself missing her whenever she wasn't onscreen . . . and I'm forced to conclude that, monstrous though she is, her jangling performance is what gives this movie its energy." Kael called her "an uncontrolled actress but a cunning force of nature" and suggested that the real text of the movie was about Taylor, "of a woman declaring herself to be what she has become."

Other critics were not so positive. Vincent Canby said the director had allowed Taylor to play the lead "as if she were the ghost of whores past, present and future, clanking her jewelry, her headbands, her earrings and her feelings behind her like someone out to haunt a funhouse." He concluded, "It is an unfortunately ridiculous perfomance." Judith Crist complained that Taylor "screams and carries on ad nauseam."

A member of the supporting cast, in the role of a London hostess who knows the scandals in everyone's life, was British actress Margaret Leighton. At the time of filming, Leighton was the fourth and final wife of Taylor's ex-husband Michael Wilding.

-Y-

The Year of the Gems

It seems that 1969 was a very good year for Elizabeth Taylor's jewelry collection. That year, she received three major pieces, all gifts from husband Richard Burton: the Cartier diamond, the Peregrina pearl, and the forty-carat sapphire pin. Burton also gave her a $100,000 diamond necklace from which to hang the diamond or the pearl as pendants.

Howard Young

Howard Young was Elizabeth Taylor's great-uncle, married to Mabel Rosemond, the sister of Francis Taylor's mother. Young was a self-made man, who left his boyhood home in Belle Center, Ohio, at the tender age of ten and quickly accumulated a fortune. He started his career as an art dealer by using a chemical process to turn family photographs into formal portraits to hang in the parlor; later he simply had the photographs copied in oil. When one of his well-heeled clients asked him to locate some other art to add to the parlor wall, Young became a full-fledged art dealer who ended up selling Old Masters to some of America's *nouveaux riches*, such as the Fords and the Fishers of Detroit.

For a time, Young owned a gallery in St. Louis, where his nephew Francis worked for him. Then Young judged the time was right to move his operation to New York, and

Francis Taylor went along with him. After Francis married Sara Warmbrodt, Young decided to send the young couple to Europe, where Francis could search for Old Masters to sell on the American market. By 1930, Young instructed his nephew to settle in London and open a gallery on Old Bond Street.

The Taylors named their first child Howard after his wealthy great-uncle, and their daughter Elizabeth was given the middle name Rosemond, which was the family name of Howard Young's wife (and that of her sister, Elizabeth's grandmother Taylor). The Taylors were frequent guests at their rich relative's various homes: the ranch in Wisconsin, the estate in Connecticut, the penthouse in Manhattan, and the winter home in Florida. Young moved in the monied set, and numbered among his friends such luminaries as Dwight D. Eisenhower. The childless art dealer died in 1972, leaving an estate of more than $20 million, which went to charity.

Z

Ardeshir Zahedi

Ardeshir Zahedi was for many years, before the revolution that toppled the shah, the Iranian ambassador to the United States. During his stay in Washington, he was known for giving lavish parties and for his flirtatious charm. In 1976, Washington rumors flew about a romance between the ambassador and Elizabeth Taylor, who had been introduced to one another by mutual friend Henry Kissinger. Zahedi, who had formerly been married to the shah's daughter, escorted Taylor to the premier of *The Blue Bird* and then invited her to be the guest of honor on Iran Air's first nonstop flight from New York to Teheran. There were reports that the two wanted to marry but that the Shah refused to agree to allow his ex–son-in-law to wed a Jewish convert. Later that year, Elizabeth met John Warner, who would become her next husband, so the question of whether she would be allowed to marry Zahedi became academic.

Zarak Kahn

In mid-1955, Michael Wilding was offered a role in a B movie called *Zarak Khan*, which costarred Victor Mature and Anita Ekberg. He initially turned it down on the grounds that he did not want to be separated from wife Elizabeth Taylor during the location shooting in Morocco.

Elizabeth, however, urged him to accept and rearranged her own schedule so she would be free to travel with him. She hoped to save their faltering marriage with a burst of togetherness, while he hoped to boost his career with one more movie to his credit. Neither hope was fulfilled.

Ardeshir Zahedi

Ardeshir Zahedi was for many years, before the revolution that toppled the shah, the Iranian ambassador to the United States. During his stay in Washington, he was known for giving lavish parties and for his flirtatious charm. In 1976, Washington rumors flew about a romance between the ambassador and Elizabeth Taylor, who had been introduced to one another by mutual friend Henry Kissinger. Zahedi, who had formerly been married to the shah's daughter, escorted Taylor to the premier of *The Blue Bird* and then invited her to be the guest of honor on Iran Air's first nonstop flight from New York to Teheran. There were reports that the two wanted to marry but that the Shah refused to agree to allow his ex–son-in-law to wed a Jewish convert. Later that year, Elizabeth met John Warner, who would become her next husband, so the question of whether she would be allowed to marry Zahedi became academic.

Zarak Kahn

In mid-1955, Michael Wilding was offered a role in a B movie called *Zarak Khan*, which costarred Victor Mature and Anita Ekberg. He initially turned it down on the grounds that he did not want to be separated from wife Elizabeth Taylor during the location shooting in Morocco.

Elizabeth, however, urged him to accept and rearranged her own schedule so she would be free to travel with him. She hoped to save their faltering marriage with a burst of togetherness, while he hoped to boost his career with one more movie to his credit. Neither hope was fulfilled.